THE BRITISH ARCHAEOLOGICAL ASSOCIATION

CONFERENCE TRANSACTIONS
For the year 1986

XII
MEDIEVAL ART,
ARCHITECTURE AND
ARCHAEOLOGY
at Rouen

Edited by
Jenny Stratford

1993

Copies of these may be obtained from W. S. Maney and Son Limited, Hudson Road, Leeds LS9 7DL

ISBN Hardback 0 901286 32 X
Paperback 0 901286 33 8

British Library Cataloguing-in-Publication Data
A catalogue record for this book is available from the British Library

PRINTED IN GREAT BRITAIN BY W. S. MANEY AND SON LIMITED
HUDSON ROAD, LEEDS LS9 7DL

CONTENTS

The British Archaeological Association
gratefully acknowledges a generous grant from
the Francis Coales Charitable Foundation
towards the cost of this volume.

PREFACE

The papers printed in this volume are based on lectures given at the Association's Annual Conference, the 15th in the present series, held in Rouen, 17–21 July 1989. The conference, attended by some 75 members from France, Germany, Great Britain and North America, was a major event in the Association's activities. On the one hand, it demonstrated the success of the academically-concentrated conferences studying important medieval buildings and their associated art and archaeology in a cathedral city or town, which had been initiated by Dr R. D. H. Gem at Worcester in 1975, and, on the other, it was our only conference on the Continent since the Association's first congress in 1844.

The organisation of any conference is a demanding and time-consuming task. That this conference was a success is due to the single-handed efforts of Dr L. M. Grant, who shouldered all the domestic, social and academic arrangements, while adding to her burden by delivering a lecture as well. We are greatly in her debt.

The Association is especially indebted to Dr J. Stratford for bringing together the papers in this volume and for editing them. The publication schedule, or the fact that some papers will be published elsewhere, has meant that, of the 20 lectures delivered, 13 were available to be published here. Our printer, W. S. Maney and Son, and Ms Linda Fish, have taken great care with the production of the volume, for which we are most grateful.

Visits were made to Jumièges, Caudebec and Saint-Georges-de-Boscherville (18 July), Château-Gaillard, Gisors and Écouis (19 July), the Bibliothèque municipale, the Cathedral, Saint-Maclou and Saint-Ouen in Rouen, and to the Petit-Quévilly (20 July): our grateful thanks are due to all those who acted as guides, stimulating and leading discussion, particularly M. J. Le Maho, who guided us around his excavations at the Cathedral and explained his discoveries at Saint-Georges-de-Boscherville, and Mlle M.-F. Rose, Conservateur, Bibliothèque municipale, Rouen, who kindly arranged a special viewing of illuminated manuscripts in her care.

Throughout the conference we were helped considerably by Dr P. Périn, Conservateur en Chef du Patrimoine and Directeur des Musées et Monuments départementaux, Seine-Maritime, and by members of the Sociétés Savantes de Rouen, in whose rooms our meetings were held. M. Y. Lescroart, Conservateur Régional des Monuments Historiques greatly helped the planning of our programme.

Through the kindness of Dr Périn and his colleagues we were able to visit the Musée des Antiquitées, where we were given a reception by the Direction de la Culture, Conseil Général de la Seine-Maritime, and Saint-Georges-de-Boscherville, where we organised a *fête-champêtre* in the cloister, attended by the Président and Directeur Général of the Conseil Général.

Arrangements made by Dr R. K. Morris enabled three student scholarships to be awarded from funds generously made available by the Charles Robertson Charitable Trust.

This volume is a fitting reminder of a memorable conference; a forum for a fresh examination of some aspects of the art, architecture and archaeology of Rouen, on which the papers printed here will surely generate further research, while, at the same time, making a significant contribution to the study of Rouen.

Laurence Keen, *President*
April 1993

LIST OF ABBREVIATIONS AND SHORTENED TITLES

AA SS OSB	*Acta Sanctorum Ordinis Sancti Benedicti*, ed L. d'Achery and J. Mabillon (Paris 1668–1701)
Antiq. J.	*Antiquaries Journal*
ADSM	Archives départementales de la Seine-Maritime
BAA CT	*British Archaeological Association Conference Transactions*
BCDA	*Bulletin de la Commission départementale des Antiquités de la Seine-Inférieure*
BEC	Bibliothèque de l'Ecole des Chartes
BL	British Library
BM	Bibliothèque municipale
BN	Bibliothèque nationale
Bull. mon.	*Bulletin monumental*
CA	*Congrès archéologique*
CVMA	Corpus Vitrearum Medii Aevi
Fauroux, *Recueil*	*Recueil des actes des ducs de Normandie de 911 à 1066*, ed. M. Fauroux (*MSAN*, xxxvi, Caen 1961)
JBAA	*Journal of the British Archaeological Association*
JWCI	*Journal of the Warburg and Courtauld Institutes*
MSAN	*Mémoires de la Société des Antiquaires de Normandie*
PRO	Public Record Office
RCHM	Royal Commission on Historical Monuments
RS	Rolls Series
SHF	Société de l'histoire de France
SHN	Société de l'histoire de Normandie

Rouen from 900 to 1204: From Scandinavian Settlement to Angevin 'Capital'

By David Bates

Rouen's size increased dramatically during these three centuries, as did its importance as a centre of trade. In these respects, the town's history is no different from that of any major northern European town in a period generally noted for urban development. Its uniqueness of course lies in its political history and its association with the rise of Norman power. A succession of references describe it as the chief town of the territorial principality which from the early 11th century was known as *Normannia*. As Orderic Vitalis, writing in the first half of the 12th century, accurately remarked: all Normandy had acknowledged its domination from ancient times.[1] In pursuit of the same idea, a mid-12th-century poet indulged in a laborious play on words by highlighting the fact that if you remove the middle syllable from 'Rouen' (*Rothoma*), you have Rome (*Roma*). Rouen, he went on, was adorned by imperial dignity, served by conquered Britain, and adored by the English, Scots and Welsh who paid their tributes.[2] In the second half of the 12th century, the town's status was more prosaically, but even more remarkably, acknowledged in formal treaties between Henry II and the French kings, Louis VII and Philip Augustus, which placed it on a par with Paris, thereby identifying it as the chief town of the Angevin lands in France.[3]

The earliest description of the town is given by Dudo of Saint-Quentin, who wrote an imaginative and tendentious history of the first Norman rulers in the early 11th century. According to him, Rouen was already a rich and cosmopolitan city at that date; he names Greeks, Indians, Frisians, Bretons, Danes, English, Scots and Irish among those who frequented the town.[4] This list has been shown not to be as fanciful as it might at first sight appear, even if the visits of the more exotic of the peoples named were extraordinary, rather than regular, occurrences.[5] The first physical description of the town is supplied by Orderic Vitalis. He described a wealthy, beautiful and populous city, flourishing because of its trade, by the side of the river Seine and bounded on the east by the Aubette and the Robec and on the west by the river Maromme. It was surrounded on all sides by hills and forests, and was rich in fruit, fish, and all kinds of goods.[6] Another description, dating from the late 12th century, is by the English canon, William of Newburgh. He again emphasised Rouen's trading connections with many lands, its wealth, and its great natural strength. In describing the siege conducted by the French king, Louis VII, in 1174, he commented that it was only possible for a besieging army to encompass about one-third of the town and that supplies could always be moved in and out across the bridge over the Seine. He was therefore by implication saying that the river was not just the route which brought most of its trade to the city, but also a great natural moat which made it almost impregnable. He thought Rouen was one of the great cities of Europe, an opinion which — with the greatest respect, since William was an exceptionally well informed historian — must in some measure derive from the perspective of an English provincial.[7] However, when 13th-century sources permit an estimate of population, scholars have arrived at a figure of between 30,000 and 40,000.[8] This makes it the second largest town in 13th-century France after Paris, and significantly larger than any contemporary English town, with the exception of London. In northern European terms, Rouen was indeed a great town.

Rouen's topography is discussed by Jacques Le Maho and Bernard Gauthiez in their papers. I will therefore merely add some details to illustrate the town's growth in the 11th and 12th centuries. The gate on the river Seine, the Porte Saint-Martin, is mentioned in the early 11th century, as also is the Porte Saint-Clément, which probably lay near the Carolingian comital residence at the west end of the town.[9] The eastern boundary probably lay at the Robec, as Orderic suggests, and can therefore be located between the cathedral and the church of Saint-Maclou.[10] The abbey of Saint-Ouen was in an outlying *bourg* in the 11th and 12th centuries. Its inclusion within a single urban area through the construction of new walls finally took place in the late 12th century in a process which Professor Lucien Musset has described as 'mal connue',[11] and which will be further illuminated by Bernard Gauthiez's work. It can be said, however, that the area covered by houses appears already to be moving towards, and perhaps to have reached, the line of the later medieval walls and the most northerly medieval gate, the Porte Beauvoisine (or Porte Saint-Ouen), in the 11th and 12th centuries, since in 1136 a fire spread directly from the city to the *bourg*. Likewise, a reference from the 1020s to the church of Saint-Laurent, which lay on a direct east–west line from the abbey of Saint-Ouen to the town's most westerly medieval gate, the Porte Cauchoise, which is first mentioned in the 1090s, described it at that date as being *in suburbio*.[12]

There are numerous references in the sources to the city's walls, although the fact that there was only a palisade by the Seine in 1202 suggests that they did not even then extend to the river side of the city.[13] It is clear that the walls were rebuilt several times during the period under discussion as the urban area expanded. The fact that the church of Saint-Sauveur in the Place du Vieux-Marché is described as being outside the walls in a charter dating from shortly after 1066, has led Bernard Gauthiez to suggest the construction of the new wall on the line of the Porte Cauchoise in the last years of the Conqueror's reign, as well as a further rebuilding late in Henry II's reign.[14] The bridge across the Seine is first mentioned in a charter of the 1020s and may well have been built in the later 10th century.[15] It was a wooden structure, which Bernard Gauthiez suggests lay at the west of the urban area near the residence inherited from the Carolingian counts.[16] It was either superseded or supplemented by a stone bridge in the 1140s, which lay at the end of the modern Rue du Grand-Pont. Access was through the Porte Saint-Martin.[17] A document of 1138 describes a house within the town as having been a fortified stone tower, a kind of dwelling which also existed at contemporary Bayeux.[18] The ducal palace was at the extreme south-east of the town, on the site described on old maps as the 'Haute Vieille Tour'. The first stone structure there was attributed to count Richard I by Robert of Torigny, although Bernard Gauthiez now suggests that its construction was organised by Richard II.[19] Its location on the eastern side of the town, facing towards 'France', is an interesting commentary on the strategic perceptions of the late 10th- and early 11th-century Normans. The residence of the Carolingian counts had traditionally been at the other end of the town, guarding the approach from the sea.

Tenth-century Rouen was one of the great Viking towns of north-western Europe. Before the Scandinavian settlements in what became the duchy of Normandy, it obviously could not have possessed the political importance it acquired when a territorial principality was created around it. The sheer range of the references in the sources for the Carolingian period, combined with recent archaeological work, none the less suggest a centre which was of considerable social and economic significance from at least as early as the 6th century.[20] The second half of the 9th century looks to have been an unhappy period in the town's history, for, once Viking fleets began to sail up the Seine from 841 onwards, its position was consistently an insecure one. Charles the Bald's decision in the 860s to construct the fortified bridge upstream at Pont-de-l'Arche suggests that the town was seen as intrinsically indefensible against attacks down the river from the sea. Even if there was still a resident

Frankish archbishop of Rouen in the early 10th century and — very improbably — still a count exercising some authority in 905 in the name of the king of the Franks, their situation was by then an exceptionally precarious one.[21] Much controversy surrounds the subject of the origins of Normandy, and Rouen's history has to be placed within these discussions. None the less, two incontrovertible facts require emphasis; namely, that Rouen was at the heart of the territory granted to Rollo and his followers,[22] and that the earliest Norman rulers were described by contemporaries as either chieftains of the men from the North or counts of Rouen.[23] Everything points to the town already possessing great potential as a centre of political and economic power even before the arrival of the Vikings.

What the Vikings have left behind in Rouen is among the greater mysteries of medieval archaeology. Excavation *ought* to yield riches in their way comparable to those of York or, to a lesser extent, Dublin. Yet the only discoveries to have been made are of weapons found in the river Seine.[24] There is, as a result, a school of thought which rejects Dudo of Saint-Quentin's image of a devastated town revived by Rollo, and argues instead that Rouen remained essentially a Frankish town throughout the settlement period; while its location within the Scandinavian settlements had decisive political consequences, its internal life was relatively undisturbed by the newcomers.[25] This is based on Dudo's suggestion that Rollo granted laws to the people of the town, on the lack of archaeological finds, and on the absence in later centuries of the kind of Scandinavian socio-cultural evidence which we might conventionally expect, such as street-names containing Scandinavian elements, Scandinavian personal names among the 12th- and 13th-century citizens, and Scandinavian church dedications.[26] Dudo's apparent belief that a good Scandinavian education could not be had at Rouen as early as the 940s and the manner in which the town admitted the Frankish king, Louis IV, without any resistance, when he invaded the Norman territories in 942, can also be cited in favour of this point of view.[27]

The contrasts between Rouen and York in the quantity and quality of evidence are surprising ones, although certainly less surprising when we bear in mind that little Viking Age archaeology has been undertaken in France.[28] However, despite the relative lack of material from Rouen, 'continuity under new management' does not do full justice to the known facts. It is certain that there was a definite and conscious attempt by the Scandinavian newcomers to assimilate with Frankish institutions within the town. Rollo both recalled the archbishop of Rouen to his church and was later buried in the cathedral. The Rouen mint was revived under his successor William Longsword and produced coins in a basically Carolingian style in his name and in that of his son count Richard I (942–96).[29] Yet in recent years, scholars have increasingly exposed the supposed Christianity of the early Norman rulers as a literary sham created in the late 10th and early 11th centuries;[30] it is, for example, doubtful whether Rollo did sponsor the refoundation of the abbey of Saint-Ouen, as has traditionally been believed.[31] There is also impeccable evidence that there was still a Viking slave-market at Rouen until the late 10th century.[32] The poem, written late in the 10th century by Garnier of Rouen, which mentions the Rouen slave-market, also describes the travels of an Irishman named Moriuht. Taken along with the presence of Rouen coins in many northern coin-hoards, this material shows very clearly Rouen's economic orientation towards the world of the Scandinavian North and Scandinavian Britain and Ireland until the early years of the 11th century.[33] The sources are mostly silent about what conditions were like within the town, although in *c*. 914 its archbishop complained about Scandinavians who had lapsed back into paganism.[34]

It is reasonable to conclude that Rouen must have had its full share of the instability which characterised the history of the future duchy of Normandy in the period up until the 960s.[35] In all probability, its population would have been mostly Franks, whose political masters were Scandinavians trying to an extent to assimilate to Frankish ways, but whose wealth was in considerable measure based on contacts with the North. While we should reject extreme suggestions about a drastic break in the town's history in the early 10th century, we should not underestimate the extent of change. The 'continuity' which is evident may well in part be explained by the interesting suggestion that Rouen was so decisively taken over by the Vikings during the later 9th century that it ceased relatively early to be the victim of plundering raids and was preserved and developed as a base for expeditions deeper into *Francia*.[36] Another point is that it is noticeable that the strong indications of Frankish influence and characteristics at Rouen date from some decades after the initial settlement. The reign of William Longsword in the 930s and early 940s may well be the period when there was a significant resumption of Frankish ways of life within the town. If major building works are a sign of stability and growth, then the construction of a ducal palace under either Richard I or II, and of a bridge across the Seine under Richard I, indicate great prosperity from the second half of the 10th century. It is possible that the 'great leap forward' in Rouen's economic and social history began at that time, and not during the Scandinavian settlements.

Rouen's political importance during the 11th and 12th centuries is so obvious that it scarcely needs emphasising. It was to Rouen that William the Conqueror brought earl Harold of Wessex during his curious mission of either 1064 or 1065. When William's eldest son Robert rebelled against his father in either late 1077 or early 1078, his first action was to try to take the castle at Rouen by surprise.[37] This was also a great period for church-building within and outside the town, with the foundation of the abbeys of La Trinité-du-Mont and Saint-Amand, the priories of Saint-Gervais and Notre-Dame-du-Pré, and the construction of the great Romanesque cathedral. The town's importance was such that the citizens tried on occasion to influence the political future of the duchy, apparently siding with the rebellion which almost overthrew the young duke William in 1047, and, in 1090, dividing into factions in support of one or other of his two sons as they struggled to control Normandy.[38] The town's independence may even have been a factor in persuading William the Conqueror to develop an alternative centre of power at Caen. After 1066, William does not seem to have been an especially frequent visitor to Rouen. On the other hand, the struggle to control his newly acquired lands in considerable measure determined his itinerary; references to visits in 1067, 1074, 1080 and 1084, that is, during the few episodes of relative peace which he enjoyed, suggest that the town had lost little, if any, of its political importance.[39]

Although the Conqueror's patronage of Caen had a permanent effect on Normandy's government, because it was there that the Exchequer was established in the 12th century, the duchy's centre of political gravity remained at Rouen after 1106. Henry I was a regular visitor and indeed went to Rouen during each one of his visits to the duchy; sometimes more than once.[40] He added a curtain wall to the ducal castle, strengthened the tower and built a hall within the wall.[41] He also built a residence across the Seine close to the priory of Notre-Dame-du-Pré, where, according to Stephen of Rouen, he usually stayed when he visited the town.[42] This residence's importance for his family is demonstrated by the fact that it was there that his daughter, the empress Mathilda, spent her 'retirement' from 1148 to 1167.[43] In 1144 the town and its castle fell to her husband Geoffrey, count of Anjou, after it had been effectively isolated within Normandy after his years of campaigning against Stephen and his Norman supporters. The town's formidable defensive capabilities — and perhaps also its loyalty to the reigning Norman dukes — are shown by its being almost the last place in the duchy to surrender in both 1144 and 1204. It is a clear indication of its dominant status within the duchy that Robert of Torigny said that Geoffrey became duke of the Normans from the moment of its fall.[44] Geoffrey is said to have repaired the castle after capturing it and, in 1145, to have begun the construction of the first stone bridge across the Seine, a project to which Mathilda is said to have contributed lavishly.[45] Charles Homer Haskins believed that Geoffrey made Rouen into a kind of capital.[46]

Although I have used the word 'capital' in my title, it is a term which needs to be used with care. Rouen was not, for example, a true centre of government, since kingship was still itinerant, and a vital part of Norman administration, the Exchequer, was based elsewhere, at Caen. However, the way in which Rouen was placed on a par with Paris in treaties from 1177 onwards, the construction of new walls and the other building work which went on there, all suggest that Rouen's development was being guided along a path analogous to that of Capetian Paris, and that its 13th-century history might have been similar, but for the collapse of 1203–4.[47] Henry II treated the town exceptionally generously before he became king of the English, granting it a charter of liberties in 1150–1, a document which provided a model for urban privileges throughout the Angevin lands in France.[48] It was the place at which the Angevin rulers tended to receive important visitors.[49] The Angevins also used Rouen Cathedral's status as *metropolis* to emphasise the continuity of their rule from that of the first Norman dukes. This contrived continuity appears first in Robert of Torigny's interpolation into the *Gesta Normannorum Ducum* where he has Henry I try to persuade his daughter Mathilda to agree to being buried in the cathedral.[50] Although Mathilda resisted persuasion and was eventually buried at Le Bec, her son William was buried there in 1164 and then, after an argument with the clergy of Le Mans, so was Henry II's son, the young King Henry, in 1183.[51] In a remarkable writ, dating from 1202, King John spoke of Rouen Cathedral as a church he held in special affection because his brothers and the early Norman dukes were buried there.[52] Recent archaeological discoveries at Boscherville have shown that the term *metropolis* was used on money minted at Rouen, whose date has been suggested as *c.* 1150.[53] The use of *metropolis* in the sources is so frequent that there looks to be a strong case for arguing that it is used as much with its classical meaning of 'provincial capital' as with its normal medieval one of 'the site of a metropolitan church'.[54]

When we turn to the social and economic substructure, two basic themes recur again and again, the royal/ducal court and the river Seine. After the early years of the Conqueror's reign, when, as we have seen, the citizens favoured a rival claimant to the duchy, and after the divisions caused by the wars in Robert Curthose's time, relations between successive Norman dukes and the town appear to have been good. The privileges described in the charter granted by Henry II in 1150–1, the earliest text of the so-called *Etablissements de Rouen*, were generous ones. They included the right for any citizen accused of a criminal offence not to be tried by anyone other than a ducal justice, with the trial taking place in the vicinity of Rouen, exemption from all ducal tallages and demands for taxation except with the citizens' consent, freedom from all customary exactions in fairs and markets in England and freedom from all customs on wine and blubber-fish in London. They also comprised complete control over trade passing through Rouen, with all transactions having to be conducted in the presence of a Rouen merchant, no one other than a merchant from Rouen being permitted to bring wine to a cellar in the town and no merchant who was not a citizen of the town allowed to transport goods through it.[55] The charter stated that these were the customs which had existed in the time of Henry I, and there are compelling reasons to believe that some of them were much older.[56] The town followed an evolution familiar to English urban historians whereby the chief official in the town of the duke's government, the *vicomte*, was, by the middle of the 12th century, a member of one of the town's leading families.[57] The surviving Norman Pipe Rolls show large parts of the farm unpaid, up until 1198, when a massive financial effort was made in the war against Philip Augustus. The town then not only paid the farm of 3,200 *livres angevins* in full, but also consented to tallages and other payments totalling almost £7,000.[58] In both the 11th and 12th centuries, several wealthy citizens can be shown to have become heavily involved in financial dealings with Norman, and later Anglo-Norman, government.[59]

A significant Jewish community existed in the city before 1066, although the earliest direct literary and archaeological evidence is post-Conquest. The building recently discovered, and commonly thought to be a synagogue, has been dated to before 1116, and, in the 12th century the Jewish quarter lay nearby, close to the modern Rue du Gros-Horloge.[60] Such was Rouen's pull as a centre of power that numerous ecclesiastical houses can be shown to have acquired property there, presumably to enable their representatives to attend the ducal court; these — quite remarkably — include the English abbey of Bury St Edmunds, which was given a house there in 1135, and also the archbishopric of York.[61] A perhaps inevitable consequence of Rouen's status was the existence there of an officially recognised and organised brothel by the 1160s, supervised by a member of the ducal household who was also responsible for the duke's prison and the gate-house of the castle.[62]

Rouen's position on that busy waterway, the river Seine, was the basis of its trade. As we have seen, Henry II's charter of privileges shows that the town's merchants had established a stranglehold on commercial traffic through Rouen, since only they could take goods through the town without paying toll.[63] The patterns of trade discernible in the 12th century were clearly a continuation of contacts established and built up during the 10th and 11th centuries. Trade with England was sufficiently important before 1066 for Rouen merchants to be given their own wharf in London by Edward the Confessor. An earlier text from the reign of King Aethelred the Unready states that the two basic commodities of Rouen's commerce were wine and blubber-fish, that is, whale-meat and associated products, a well-established Norman industry in the 11th century.[64] In the 12th century, the texts reveal both the continued existence and the further development of the far-flung trading connections implied by Dudo of Saint-Quentin and that basic commodities were transported into the town from other parts of Normandy.[65] There was, for example, a coastal trade which supplied corn from the cereal-growing region of the plain of Caen.[66] An inquest into the customs of the mills of Rouen, dated 28 September 1199, shows that bread was regularly brought into the town by water and sold at its markets.[67] All the trade was supported by a certain amount of local industry; the guild of the cordwainers, for instance, is first mentioned during Henry I's reign.[68] It is finally worth mentioning that Rouen's merchants had a monopoly of Normandy's trade with Ireland, with the exception that one boat per year went to Cherbourg.[69]

Far and away the most important commodity in Rouen's commerce looks to have been wine. The town would appear to have been one of the greatest centres of the wine trade in western Europe. In both 1180 and 1195, for example, more than 100 *livres angevins* out of the farm of Rouen were devoted to the purchase of wine for the royal court.[70] Wine apparently came to Normandy by ship from Poitou, Gascony and Anjou, across land from Berry and Anjou, and by river from the Ile-de-France, as well as from the great Norman vineyards down the Seine towards Paris.[71] Given this network of communications, it is reasonable to think of Rouen as the centre of distribution for wine throughout Normandy, and probably for much of southern and eastern England as well. This was probably the case from a relatively early date, since, as we have seen, a regular trade in wine between Rouen and London existed in c. 1000, and since the abbey of Saint-Etienne of Caen received a cellar on the Seine at Rouen in the 11th century, the abbey of Cerisy was given an allowance of wine there in 1034, and Henry I inaugurated an annual grant of wine from Rouen to the abbey of Le Bec in 1122.[72] The 13th-century evidence — when the town's trade with

England was affected by political conflict and might have been expected to be declining —
shows the town's merchants visiting all kinds of places.[73] The wine was also evidently highly
prized, since in 1200 King John reserved to himself the right to select two barrels of wine
from every ship from Rouen which docked in London.[74]

The first part of this article supported the well-established view that it was the Scandinavian settlements which made Rouen into a great and prosperous city. The matter is one
which has been much discussed, even if it remains controversial. I do not myself share the
extreme 'Scandinavian' theories recently advanced by Professor Eleanor Searle, but neither
is 'continuity' an entirely sufficient description of the town's history. It is evident that
growth took place from a substantial existing base. An important topic which has been
much less discussed is Rouen's place within the union of Normandy and England. The only
modern discussions appear in some important studies by Professor Lucien Musset. What
emerges from Musset's work is the contention that the citizens of Rouen did not play a
major part in the colonisation of Britain and did not establish a significant commercial base
in the English kingdom — the Jews possibly excepted. The most famous migrant from
Rouen to England was of course Gilbert Becket, the father of St Thomas, but he was one of
Rouen's failures, not someone who was enterprisingly expanding his business from a strong
base within the Norman town. Some of the richest Rouen families were for a time associated
with the operation of England's government under Henry I and under the Angevins, but the
associations were brief and the business apparently neither especially profitable nor worth
maintaining.[75] There was, in fact, a trend in the later 12th century whereby Englishmen
became established in the upper reaches of Rouen society; an original writ of Henry I
addressed to 'all my faithful French and English of Rouen' may well represent the formulaic
carelessness of a chancery scribe, but by the late 12th century, the English 'Hampton' family
had certainly established a base in Rouen.[76] Professor Musset censures his fellow Normans
for complacency and especially for their failure to compete with the Flemings for the trade
of 12th-century England.[77] This seems to me rather unfair. We should not expect miracles
from the medieval citizens of Rouen. The Rouennais in truth did very well out of the
Anglo-Norman connection, and they did this without needing to establish formal cross-
Channel trading links or engage in commercial colonisation. We need also to remember that
the great Norman migration to England was over by 1100 at the latest and that it never
included many whose power and wealth were securely founded in the duchy, and whose
reasons for not taking part were complex, but entirely rational ones.[78] Eleventh- and
12th-century Rouen was an exceptionally prosperous city on the basis of its situation on the
Seine. It was, perhaps, more a centre of power and trade than a dynamic force for unification
across the seas or for the economic development of the union of Normandy and England.
The trading connection of England and Flanders was well established before 1066 and the
12th-century Flemings became formidable commercial competitors. The currents of economic development and change do not necessarily follow the same course as political ones.[79]

On 24 June 1204 the town fell to the army of the French King Philip Augustus. This event
signified the effective end of the union of Normandy and England. Thereafter Rouen lost the
political importance which it had derived from its place at the heart of Norman and Angevin
power. Professor Musset is censorious; the citizens preferred a quiet life to making a fight to
the end.[80] This is again surely unfair. As we saw above, the 1198 Norman Pipe Roll shows
the town making a substantial contribution to the defence of the beleaguered province,
despite the fact that its charter of liberties indicates that it was under no obligation to do so;
the loss of the equivalent Rolls from other years is likely to conceal other major grants.[81]
The defences of Normandy had already collapsed by the beginning of June 1204. Many
Norman nobles had come to Rouen to make a last stand. Their ruler, King John, had retired

to England. An assembly sought his assistance, but none was forthcoming. Only after this did the citizens bow to the inevitable and surrender on terms. As in 1144, the town capitulated after the rest of Normandy had fallen; in 1174 and 1193 when direct assaults had been made by the French, they had been beaten off.[82] In 1204 there was no hope left. One of Philip Augustus's acts during the years which followed was to destroy the castle of the duke of Normandy within the town, and replace it with a large new castle of his own on a site which dominated Rouen from above. Security was surely not the only consideration which influenced this change. He was also demonstrating symbolically that an era truly had come to an end.[83]

ACKNOWLEDGEMENTS

I would like to thank Lindy Grant who encouraged me to give this survey of Rouen's history to the Conference, Bernard Gauthiez for his helpful comments and for allowing me to consult his *thèse de doctorat* which will be the basis for a major contribution to our understanding of the history of medieval Rouen, and Vivienne Miguet of the Archives départementales de la Seine-Maritime for sending me several maps of Rouen which have proved extremely useful.

REFERENCES

1. *The Ecclesiastical History of Orderic Vitalis*, ed. and trans. M. Chibnall, 6 vols (Oxford 1969–80), IV, 224.
2. For a convenient printed text of the part of the poem which refers to Rouen, C.H. Haskins, *Norman Institutions* (Cambridge, Mass. 1918), 144, n. 72. For the full text, C. Richard, *Notice sur l'ancienne bibliothèque des échevins de Rouen* (Rouen 1845), 37. Rouen's Roman origins feature in other 12th-century literary sources, *Orderic*, VI, 280–2; Stephen of Rouen, *Draco Normannicus: Chronicles of the Reigns of Stephen, Henry II and Richard I*, 4 vols, ed. R. Howlett (RS, LXXXII, 1884–9), II, 601–2.
3. The treaties of 1177 and 1180 are conveniently printed in *Recueil des actes de Henri II, roi d'Angleterre et duc de Normandie*, ed. L. Delisle and E. Berger, 4 vols (Paris 1909–27), II, nos DVI, DL, with references there to other printed texts. The crucial passage is: ... *ita quod illi quos Henricus rex Anglie prefecero ad gubernandum terras meas, cum omni posse suo iuvabunt ad defendum terras Lodovici regis Francie domini mei, quemadmodum terras meas defenderent si civitas mea Rothomagi obsessa esset, et eodem modo ...*, with a similar passage referring to Paris following on. See also, J.C. Holt, 'The End of the Anglo-Norman Realm', *Proceedings of the British Academy*, LXI (1975), 244.
4. Dudo of Saint-Quentin, *De Moribus et Actis Primorum Normannie Ducum*, ed. J. Lair (Caen 1865), 127.
5. L. Musset, 'La Seine normande et le commerce maritime du IIIᵉ au XIᵉ siècle', *Revue des sociétés savantes de Haute-Normandie*, no. 53 (1969), 10. See also, *idem*, 'Rouen au temps des Francs et sous les Ducs (Vᵉ siècle–1204)', *Histoire de Rouen*, ed. M. Mollat (Toulouse 1979), 42–3.
6. *Orderic*, III, 36.
7. William of Newburgh, *Historia Rerum Anglicarum*, in *Chronicles of the Reigns of Stephen, Henry II and Richard I*, I, 190–1.
8. A. Sadourny, 'L'époque communale (1204–début XIVᵉ siècle)', in Mollat, *Histoire de Rouen*, 78–9.
9. For the Porte Saint-Martin, 153, describing an incident which he wishes to attribute to the early 10th century. For the Porte Cauchoise, Fauroux, *Recueil*, no. 34.
10. *Orderic*, III, 36. Note also that Orderic says that duke Robert Curthose left the town by the east gate in order to reach the district of Malpalu, which is around the church of Saint-Maclou, ibid., IV, 222.
11. Note that Dudo, 170, says that the abbey of Saint-Ouen was *in suburbio civitatis*. For the enlargement of the walls, Musset, 'Rouen', 54.
12. *Orderic*, VI, 466; Fauroux, *Recueil*, no. 52.
13. For the palisade, Musset, 'Rouen', 54.
14. ADSM, 14 H 18, p. 230; B. Gauthiez, 'Hypothèses sur la fortification de Rouen au onzième siècle. Le donjon, la tour de Richard II et l'enceinte de Guillaume', *Anglo-Norman Studies*, XIV (1992), 74–6.
15. Fauroux, *Recueil*, no. 36. It is unlikely that a bridge could have existed during the period that Viking ships were sailing up and down the river.
16. B. Gauthiez, 'La logique de l'espace urbain. Formation et évolution: le cas de Rouen', 2 vols (Thèse de doctorat nouveau régime, Ecole des Hautes Etudes en Sciences Sociales, 1991), I, 133–5.

17. For the stone bridge, 'The Chronicle of Robert of Torigni', in *Chronicles of the Reign of Stephen, Henry II and Richard I*, IV, 151, 233.
18. *Chartes de l'abbaye de Jumièges (v. 825 à 1204) conservées aux archives de la Seine-Inférieure*, 2 vols, ed. J.-J. Vernier (Rouen and Paris 1916), I, no. LXI. For fortified towers at Bayeux, 'Vita beati Gaufridi secundi abbatis Saviniacensis', ed. E. P. Sauvage, *Analecta Bollandiana*, I (1882), 392–5. For the suggestion that scholars have been too accepting of this source's value for 11th-century conditions, D. Bates, 'Notes sur l'aristocratie normande: I. Hugues, évêque de Bayeux (1011 env.–1049)', *Annales de Normandie*, XXIII (1973), 19.
19. 'The Chronicle of Robert of Torigni', 106; Gauthiez, 'Hypothèses sur la fortification de Rouen', 63–70.
20. The excavations of Jacques Le Maho will make a major contribution to our knowledge of early Rouen. There is a good survey of the state of knowledge in the late 1980s in N. Gauthier, 'Rouen pendant le haut Moyen Age (650–850)', *La Neustrie. Les pays au nord de la Loire de 650 à 850. Colloque historique international, Rouen, 1985*, 2 vols (Sigmaringen 1989), I, 1–19. On the early history of Rouen, see also, Musset, 'La Seine normande', 8, and *idem*, 'Rouen', 37–44.
21. The extent of Frankish control in late 9th- and early 10th-century Rouen is now controversial. For the optimistic assessment, see *inter alia*, Musset, 'Rouen', 38; D. Bates, *Normandy before 1066* (London 1982), 10–11. The fragility of the evidence has been stressed by E. Searle, *Predatory Kinship and the Creation of Norman Power* (Los Angeles and Berkeley 1988), 3–4, where the notion that there was still a Frankish count at Rouen is rejected.
22. Thus, the grant of 'certain districts (*pagi*) bordering the sea-coast, along with the city of Rouen' mentioned in Flodoard, *Historia Remensis Ecclesiae*, in *Monumenta Germaniae Historica, Scriptores*, XIII (1881), 577. Dudo consistently treats Rouen as the political centre of 10th-century Norman power, e.g. Dudo, 183, 185, 188, 193, 194, 200.
23. K. F. Werner, 'Quelques observations au sujet du début du "duché" de Normandie', *Droit privé et institutions régionales: Etudes historiques offertes à Jean Yver* (Paris 1976), 696–9.
24. Musset, 'Rouen', 40; P. Périn, 'Les objets vikings du Musée des Antiquités de la Seine-Maritime', *Recueil d'études en hommage à Lucien Musset* (Cahiers des Annales de Normandie, XXIII, Caen 1990), 161–88.
25. 'Rouen resta une ville franque, mais incorporée à une formation politique dont la classe dirigeante était scandinave: cela orienta de manière décisive l'histoire normande', Musset, 'Rouen', 40.
26. In general, Musset, 'Rouen', 40. Also, L. Musset, 'Pour l'histoire sociale d'une habitude onomastique. Essai sur l'apparition des noms de rues dans les villes normandes (XIe–XIIIe siècles), L. Musset *et al.*, *Aspects de la société et de l'économie dans la Normandie médiévale (Xe–XIIIe siècles)* (Caen 1988), 133–5, 139.
27. Dudo, 221; *Les annales de Flodoard*, ed. P. Lauer (Paris 1906), *s.a.*, 943.
28. See the eloquent appeal in Périn, 'Les objets vikings', 184.
29. For a convenient summary, Bates, *Normandy before 1066*, 12, 28–30, relying on F. Dumas-Dubourg, *Le trésor de Fécamp et le monnayage en Francie occidentale pendant la seconde moitié du Xe siècle* (Paris 1971), *passim*.
30. L. Shopkow, 'The Carolingian World of Dudo of Saint-Quentin', *Journal of Medieval History*, XV (1989), 28–9.
31. O. Guillot, 'La conversion des Normands peu après 911', *Cahiers de civilisation médiévale*, XXIV (1981), 216–17.
32. L. Musset, 'Le satiriste Garnier de Rouen et son milieu (début du XIe siècle)', *Revue du Moyen Age latin*, X (1954), 252–3. In general, Musset, 'La Seine normande', 9.
33. Musset, 'Garnier de Rouen', 249–54. On the distribution of coins, L. Musset, 'Les relations extérieures de la Normandie du IXe au XIe siècle, d'après quelques trouvailles monétaires récentes', *Annales de Normandie*, IV (1954), 31–8. The theme of migration between the Scandinavian colonies in N.W. Europe has recently been re-emphasised by G. Fellows Jensen, 'Scandinavian Personal Names in Foreign Fields', *Recueil d'études en hommage à Lucien Musset*, 149–59.
34. See the evidence surveyed in Guillot, 'La conversion des Normands', 101–16.
35. Bates, *Normandy before 1066*, 13–15; Searle, 79–86.
36. Périn, 'Les objets vikings', 173–4.
37. *Orderic*, II, 358.
38. *Guillaume de Poitiers, Gesta Guillelmi Ducis Normannorum et Regis Anglorum*, ed. R. Foreville (Paris 1952), 20; *Orderic*, IV, 220–6.
39. A visit to Rouen can be assumed in 1067 since William is known to have visited Jumièges (*Annales de Saint-Pierre de Jumièges*, ed. Dom. J. Laporte (Rouen 1954), 57), Le Vaudreuil (*Regesta Regum Anglo-Normannorum*, I, ed. H. W. C. Davis (Oxford, 1913), no. 6a) and Lyons-la-Forêt, BN, MS latin 12878, ff. 230–231. For 1074, *Regesta*, I, no. 75; F. Lot, *Etude critique sur l'abbaye de Saint-Wandrille* (Paris 1913), recueil des chartes, no. 38. For 1080, *Regesta*, I, no. 123. For 1084, *Chartes de Jumièges*, I, no. 33; ADSM, 14 H 344.

40. *Regesta Regum Anglo-Normannorum*, II, ed. C. Johnson and H. A. Cronne (Oxford 1956), xxx.

41. 'The Chronicle of Robert of Torigni', 106.

42. Stephen of Rouen, *Draco Normannicus*, II, 713.

43. See now, M. Chibnall, 'The Empress Matilda and Bec-Hellouin', in *Anglo-Norman Studies*, X (1988), 43–5; *idem*, *The Empress Matilda* (Oxford 1991), 151–3. Also, Delisle, introduction to *Recueil des actes de Henri II*, I, 139–44, 169–71.

44. ... *reddiderunt se et turrem, videlicet Gaufrido antea Andegavenisi comiti, iam exinde Normannorum duci*, 'The Chronicle of Robert of Torigni', 148.

45. Ibid., 151, 233.

46. Haskins, *Norman Institutions*, 143–4. He bases this assertion on the increased number of charters issued at Rouen.

47. This theme receives more extensive development in Dr Lindy Grant's paper. It is worth noting that Rouen's importance under the Angevins has long been recognised. Note, for example, the description of the period from 1145 to 1204 as 'les soixante plus belles années de l'histoire de Normandie' and as the time when 'Rouen parvient à l'apogée de sa puissance', E. de Fréville, *Mémoire sur le commerce maritime de Rouen depuis les temps les plus reculés jusqu'à la fin du XVIᵉ siècle*, 2 vols (Rouen and Paris 1857), I, 107.

48. *Regesta Regum Anglo-Normannorum*, III, ed. H. A. Cronne and R. H. C. Davis (Oxford 1968), no. 729. The classic study of its dissemination throughout the Angevin lands and also of the complex diplomatic problems which it and later versions pose is A. Giry, *Les Etablissements de Rouen*, 2 vols (Paris 1883).

49. It is obvious from Delisle and Berger, *Recueil des actes de Henri II*, that far more charters were issued at Rouen by Henry II than anywhere else. For meetings with neighbouring princes at Rouen, see 'The Chronicle of Robert of Torigni', 186, 224.

50. Robert of Torigni's interpolations in *Guillaume de Jumièges, Gesta Normannorum Ducum*, ed. J. Marx (Rouen and Paris 1913), 304–5.

51. 'The Chronicle of Robert of Torigni', 221, 306. The description of the young King Henry's reasoning is especially interesting: *Disposuerunt ante mortem suam, ut corpus eius sepeliretur, ubi iacent primi antecessores eius, id est Rollo et Willelmus Longa Spata, filius eius, duces Normannorum*, ...

52. *Rotuli Litterarum Patentium in Turri Londiniensi asservati*, ed. T. Duffus Hardy (London 1835), 19.

53. J. Pilet-Lemière, 'Deniers inédits de Rouen à la légende METROPOLIS', *Bulletin de la Société française de numismatique*, V (1985), 639–40.

54. Thus William of Poitiers calls Rouen *sui principatus caput* and *in metropolim suam*, *Guillaume de Poitiers*, 102, 256, with a discussion of the subject at p. 20 n. 2. Dr Marjorie Chibnall indicates that Orderic uses *metropolis* in the sense of both 'metropolitan city' and 'chief city', *Orderic*, I, 322, and it is certainly used with the second meaning to describe Rouen in ibid., IV, 220, 226; VI, 222, 282. See also, Robert of Torigni in *Gesta Normannorum Ducum*, 304–5.

55. *Regesta*, III, no. 729.

56. Giry, *Les Etablissements*, I, 25, dated them back to William the Conqueror. Gauthiez, 'Rouen', 148–51, suggests that many may have originated in the time of duke Richard II.

57. L. Musset, 'Une aristocratie d'affaires anglo-normande après la conquête', *Etudes Normandes*, XXXV, no. 3 (1986), 10–11, summarises knowledge of the careers of William Trentegerons and Emma the *vicomtesse*.

58. *Magni Rotuli Scaccarii Normanniae sub Regibus Angliae*, 2 vols, ed. T. Stapleton (London 1840), I, 70–1; II, 154–5, 304–5, 306–8. I am grateful to Vincent Moss for a discussion of the Rouen entries on the Norman Pipe Rolls.

59. L. Musset, 'A-t-il existé en Normandie au XIᵉ siècle une aristocratie d'argent?', *Annales de Normandie*, IX (1959), 290–2; *idem*, 'Une aristocratie d'affaires anglo-normande', 9–12.

60. The basic account of this remarkable discovery is B. Blumenkranz, 'Un ensemble synagogal à Rouen: 1096–1116', *Comptes rendus de l'Académie des inscriptions et belles-lettres* (1976), 663–87, which also contains an account of the Jewish community in Rouen. See also, M. Chibnall, *The World of Orderic Vitalis* (Oxford 1984), 152–61.

61. On Norman bishoprics and religious houses, Musset, 'Rouen', 47. See also, *Regesta*, II, no. 1913; Gauthiez, 'Rouen', 130, citing Rouen, BM, MS 1193 (Y.44), no. 228.

62. *Recueil des actes de Henri II*, I, no. CCXII.

63. *Regesta*, III, no. 729.

64. On these developments, see Musset, 'La Seine normande', 11. For Edward the Confessor's grant, *Regesta*, III, no. 729.

65. There is a useful collection of references to long-distance trading connections in S. Deck, 'Les marchands de Rouen sous les Ducs', *Annales de Normandie*, VI (1956), 252. For Dudo, above, p. 1.

66. 'Miracula sancti Wulfranni', *Acta Sanctorum*, ed. J. Bollandus *et al.* (Antwerp and Brussels 1643–), March, III, 151.

67. A. Teulet, *Layettes du Trésor des Chartes*, I (Paris 1863), no. 500.

68. *Regesta*, II, no. 1695; Musset, 'Rouen', 67–8.

69. *Regesta*, III, no. 729.

70. *Magni Rotuli*, I, 69–70; II, 153–5.

71. The regions from which wine was transported are made clear by the economic blockade imposed by Philip Augustus, *Recueil des actes de Philippe-Auguste*, 4 vols, ed. H.-F. Delaborde, J. Monicat *et al.* (Paris 1916–79), II, no. 864; Musset, 'Rouen', 69–70.

72. *Les actes de Guillaume le Conquérant et de la reine Mathilde pour les abbayes caennaises*, ed. L. Musset (Caen 1967), no. 10; Fauroux, *Recueil*, no. 64; *Regesta*, II, no. 1290.

73. A. Sadourny, 'Les marchands normands en Angleterre au lendemain de la conquête de 1204', *Cahiers d'études médiévales*, I (1979), 138.

74. See the text cited in De Fréville, *Mémoire sur le commerce maritime de Rouen*, I, 119, n. 1.

75. See especially, Musset, 'Rouen', 59–61; *idem*, 'Une aristocratie d'affaires anglo-normande', 9–12, 15–17.

76. *Regesta*, II, no. 1964; Musset, 'Une aristocratie d'affaires anglo-normande', 11–12.

77. Ibid., 17.

78. On this theme, D. Bates, 'Normandy and England after 1066', *English Historical Review*, CIV (1989), 853–7.

79. Note the observations of R.-H. Bautier, '"Empire Plantagenêt" ou "Espace Plantagenêt". Y-a-t-il eu une civilisation du monde Plantagenêt?', *Cahiers de civilisation médiévale*, XXIX (1986), 140.

80. Musset, 'Rouen', 46: 'Ce fut la fin de l'indépendance normande et du rôle de Rouen comme capitale. On peut s'étonner de la facilité avec laquelle ils y renoncèrent: leur lassitude, leur exaspération leur firent préférer la paix à tout'.

81. Above, p. 6.

82. For clear accounts of the sieges of 1174 and 1193, W. L. Warren, *Henry II* (London 1973), 135–6; F. M. Powicke, *The Loss of Normandy* (2nd edn, Manchester 1960), 96–7.

83. For the political context, L. Musset, 'Quelques problèmes posés par l'annexion de la Normandie au domaine royal français', R.-H. Bautier (ed.), *La France de Philippe Auguste: Le temps des mutations* (Paris 1982), 299–300.

La ré-occupation planifiée de la Cité de Rouen au haut Moyen Age*

Par Bernard Gauthiez

Le plan de la partie centrale de Rouen, autour de la cathédrale, est parfois présenté comme un exemple de persistence de tracés de rues antiques, du fait de l'organisation des rues suivant une trame orthogonale. Dans son état actuel, ce quartier a toutefois une forme assez différente de ce qu'elle fut jusqu'au début de notre siècle, la Reconstruction après 1945 n'ayant pas respecté les tracés antérieurs (Fig. 1).

La disposition médiévale des rues à l'intérieur du *castrum* de Rouen, telle que nous la donne pour l'essentiel le plan cadastral de 1827, présentait une physionomie étonnamment régulière (Fig. 2). Deux axes structuraient cette partie de la ville. L'un, nord–sud, était formé des rues Grand-Pont et des Carmes. L'autre, est–ouest, est la rue du Gros-Horloge. De part et d'autre de ce dernier axe étaient, et sont encore pour certaines, placées symétriquement des rues parallèles, à des espacements rigoureusement identiques. Il en est ainsi des rues aux Juifs et aux Ours, à 88 m au nord et au sud de la rue du Gros-Horloge, et des rues Saint-Lô, dans son prolongement vers l'est, et du Fardeau à 145 m. Dans la partie est du *castrum*, la symétrie est respectée par les rues Saint-Nicolas et de la Madeleine à 115 m au nord et au sud de l'axe; enfin les rues du Change et Saint-Romain, dans son prolongement restitué vers l'ouest, sont un peu moins précisément disposées à environ 44 m de l'axe de la rue du Gros-Horloge. Les mesures sont prises au débouché des rues sur l'axe rue des Carmes–rue Grand-Pont.

La régularité de ce schéma ne peut être due au hasard. Elle implique une mise en place volontaire en un temps limité.

Elle n'est pas antique. En effet la rue du Gros-Horloge n'existait pas à cette époque; des murs gallo-romains qui la traversaient ont été rencontrés.[1] De même, la partie nord de la rue des Carmes, que l'enceinte du IVe siècle recoupait, ce qui montre qu'il n'y avait pas de porte antique en ce point, ne correspond pas non plus à une rue antique.[2] Des autres rues de la cité, seule la rue Saint-Nicolas correspond sans doute à une voie gallo-romaine. C'est très peu, et ce que l'on peut restituer du réseau des rues gallo-romaines montre qu'il ne peut pas être à l'origine du réseau des rues médiévales (Fig. 3).[3]

Par ailleurs, la création des rues du Gros-Horloge et du nord de la rue des Carmes fut nécessairement accompagnée d'une part de leur prolongation à l'extérieur du *castrum*, la rue du Gros-Horloge jusqu'à rejoindre la rue Cauchoise, et la rue des Carmes avec la rue Beauvoisine, et d'autre part du percement de portes dans le mur d'enceinte.

L'ensemble paraît d'autre part lié à la cathédrale antique. Les fouilles de Jacques Le Maho au nord de la cathédrale actuelle ont livré les restes d'un édifice du IVe siècle faisant partie de la cathédrale primitive.[4] Des fouilles plus sommaires menées antérieurement par Georges Lanfry avaient rencontré, semble-t-il, d'autres éléments de cette cathédrale, peut-être appartenant à un édifice construit par l'évêque Victricius à la fin du IVe siècle.[5] L'ensemble était donc certainement organisé en deux basiliques, réunies par un *atrium* dont des vestiges ont été mis au jour (Fig. 4). Une voie antique a été supprimée lors de la construction de cet *atrium*. Son axe est proche de celui de la rue du Gros-Horloge, mais cependant suffisamment décalé vers le sud pour que l'on puisse exclure qu'elle en soit à l'origine. L'axe central de la cathédrale double primitive est donc très proche de l'axe est–ouest de la composition, axe à

FIG. 1.   La partie centrale de Rouen vers 1980. L'emplacement du mur du Bas-Empire
est indiqué par un trait épais, et celui des portes probables par des ronds

partir duquel les nouvelles rues et des portes leur correspondant ont été positionnées, et le
castrum de Rouen ré-occupé. Ceci semble indiquer une volonté de composition par rapport
à un édifice préexistant.

DATATION

La régularité de l'ensemble montre qu'il a été mis en œuvre en un temps relativement court.
De ce fait, une datation relative à un élément topographique étroitement associé peut nous
renseigner sur la datation de l'ensemble. Les indices à notre disposition sont cependant peu
concluants, et font cruellement regretter l'absence de fouilles, tout du moins sur les rues de la
partie ouest du *castrum*.

Cette intervention ne peut être antique, on l'a vu, du fait de son indépendance par rapport au réseau des rues gallo-romaines.

Sa symétrie axiale montre qu'elle est vraisemblablement antérieure à la reconstruction de la cathédrale sur le site actuel, à l'époque romane, car celle-ci brise la symétrie de l'ensemble initial. Construite à partir de la fin du Xe siècle sur un axe reprenant celui de l'édifice sud de la cathédrale double primitive, la cathédrale romane, qui précède sur son site l'édifice que nous connaissons et amène la destruction de la basilique nord, est consacrée en 1063 (Fig. 4).[6] Les portes de la ville associées à l'opération[7] sont mentionnées peut-être dès 946 pour la porte Beauvoisine,[8] rue des Carmes, et pas avant le XIIIe siècle pour la porte

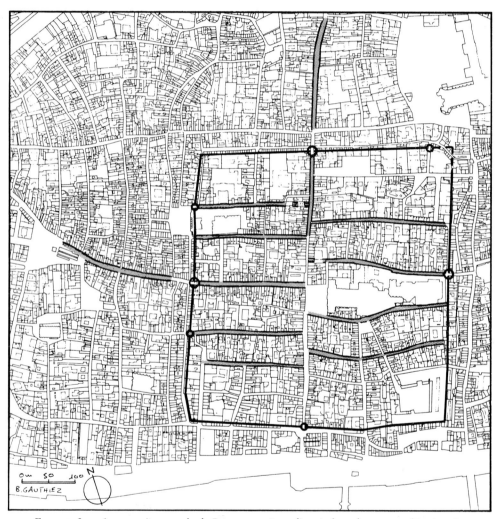

FIG. 2.   La même partie centrale de Rouen en 1827, d'après le cadastre napoléonien. Le réseau des rues à l'intérieur du *castrum*, organisé symétriquement par rapport à l'axe constitué par la rue du Gros-Horloge, est indiqué en grisé. Les nouvelles portes induites par ce réseau prennent place au centre des côtés de l'enceinte, à l'ouest, au nord à l'est

Massacre rue du Gros-Horloge, alors qu'elle n'a plus de fonction militaire.[9] La porte rue Saint-Romain, à l'est, est mentionnée vers 1042.[10] Le patronage de la paroisse Saint-Michel, au débouché de la rue du Gros-Horloge sur la place du Vieux-Marché, est confirmé en 1179 par le pape Alexandre III.[11] Il pourrait avoir été donné en dotation à l'abbaye du Mont-Saint-Michel après sa fondation en 709, ou à l'occasion de sa refondation vers 965. Des éléments de l'église paroissiale Saint-Herbland à la croisée des deux axes principaux, datant du XIᵉ siècle, ont été reconnus en fouille en 1977.[12] L'église porte le nom d'Hermeland, moine de Jumièges, fondateur de l'abbaye d'Aindre, mort vers 720.[13]

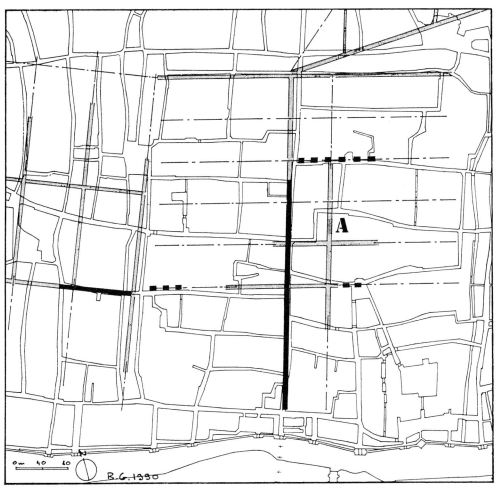

FIG. 3. Superposition de la trame viaire antique sur le réseau des rues en 1730. En noir sont indiqués les segments de rue dont l'emplacement n'a pas varié depuis l'Antiquité, attestant ainsi d'une permanence, au moins relative, de l'habitat. En A, la rue ne disparaît qu'au Xᵉ siècle. Cette figure montre qu'à l'évidence la période qui suit l'Antiquité a vu une extrème réduction de l'habitat, et que le plan de la ville médiévale doit bien peu aux tracés gallo-romains

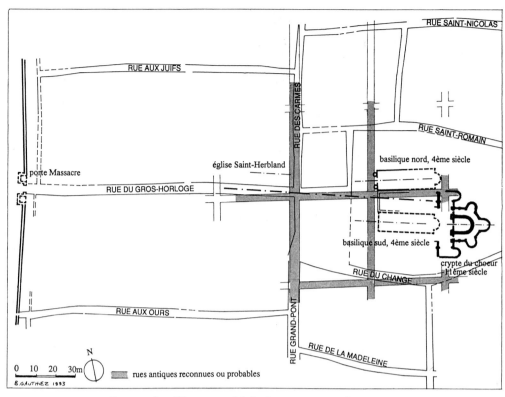

FIG. 4. Les éléments archéologiques au centre du *castrum*

La datation pourrait donc se situer entre 720, date de la mort d'Hermeland, et 946, première mention de la porte Beauvoisine. On peut d'autre part raisonnablement écarter l'hypothèse d'une réalisation lors des raids vikings, entre environ 840 et le début du Xe siècle.

L'opération a donc pu être réalisée soit entre environ 720 et 840, soit par l'un des premiers ducs normands.

D'autres arguments, d'ordres historique et architectural, plaidaient, avant de récentes découvertes, pour la première période.

Jacques Le Maho a rencontré au nord de la cathédrale un édifice qui paraît avoir été une salle commune du chapitre. Il fut, semble-t-il, construit à l'occasion de la réforme canoniale, introduite par l'archevêque de Metz, Chrodegang, vers 742–66.[14] Les abords de la cathédrale furent l'objet, au milieu du VIIIe siècle, d'autres réaménagements importants, avec notamment la construction de grands *claustra* au nord et au sud de l'ensemble double du IVe siècle. Or, entre 753–5 et 771–2, l'évêque métropolitain de Rouen est Remigius, fils de Charles Martel.[15] Il y est chargé de la mise en place de la réforme canoniale. On sait aussi qu'il était très proche de Chrodegang.[16] Il est remarquable, dans ce contexte, que le plan de la ré-occupation du *castrum* de Rouen soit si proche de celui de l'abbaye de Lorsch, dont Chrodegang participe étroitement à la fondation en 760–4.[17] Il est difficile de ne voir là qu'une coïncidence. On est tenté de penser que l'on a pu reprendre à Rouen un schéma type de l'architecture religieuse carolingienne, notamment avec la forme de la croix. Dans cette hypothèse, où les plans de l'abbaye de Lorsch et des rues de la cité de Rouen partageraient une commune conception symbolique, la datation de l'opération, ou du début de sa réalisation, paraissait pouvoir être contemporaine de Chrodegang et de Remigius à Rouen, vers 753–66. On a vu d'autre part que Remigius était le frère de Pépin le Bref, par ailleurs gouverneur de Neustrie entre 741 et 751. L'implication du roi était donc possible.[18]

Cette hypothèse paraissait d'autant plus plausible que ce développement de Rouen pouvait s'insérer dans un contexte international cohérent, qui lui donnait sa logique.

En effet, un certain nombre de villes portuaires des rives de la mer du Nord et de la Manche connaissent à partir du VIIe siècle un développement sensible, comme par exemple Dorestad, Quentovic,[19] ou encore Ipswich,[20] Londres,[21] et surtout Hamwic, fondée vers 688–726, située en face de Rouen.[22] Les produits dont la trace a été rencontrée dans les fouilles d'Exeter et d'Hamwic suggèrent d'autre part un lien privilégié avec la France du nord-ouest, et particulièrement avec Rouen.[23] Après un apogée au début du IXe siècle ces villes disparaissent sous les coups des vikings avant la fin de ce même siècle.

Il était, de plus, suprenant qu'aux ports anglais attestés sur la Manche ne correspondait sur le Continent que Quentovic comme établissement de taille comparable. Le *portus* Rouen existait très vraisemblablement dès le VIIe siècle,[24] mais était de taille modeste. La recherche historique à venir nous dira si, par exemple, il n'y a pas eu parmi les ports normands mentionnés au XIe siècle des antécédents plus précoces, tel Caen, qui pouvait être le *portus* de Bayeux.[25]

Quant à la période des premiers ducs normands, qui correspondait à la deuxième hypothèse pour la datation de l'opération, aucun élément ne plaidait directement en sa faveur. Le parallèle avec York, et dans une moindre mesure Dublin, était cependant possible. Il faut d'autre part garder à l'esprit l'absence de données archéologiques jusqu'il y a peu.

ETAT DE LA QUESTION EN 1992

Nous disposons maintenant de nouveaux éléments pour la datation de la ré-occupation planifiée du *castrum* de Rouen, il s'agit de résultats obtenus par Jacques Le Maho à l'occasion de ses fouilles autour de la cathédrale, et particulièrement sur la date à laquelle les rues Saint-Romain et du Change, directement au nord et au sud de la cathédrale, et donc partie de la composition régulière des rues à l'intérieur du *castrum*, auraient été percées. Dans l'attente d'une publication complète, et avec l'accord de Jacques Le Maho que je dois ici remercier, il est possible d'annoncer cette date: le deuxième quart du Xe siècle.

Cette datation concerne non pas les rues elles-mêmes, mais l'apparition de lotissements sur leur côté. Par ailleurs, seuls des éléments de datation concernant les rues de part et d'autre de la rue du Gros-Horloge, à l'ouest du *castrum*, permettraient de s'assurer de la datation de l'ensemble de l'opération.

Les éléments qui renvoient à une possible origine carolingienne de sa conception gardent cependant peut-être une partie de leur sens. Le concepteur de l'ensemble de l'opération, au début du Xe siècle, a pu s'inspirer de modèles carolingiens, ce qui ne serait pas si surprenant, et irait dans le sens de l'opinion de Lucien Musset sur cette époque.[26]

Pour conclure, le *castrum* de Rouen fut l'objet au cours du haut Moyen Age d'une opération de ré-occupation planifiée, concernant la plus grande part de son étendue, organisée suivant une forme symétrique. Sa remarquable régularité implique un fort volontarisme. Elle implique aussi à la fois une maîtrise foncière de la zone concernée, et des terrains assez dégagés. Les données archéologiques les plus récentes permettent d'avancer une datation du deuxième quart du Xe siècle.

Les implications historiques d'un tel évènement, en pleine époque viking, sont considérables, notamment en termes de parallélisme avec York et Winchester, de l'autre côté de la Manche. Les recherches en cours visent à mieux mettre en parallèle cette importante opération d'urbanisme, véritablement fondatrice du Rouen médiéval, avec d'une part les données archéologiques issues des fouilles sur la cathédrale, et d'autre part une relecture des textes portant sur ces périodes. C'est une histoire plus circonstanciée de la période viking qui se dessine, et devrait prochainement faire l'objet de publications.

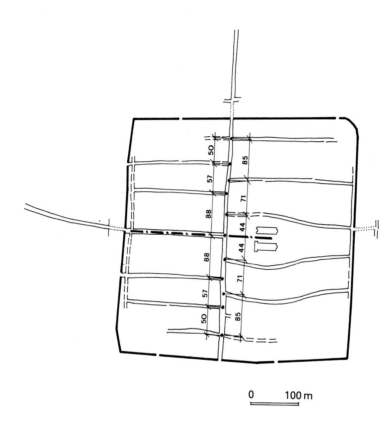

FIG. 5.   Structure des rues à l'intérieur du *castrum* de Rouen. L'axe majeur de la composition est constitué de la rue du Gros-Horloge, dont c'est là l'origine. Il est probablement déterminé par les dispositions architecturales de l'ensemble cathédral. Les intervals des rues disposées symétriquement de part et d'autre de la rue du Gros-Horloge sont donnés en mètres

Plan B. Gauthiez

0   100 m

REFERENCES

*   La majeure partie de la matière de cet article a été réunie dans le cadre de ma thèse, en cours en 1989, maintenant achevée: 'La logique de l'espace urbain, formation et évolution; le cas de Rouen', Ecole des Hautes Etudes en Sciences Sociales (Paris 1991).

1.   Ces murs ont été rencontrés de manière douteuse à proximité du Gros-Horloge, mais assurément aux alentours de l'ancienne église Saint-Herbland, *Journal de Rouen*, 20 janvier 1929; J.-M. Thaurin, *BCDA*, I (1868), 326.

2.   B. Gauthiez et al., *Rouen Gallo-Romain*, catalogue de l'exposition, Musée des Beaux-Arts (Rouen 1982), 29–34. Voir aussi *BCDA*, v (1879), 104; J.-M. Thaurin, 'Le vieux Rouen et ses monuments' (*MSAN*, XXIV, 1859), 269.

3.   Gauthiez (1991), 77–80, fig. 27. Cette indépendance des réseaux de rues antiques et médiévales est un argument décisif en faveur d'une planification médiévale, voir notamment à ce sujet M. Biddle et D. Hill, 'Late Saxon Planned Towns', *Antiq. J.*, LI (1971), 71–85.

4.   Jacques Le Maho, *Cathédrale Notre-Dame de Rouen, fouilles de la cour d'Albane*, plaquette des Musées départementaux de la Seine-Maritime et le Groupe de Recherche archéologique du Pays de Caux (Rouen 1988).

5.   G. Lanfry, 'La cathédrale dans la Cité romaine et la Normandie ducale', *Les Cahiers de Notre-Dame de Rouen*, numéro spécial (1956).

6.   Orderic Vital, 'Histoire écclésiastique', traduction publiée dans *Collection des mémoires relatifs à l'histoire de France*, éd. J. P. F. Guizot, 31 vols (Paris 1823–35), XXVI, 363. Dudon de St Quentin, *De moribus et actis primorum Normanniae ducum*, éd. J. Lair (*MSAN*, XXIII, Caen 1865), 171.

7.   La porte au sud de la ville, située près de l'église Saint-Martin-du-Pont attestée au VIe siècle, sur une rue antique conservée, est vraisemblablement antique.

8.   Dudon, 236, 254, 255.

9.   Bibliothèque municipale de Rouen, Tiroir 52, 1219.

10.   Fauroux, *Recueil*, no. 62, 187.

11.   *Chronique de Robert de Torigni*, éd. L. Delisle, 2 vols (SHN, Rouen 1872–3), II, 316.

12.   G. Dubois, *BCDA*, XXIX (1977), 96, 105, voir aussi *Gallia*, XXXVI (1978), fasc. I, 311–12.

13.   Dom J. Laporte, 'Saint-Hermeland', *L'abbaye de Saint-Wandrille de Fontenelle*, XV (1965), 8.

14.   N. Gauthier, 'Metz', *Province ecclésiastique de Trèves (Belgica Prima) (Topographie chrétienne des Cités de la Gaule des origines au milieu du VIIIe siècle*, I) (Paris 1986), II, 42.

15.   H. Platelle, 'Remigio', *Bibliotheca Sanctorum*, XI (Rome 1970), cols 113–14.

16.   Ils vont chercher en 753–4 des clercs de chant en Italie de façon à introduire le chant grégorien dans le royaume franc. Deux écoles, précisément à Metz et à Rouen, seront fondées. G. Hocquard, 'Chrodegang', *Catholicisme*, encyclopédie, ed. G. Jacquement, II (Paris 1949), cols 1094–6.

17.   La composition du plan est identique à Rouen et à Lorsch, où l'on retrouve deux axes, à peu près nord–sud et est–ouest. Une porte répond à chaque branche de la croix ainsi formée. A Rouen, l'intersection des axes se fait sur le parvis devant la cathédrale qui occupe la branche est. L'église paroissiale Saint-Michel occupe un emplacement à l'extrémité de la branche ouest. L'ensemble est de même symétrique par rapport à l'axe est–ouest. Le plan de l'abbaye de Lorsch est donné par C. Heitz, *L'architecture religieuse carolingienne* (Paris 1980), 44.

18.   J. Dubois, 'Numismatique mérovingienne et hagiographie', *Mélanges numismatiques d'archéologie et d'histoire offerts à Jean Lafaurie* (Paris 1980), 209.

19.   *Histoire de la France urbaine*, I (Paris 1980), 537. De récentes découvertes ont localisé le site de Quentovic. D. Hill et al., 'Quentovic defined', *Antiquity*, LXIV (1990), 51–8.

20.   D. A. Hinton, 'The Towns of Hampshire', *Anglo-Saxon Towns in Southern England*, éd. J. Haslam (Chichester, 1984), 162.

21.   T. Dyson and J. Schofield, 'Saxon London', *Anglo-Saxon Towns*, éd. Haslam, 290–6.

22.   Hinton, 'The Towns of Hampshire', 160, et P. Holdsworth, 'Saxon Southampton', *Anglo-Saxon Towns*, éd. Haslam, 331, 337. Sur la superficie de la ville, voir la communication récente de Mark Brisbane, 'Un centre d'activité portuaire et économique au VIIIe siècle: Hamwic', Colloque de la Société d'Archéologie Médiévale (Douai, 27 septembre 1991), à paraître.

23.   J. Allan, C. Henderson et R. Higham, 'Saxon Exeter', *Anglo-Saxon Towns*, éd Haslam, 405.

24.   Gauthiez (1991), 82–3.

25.   L'existence d'un *vicus* peut être considérée comme certaine à la suite des découvertes de ces dernières années à Caen, son étendue pouvant avoir dépassé 10 ha. Situé en bordure d'un fleuve navigable, à proximité de la mer, cet établissement a probablement eu une fonction de *portus*.

26.   L. Musset, 'Rouen au temps de Francs et sous les Ducs', *Histoire de Rouen*, ed. M. Mollat (Toulouse 1979), 40.

Le groupe épiscopal de Rouen du IVᵉ au Xᵉ siècle

Par Jacques Le Maho

Depuis 1985, un programme de recherches archéologiques est en cours sur le site de l'ancien groupe épiscopal de Rouen. Les investigations ont d'abord porté jusqu'en 1989 sur l'emplacement du cloître du chapitre, nommé 'cour d'Albane', au côté nord de l'église cathédrale. A la fin de l'année 1989, un second chantier de fouilles a été ouvert au côté sud de l'église, dans l'ancien 'aître Saint-Etienne', aujourd'hui connu sous le nom de 'cour des maçons'.

Ces recherches ont livré d'ores et déjà un nombre considérable d'informations sur l'histoire et la topographie du groupe épiscopal depuis l'Antiquité Tardive. L'analyse des données du terrain de même que l'étude du mobilier sont encore loin d'être achevées et quantités d'hypothèses ou d'interprétations restent à préciser. Il n'a donc pas paru possible de présenter ici autre chose qu'un descriptif sommaire des différentes séquences architecturales mises au jour. D'autre part, il a fallu limiter cette note à l'exposé d'une partie seulement des périodes représentées sur le site. C'est pourquoi nous nous bornerons à décrire l'évolution du groupe épiscopal depuis sa mise en place à la fin du IVᵉ siècle jusqu'à sa reconstruction au Xᵉ siècle.

Du IIIᵉ au début du IVᵉ siècle

Le secteur actuel de la cathédrale était occupé vers le milieu du IIIᵉ siècle par un quartier d'habitation constitué de maisons de pierre, de bois et de torchis s'étageant sur la pente de la terrasse alluviale.[1] Au cours du dernier tiers du IIIᵉ siècle, un grand incendie détruisit ce quartier ainsi que la plus grande partie de la ville antique. Sur les décombres de l'incendie furent mis en place peu après un ensemble de bâtiments à claire-voie de très vastes dimensions ouvrant sur des cours quadrangulaires et pourvus de ruelles d'accès empierrées. Ce complexe, qui s'étend au minimum de la rue Saint-Romain actuelle jusqu'à la rue du Change et du transept de la cathédrale jusqu'à la rue des Carmes, pourrait être lié à la construction du *castrum* et à l'installation d'un entrepôt de l'annone ou de quartiers militaires au centre de la ville close où, selon la *Notitia Dignitatum*, aurait séjourné une garnison d'*Ursarii*.

Vers 340–380

Les bâtiments à claire-voie sont en grande partie réoccupés par des installations privées. Les claires-voies sont obturées par des cloisons de bois et d'argile, on ajoute des murs de refend sur poteaux plantés. Dans le secteur nord (cour d'Albane), un tronçon de bâtiment est abattu pour l'édification d'un petit balnéaire comprenant un *praefurnium*, une salle chaude à chevet rectangulaire, une salle tiède à abside semi-circulaire, un vestibule et deux piscines froides avec un tuyau d'évacuation en plomb.[2] Ces thermes occupent l'extrémité de la cour d'une maison de bois et de torchis accompagnée d'un petit bâtiment de pierre légèrement excentré à usage de four, et derrière cette demeure s'étend un jardin avec un puits.

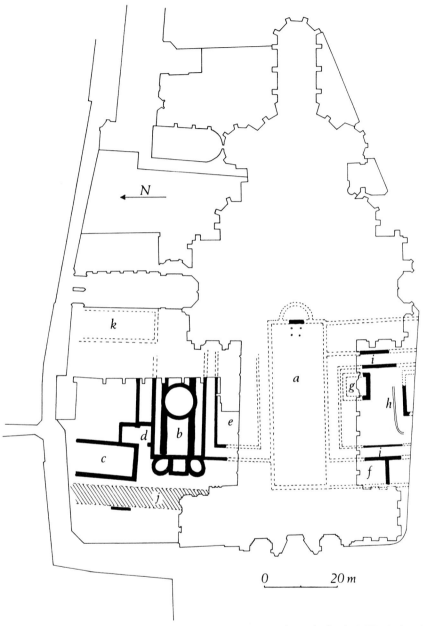

N

0   20 m

FIG. 1. Rouen, cathédrale Notre-Dame. Le groupe épiscoal vers la fin du VIIIe siècle et le début du IXe siècle. En (a) emplacement présumé de la basilique sud (église Notre-Dame); (b) basilique nord (église Saint-Etienne), le Westbau occupe l'emplacement du balnéaire du IVe siècle; (c) salle commune des chanoines (chauffoir?); (d) vestibule; (e) ancien *atrium* paléochrétien; (f) emplacement présumé de l'hôtellerie; (g) tour des archives(?); (h) aqueduc; (i) portiques; (j) rue; (k) cellier et réfectoire, bâtiment reconstruit au XIe siècle

Vers 395–396

Les données fournies par un abondant matériel monétaire ainsi que par les textes permettent de placer dans les dernières années du IVe siècle l'édification dans le secteur sud de la cour d'Albane d'un vaste édifice d'orientation est–ouest, identifiable selon toute probabilité avec la *basilica* élevée sur le site de la cathédrale de Rouen par l'évêque *Victricius* aux environs de 396.[3]

Les fouilles ont permis de dégager la partie occidentale de la nef de cet édifice sur toute sa largeur et sur une longueur de 25 m, le reste de la construction disparaissant vers l'est sous le corps de bâtiment gothique du chapitre. Les murs composés d'un petit appareil de calcaire et d'assises de briques, avec un massif de fondation à ressauts reposant sur une assise de pierre de libage, sont conservés au sud sur une hauteur de près d'1,50 m. L'intérieur du bâtiment était divisé en trois nefs par des colonnes de marbres reposant sur des murs de chaînages constitués de gros blocs de pierres calcaires insérés dans un tranchée.

La basilique fut élevée sur l'emplacement d'une maison du IVe siècle (cf. ci-dessus: *Vers 340–380*) dont ne fut conservé que le balnéaire, l'édifice chrétien venant s'insérer dans l'espace libéré par la démolition d'une aile de la demeure et sans doute de la galerie qui reliait originellement la partie résidentielle de cette maison aux bains. Les constructeurs de la basilique supprimèrent le mur oriental du balnéaire pour élever à cet endroit la façade occidentale de la nef, procédant ensuite à un raccord entre les deux constructions, à un réaménagement partiel de l'hypocauste et à la mise en place d'un petit emmarchement permettant de descendre du *tepidarium* dans la nef centrale de la basilique. Ce dernier détail montre que le souci de conserver le corps du bâtiment thermal répondait à une nécessité fonctionnelle et que les bains étaient destinés à devenir une annexe de l'édifice chrétien. Ils n'en continuèrent pas moins à assurer par la suite leur fonction thermale, comme l'indique une forte rubéfaction des soubassements de la basilique exposés à la chaleur de l'hypocauste. Ceci pose un problème d'interpétation. Sommes-nous en présence des thermes de l'évêque ou des clercs — ce qui soulèverait d'autres problèmes, l'édifice étant placé entre la basilique et la rue, à l'écart de tout bâtiment d'habitation — ou plutôt d'un complexe de salles destinées aux bains rituels avant le baptême, ce qui expliquerait sa liaison directe avec la nef de la basilique?[4]

Une des sources majeures de l'histoire de Rouen aux temps paléochrétiens est le *De Laude Sanctorum*, sermon qui fut prononcé par l'évêque Victrice en 395–6 lors d'une cérémonie qui s'était déroulée à la cathédrale pour célébrer l'arrivée d'un lot de reliques italiennes.[5] Le texte est non seulement essentiel pour l'étude des débuts du culte des reliques en Gaule septentrionale à la fin du IVe siècle, mais il fournit aussi pour Rouen des indications précieuses sur l'histoire des bâtiments. Victrice fait allusion en plusieurs endroits à des travaux de construction en cours sur le site de la cathédrale en 396. Il semble que les locaux existants étaient jugés trop petits et que l'on procédait alors à des travaux d'agrandissement, ou plus exactement à la construction d'une nouvelle basilique (*basilica, aula*). Victrice se félicite de l'achèvement prochain de cet édifice qui allait accueillir une partie au moins des reliques nouvellement arrivées dans la cathédrale, et se dit ainsi récompensé des efforts qu'il avait lui-même déployés pour acheter le terrain. Le chantier se déroule dans une atmosphère de grande ferveur religieuse, l'évêque n'hésitant pas à porter lui-même de lourdes pierres sur ses épaules: 'Que la terre boive notre sueur' ... 'Nous avons posé des fondements, nous avons tracé les murs en longueur' ...[6]

Comme on l'a signalé précédemment, la date de construction de la basilique de la cour d'Albane coïncide avec celle des travaux mentionnés dans le *De Laude Sanctorum*, et tout permet de penser que l'édifice mis au jour correspond à la *basilica* édifiée par l'évêque

Victrice. Ce bâtiment ne saurait cependant avoir été le premier lieu de culte du groupe épiscopal de Rouen. Un évêque de cette ville est mentionné dès 314 au concile d'Arles, et tout le contexte évoqué dans l'homélie de Victrice indique qu'il existait déjà un sanctuaire sur le site de la cathédrale en 395–6. C'est dans ce premier lieu de culte que se déroule la cérémonie de l'*adventus* des reliques, le nouvel édifice étant encore en travaux. Cette basilique primitive contient un certain nombre de reliques ou de *brandea* données à Rouen au cours des années précédentes, notamment une relique des saints Gervais et Protais reçue de saint Ambroise de Milan lors d'une entrevue à Vienne (Rhône) vers 386, où l'évêque de Rouen s'était rendu en compagnie de Martin de Tours.[7]

La basilique construite par Victrice vers 395–6 ne peut donc correspondre qu'à la seconde église du groupe épiscopal. L'hypothèse la plus probable paraît être celle d'un couple de basiliques élevées parallèlement l'une à l'autre, l'église la plus ancienne étant celle du sud, à l'emplacement de la nef de la cathédrale actuelle (cf. ci-après). L'œuvre de Victrice aurait donc consisté à bâtir une seconde basilique au côté nord de l'*ecclesia prima*, l'évêque de Rouen poursuivant ainsi la réalisation du groupe épiscopal suivant un schéma similaire à celui des églises jumelles de la cathédrale de Trèves par exemple, où le premier sanctuaire daterait de la période constantinienne, la seconde de la fin du IVe siècle.[8] Ce programme resta inachevé. Ce n'est qu'au cours du Ve siècle, sans doute bien après l'épiscopat de Victrice, que les deux basiliques seront réunies par un *atrium* (cf. ci-après).

Début du Ve siècle

Un violent incendie provoque la destruction des charpentes de la basilique, d'un petit bâtiment de bois situé au nord de celle-ci et des dépendances de la partie sud du groupe épiscopal. L'aspect du quartier en ressort profondément modifié. La parcelle située au nord de la basilique est convertie en jardin et seul subsiste en son centre l'ancien puits de la *domus* du IIIe siècle. Une couche de terre noire se développe sur ce terrain, des fosses à compost sont creusées çà et là. Le secteur sud du groupe épiscopal connaît une transformation similaire, et l'on y voit apparaître une couche de terre végétale traversée d'une multitude de canaux de racines et plusieurs fosses à compost: la parcelle est sans doute alors convertie en potager.

La désertion d'un certain nombre d'îlots aux abords de la cathédrale vers le début du Ve siècle a sans doute facilité la réunion des deux églises du groupe épiscopal. Jusqu'à cette époque en effet, les deux édifices étaient séparés l'un de l'autre par une voie publique correspondant à l'axe central est–ouest du *castrum*. Dans le courant du Ve siècle, un portique de pierre est mis en place au-dessus du tronçon de la voie passant entre les deux églises. Ses galeries délimitent une cour centrale qui fait à la fois office d'*atrium* et de structure de liaison entre les deux sanctuaires du groupe épiscopal. Le baptistère est vraisemblablement situé à l'est de l'ensemble, aux environs du bras nord du transept de la cathédrale actuelle. Lors de la mise en place de l'*atrium*, on supprime le balnéaire adossé au mur occidental de la basilique nord. Cette modification permet l'ouverture d'une nouvelle entrée à l'ouest, par la porte qui faisait initialement communiquer la nef de l'église avec le complexe thermal.

VIe–VIIe siècle

Il ne semble pas que les deux églises du groupe épiscopal aient été l'objet de transformations importantes à l'époque mérovingienne. La basilique nord reçoit une toiture de métal destinée à remplacer la couverture primitive de *tegulae*. Plusieurs plaques de plomb intactes provenant de cette nouvelle toiture ont été recueillies dans une couche de remblai du début du IXe siècle. La basilique sud est décorée par l'évêque *Audœnus* (†684), mais, s'il faut en croire une *vita* tardive de cet évêque, l'intervention de ce personnage se serait limitée à enrichir le trésor et le décor de l'église, sans toucher semble-t-il au bâtiment élevé par ses prédécesseurs.[9]

C'est sans doute au cours de l'époque mérovingienne que se fixent définitivement les titulatures des églises du groupe épiscopal. Le plus important sanctuaire du groupe est dédié à Notre-Dame, vocable que l'on retrouve d'une part sur les monnaies émises par l'église de Rouen à la fin du VIIe siècle,[10] d'autre part dans la vie de saint Ouen, à propos d'un autel que cet évêque aurait fait placer dans la cathédrale en l'honneur de la Vierge.[11] Quant à la basilique nord, nul document n'a conservé le nom de son saint patron. Mais il y aurait de bonnes raisons d'attribuer à cette église le vocable de Saint-Etienne que la tradition rouennaise associait dès la fin du Moyen Age à un sanctuaire disparu, non situé avec précision mais voisin de l'église Notre-Dame, et dont paraît avoir primitivement dépendu la paroisse de la cathédrale (cf. ci-après: *Vers 760–770*).

Première moitié du VIIIe siècle

Au côté nord de la basilique Saint-Etienne est élevé un bâtiment de pierre longé par une galerie de bois sur poteaux plantés, avec un retour en équerre le long de la rue passant à l'ouest du groupe épiscopal. Dans un second temps, l'aile ouest de ce cloître est remplacée par un bâtiment en petit appareil de silex et une nouvelle galerie de bois est disposée autour du préau. Les deux ailes de pierre comportent plusieurs pièces séparées les unes des autres par des murs de refend. Une troisième campagne de travaux est marquée par la reconstruction des deux bâtiments de pierre sur un plan plus vaste en empiétant sur l'espace disponible dans la cour centrale. Les dispositions internes, délimitées par des cloisons de refend, reproduisent cependant à quelques détails près celles de l'état précédent.

Il est possible que ces aménagements architecturaux, datés pour les plus récents par un petit lot de deniers d'argent de la première moitié du VIIIe siècle, et situés à l'emplacement du futur cloître canonial (cf. ci-après), aient été réalisés pour les clercs de la cathédrale. Leur influence commence alors à s'accroître et il semble qu'ils aient acquis dès lors à Rouen une certaine autonomie vis-à-vis de l'évêque, notamment sous le gouvernement des évêques austrasiens de la première moitié du VIIIe siècle, qui pour la plupart d'entre eux ne résidèrent qu'épisodiquement à Rouen.[12]

Vers 760–770

L'archevêque *Remigius*, introducteur de la réforme romaine à Rouen, accorde aux clercs du chapitre en 769 un acte de partition du temporel, c'est-à-dire la constitution d'une mense canoniale qui assure désormais à ceux-ci des ressources propres.[13] On peut dater de ce moment l'installation officielle du chapitre dans l'église Saint-Etienne, son établissement en communauté selon la règle de saint Chrodegang et, ce qui en est la conséquence directe sur le plan architectural, la transformation des dépendances en édifices collectifs.

Dans le bâtiment ouest du cloître, on abat le refend central et l'on installe à la place de ce mur un grand foyer muni d'une sole en tuileaux posés de chant. Ces deux modifications semblent correspondre à la transformation du rez-de-chaussée en chauffoir, et divers indices suggèrent que la salle du premier étage est convertie dans le même temps en dortoir (v. ci-après: *Début du IXe siècle.*)

L'église Saint-Etienne, qui sert désormais aux heures canoniales (notamment, sans doute, aux offices de nuit), reçoit un nouveau mobilier liturgique. De nombreux fragments de chancels à décor d'entrelacs ont été recueillis, attestant une influence italienne que l'on pourrait mettre en rapport avec la présence à Rouen, dans les années 760, d'un groupe de clercs amenés de Rome par l'archevêque *Remigius* pour enseigner le chant romain.[14] Un four à cloches de petit module installé dans un angle du parvis indique la présence d'au moins une cloche dans l'église, fait nouveau qui est également dans la ligne de la règle de saint Chrodegang, celle-ci prescrivant la sonnerie des heures canoniales. Deux petits foyers culinaires découverts sur le pavé du parvis, en face de l'église, trouvent peut-être leur explication dans divers textes carolingiens faisant état de foules d'indigents campant devant les portes de la cathédrale pendant les périodes de famine, dans l'attente de distributions de nourriture.[15]

A cette époque, l'*atrium* ayant originellement servi de liaison entre les deux églises du groupe épiscopal commence à être subdivisé par des cloisons et des bâtisses commencent à proliférer autour de la collégiale. Une maison de bois est édifiée au côté sud du parvis (VIIIe siècle?). Dans l'angle nord–ouest du préau s'élève un second logis de bois muni d'un cellier de pierre profondément encavé (seconde moitié du VIIIe siècle). Un troisième logis pourvu d'une salle basse en pierre a pu être partiellement fouillé dans l'angle nord–est du cloître septentrional (fin VIIIe–début IXe siècle). Cette multiplication de logis dans les cours de cloîtres est le signe d'un accroissement des effectifs du chapitre et il semble bien indiquer que l'enceinte des *claustra* elle-même, espace réservé aux maisons des chanoines, est déjà saturée de constructions au début du IXe siècle (cf. ci-après: *Debut du IXe siècle*).

Dans le secteur sud (cour des maçons), les fouilles de 1990–1 ont révélé les soubassements de deux grands bâtiments en pierre d'axe nord–sud encadrant un préau bordé de portiques et datés de la fin du VIIIe siècle par un denier de Charlemagne à fleur de coin recueilli au fond d'un trou de poteau. Le bâtiment ouest, proche du portail de l'église Notre-Dame et du parvis, correspond à l'emplacement habituel de l'hôtellerie dans les abbayes et les groupes épiscopaux (cf. le plan de S.Gall). Il pourrait s'agir de la salle de distribution des aumones, *domus dispensatoria*, mentionnée dans une vie de saint Hugues de Rouen du IXe siècle comme voisine à la fois de l'église Notre-Dame et de l'Hôtel-Dieu.[16] Le rez-de-chaussée comportait au moins deux salles séparées par un mur de refend. Au-dessus s'élevait un étage sur plancher, pourvu de baies vitrées composées de petits carreaux de teinte vert-pâle ou de verre peint et de bordures rectangulaires, le tout serti de plomb. La couverture était en essentes de bois. Le bâtiment oriental du cloître était situé à la hauteur du sanctuaire de l'église Notre-Dame. De la galerie du cloître, on entrait dans cet édifice par une porte encadrée de deux colonnes adossées et précédée d'un perron, ce qui rappelle les *pogia* du cloître de Saint-Wandrille au début du IXe siècle.[17] L'appentis du cloître proprement dit était constitué d'une galerie de bois sur poutres sablières dans l'aile ouest et d'une galerie de pierre le long du bâtiment est. Dans l'angle sud–est de la cour du cloître s'élevait un petit bâtiment rectangulaire à étage, d'une structure identique à celle de l'hôtellerie. Sa fonction précise nous échappe, mais le contexte n'est pas sans rappeler celui de la bibliothèque mentionnée dans le préau du cloître de Saint-Wandrille au début du IXe siècle.[18]

Fin du VIIIe siècle — premières décennies du IXe siècle

Des travaux considérables sont effectués dans l'église Saint-Etienne. Le chancel est démonté, le sol de la nef est exhaussé de près de 50 cm, ce qui correspond peut-être à un agrandissement du chœur (les terrains situés derrière l'église primitive forment une légère surélévation). Il est possible que la rotonde de 10 m de diamètre mise au jour en 1987 à l'extrémité orientale de la nef n'ait été élevée qu'à cette époque. Surmontée d'une coupole sur tambour et peut-être d'un lanterneau, elle présentait en son centre, aménagée dans le sol de béton du début du IXe siècle, une fosse à reliques qui devait occuper le soubassement d'un autel. De semblables rotondes à autel central furent élevées dans plusieurs sanctuaires de l'empire carolingien à partir de la fin du VIIIe siècle, l'exemple le mieux connu étant celui de Saint-Riquier de Centule, au diocèse d'Amiens.[19]

La façade de l'église est prolongée par une petite tour-porche de plan quadrangulaire que cantonnent deux tourelles d'escaliers semi-circulaires desservant une tribune ou une chapelle à l'étage, le tout formant, à échelle réduite, un massif occidental comme il en existait sans doute à la même époque à Jumièges et à Saint-Wandrille. A cette phase se rattache également un four à cloche établi dans l'église même à droite de l'entrée. Ce dernier détail peut laisser supposer que la cloche, de petites dimensions, était destinée à l'une des tours de façade.

Au nord de l'église St-Etienne, l'aile sud du cloître est entièrement reconstruite ainsi que la grande salle commune occupant le côté occidental du cloître. L'orientation des deux édifices est la même que dans l'état précédent, mais leurs murs sont décalés par rapport aux tracés du VIIIe siècle. Composés de moellons de tuf disposés en assises obliques, ils reposent sur de puissants massifs de fondation en pierres de libage incluant divers réemplois gallo-romains (bases de cuves ou de bassins, un morceau de stèle funéraire à acrotères et *ascia*). Ces réemplois pourraient être issus d'un démantèlement partiel de l'enceinte urbaine comme on en a plusieurs autres exemples au début du IXe siècle, notamment à Reims.[20] Entre la salle ouest et l'église se trouve un vestibule avec une porte donnant sur le bas de la nef. Tout près de ce passage, dans l'angle du collatéral, ont été mis au jour les soubassements d'un escalier en appui sur une forte pile de maçonnerie, ce degré conduisant à l'étage du vestibule et de là sans doute à un dortoir situé au-dessus de la salle commune (cf. ci-dessus: *Vers 760–770*). Le réfectoire occupait vraisemblablement, comme dans l'abbaye de Saint-Wandrille, l'aile orientale du cloître;[21] il fut entièrement reconstruit, avec sa salle basse à usage de cellier, dans les dernières années du XIe siècle.

Dans l'angle sud–ouest du cloître, le vestibule est précédé par un pavillon d'entrée situé dans le prolongement exact de l'actuelle rue Croix-de-Fer. Cette dernière, parallèle à la rue antique passant à l'ouest du groupe épiscopal, paraît correspondre à la survivance de la voie desservant l'intérieur du clos canonial où étaient regroupées les maisons des chanoines (*claustra*). Un diplôme impérial de 822 accorde à l'archevêque de Rouen *Willebertus* un terrain du fisc pour l'agrandissement de ces *claustra* en direction d'un monastère féminin qu'il faut probablement identifier avec l'abbaye de Saint-Amand.[22] Ceci témoigne d'un accroissement notable de l'effectif des chanoines au début du IXe siècle (ils seront encore une quarantaine à Rouen en 875, plus de trente ans après les premières incursions vikings). L'élargissement des *claustra* semble avoir eu pour effet de dégager les cloîtres où deux maisons sont abattues et leur cellier comblé de terre avant les années 840 (cf. ci-dessus: *Vers 760–770*).

Au sud de l'église Notre-Dame (cour des maçons), on élève dans l'angle nord-est du cloître un bâtiment de pierre en forme de tour carrée, aux murs épais de plus d'1,50 m. Les caractéristiques architecturales de cet édifice, son implantation hors-œuvre dans un angle de la cour et la proximité du transept de la cathédrale évoquent une tour d'archives (*scrinia*), semblable à celle que l'abbé Anségise fit construire vers 820 dans le préau du cloître de Saint-Wandrille.[23] Les *scrinia* de l'église de Rouen sont mentionnés au début du IXe siècle dans plusieurs textes d'origine monastique où l'on laisse entendre que les clercs étrangers à la cathédrale avaient la possibilité d'y consulter assez librement le fonds des archives diocésaines. Cet office dépend alors directement de l'archevêque. Il en est de même de la bibliothèque située à quelques pas vers le sud, de l'hôtellerie, installée dans une aile du même cloître (cf. ci-dessus), et de l'hôpital tout proche, autre fondation épiscopale, dont l'Hôtel-

Dieu occupe sans doute encore à peu près au XVIe siècle le site primitif, à l'extrémité sud du groupe cathédral.

C'est à la phase de travaux de la fin du VIIIe siècle ou du début du IXe siècle qu'appartient également l'installation d'un aqueduc dans la cour du cloître sud. Sa conduite, de bois ou de plomb, était protégée par une gaine de maçonnerie souterraine formée de deux murets parallèles et couverte de dalles de pierre ou de terre cuite à fleur de sol. Elle traversait le préau d'Ouest en Est en passant sous les bâtiments du cloître, la source étant sans doute à rechercher en direction des quartiers nord-ouest de la ville, peut-être du côté de la 'Fontaine Notre-Dame', non loin des ruines de l'amphithéâtre. De cet endroit partaient encore au XIIIe siècle les eaux de l'aqueduc desservant l'Hôtel-Dieu de la cathédrale, suivant un tracé qui correspond pratiquement à celui de la conduite carolingienne dans la traversée de la cour des maçons.[24] La construction d'un tel aqueduc à Rouen, probablement à l'initiative de l'archevêque, rappelle les travaux édilitaires attribués à l'évêque Aldric du Mans au début du IXe siècle.

Au total, les sources archéologiques et scripturaires permettent de restituer avec une certaine précision le tracé du groupe épiscopal de Rouen à la veille des premières incursions vikings. Celui-ci forme à cette époque une enceinte longue d'environ 250 m du nord au sud, depuis l'actuelle rue Saint-Nicolas jusqu'à l'ancienne rue de la Madeleine. On y trouve successivement dans cet ordre les *claustra* regroupant les maisons des chanoines, les bâtiments communs du chapitre, la collégiale Saint-Etienne, l'ancien *atrium* central du IVe siècle (cour du baptistère?), l'église Notre-Dame, le cloître abritant l'hôtellerie et la bibliothèque, l'Hôtel-Dieu à l'extrémité sud. La répartition spatiale de ces différents offices — ceux relevant de l'archevêque au côté sud, à l'ombre de l'église Notre-Dame, ceux relevant du chapitre au côté nord, contre l'église Saint-Etienne — suggère que les dispositions observées sont consécutives au partage des manses en 769 et à la division des biens de la cathédrale entre l'archevêque et le collège des chanoines. Ce vaste complexe de bâtiments, qui occupe à lui seul une superficie notable de la cité, ne représente cependant qu'une partie de l'ensemble épiscopal. Il existait sans doute d'autres extensions comme le parvis de l'église Notre-Dame, sans doute déjà clos de murs au VIIIe siècle, avec une chapelle de porte sous le vocable de saint Hermeland d'Aindre qui pourrait dater de l'épiscopat d'Hugues († vers 732), et, élément le plus considérable en superficie, la résidence de l'archevêque à l'est, avec une chapelle de porte dédiée à saint Michel, des jardins qui s'étendent jusqu'au mur de la cité et probablement la prison dans une des tours de l'enceinte antique.

Vers 841–vers 880

Un grand incendie détruit les églises du groupe épiscopal et leurs annexes. Les traces archéologiques de ce sinistre sont nombreuses et particulièrement explicites: couche de bois carbonisé et gouttes de plomb fondu au pied de la basilique nord, pierres de parement éclatées et rubéfiées, éclats de verre à vitre déformés par la chaleur, poutres calcinées provenant de l'effondrement d'un plancher dans l'aile occidentale du cloître sud.

La chronologie relative ainsi que les recoupements fournis par divers éléments mobiliers et les analyses de Carbone 14 situent l'évènement autour du milieu du IXe siècle. Il est donc assez probable qu'il corresponde à l'incendie qui fut provoqué par le premier raid viking sur la ville de Rouen au mois de mai 841, au cours duquel selon plusieurs sources dignes de foi, en particulier un acte royal de 863, la cathédrale fut détruite par le feu avec toutes ses archives.[25]

Aucun des édifices du groupe épiscopal connus par la fouille ne sortit indemne de ce désastre et ses conséquences furent durables sur le plan matériel, même si, selon plusieurs sources, la vie reprit un cours à peu près normal jusqu'à la fin des années 870. La nef de

C

l'église Saint-Etienne fut abandonnée et son emplacement ne tarda pas à être envahi par la végétation comme en témoignent l'apparition d'une couche de terre végétale sur le béton carolingien et la présence de trous de racines. Afin de pouvoir continuer à utiliser le chœur, on isola celui-ci de la partie ruinée par un mur élevé en travers de la nef, solution similaire à celle qui fut adoptée dans les mêmes circonstances à Saint-Géry de Cambrai.[26] L'église Notre-Dame connut sans doute un sort analogue. Juste après l'incendie, le préau du cloître sud fut recouvert sur toute sa partie occidentale par une masse de décombres qui provenait sans doute de la nef de cette église (pierres de petit appareil antique portant des traces de feu, débris de chapiteaux, fragments de colonnes de grand diamètre en marbre, etc.).

Vers 880–vers 930

Au côté sud de l'église Saint-Etienne est élevée juste après l'incendie une grande salle en pierre de plus de 15 m de long, avec un foyer central de forme circulaire installé sur des briques antiques de récupération. Ses maçonneries elles-mêmes sont constituées de réemplois empruntés aux ruines voisines (moëllons de calcaire gallo-romains, silex, éléments architecturaux divers). Ce bâtiment d'assez médiocre qualité, qui sera de courte durée, sert peut-être de logis provisoire au petit groupe de chanoines resté à Rouen après 841, le reste de la communauté s'étant transportée à Gasny.[27] Le rez-de-chaussée de la tour sud de la façade de l'église abrite une petite latrine, signe que cette partie de l'édifice est désaffectée. Il est possible que l'on ait installé provisoirement, dans le porche de la collégiale ruinée, un logis de portier.

Dans le même temps apparaît un petit groupe de trois sépultures alignées sous la gouttière du cloître de Saint-Etienne. Ce sont les premières tombes connues sur le site de la cathédrale. Leur présence en ce lieu, alors qu'il n'existe encore aucun cimetière dans cette enceinte, est l'indice possible d'un repli de la cité sur elle-même et d'une désertion momentanée des espaces *extra-muros* pendant les incursions vikings. C'est sans doute à cette époque que l'on transfere les reliques de saint Romain de l'église suburbaine de Saint-Godard dans une chapelle du manoir archiépiscopal, à l'abri d'une des tours de la muraille romaine.[28]

Le squelette d'un chien mort au milieu de la salle des chanoines et l'apparition d'un mince niveau de terre végétale sur le sol de ce bâtiment semblent être les témoins d'un abandon provisoire des lieux à la fin du IXe siècle. Ceci corroborerait le témoignage des sources écrites faisant état de la fuite des chanoines à Vasseny dans le Soissonnais vers la fin des années 880 et des retraites de plus en plus fréquentes de l'archevêque de Rouen dans son domaine fortifié de Braine.

Sur l'emplacement de l'aile sud du cloître Saint-Etienne est édifiée un peu plus tard une maison de pierre, sans doute à étage, avec des murs de refend en bois sur poteaux plantés. La pièce occidentale est occupée par une latrine. Au nord de la maison (vers l'actuelle rue Saint-Romain) se trouve une petite cour intérieure contenant un appentis de bois. Un mur de pierre la sépare du passage conduisant au portail latéral nord de la collégiale, ce qui situerait la construction de ce logis après la remise hors d'eau de la nef et le rétablissement du culte dans cette partie de l'église (vers 920–5 ?).

Au sud (cour des maçons), les galeries du cloître carolingien n'existent plus mais de grands bâtiments de pierre s'élèvent encore à l'ouest et à l'est. Le rez-de-chaussée du premier d'entre eux (ancienne hôtellerie) est utilisé comme cellier.

Vers 930–vers 970

Le long de la rue Saint-Romain apparaît toute une série de latrines creusées dans des cours privées au dépens de l'ancienne salle commune des chanoines et de la rue antique longeant le côté ouest du groupe épiscopal. Un phénomène analogue se manifeste au même moment de l'autre côté de la cathédrale, en bordure de la rue du Change (plus de huit fosses). Il est probable que c'est à ce moment que sont tracées les rues Saint-Romain et du Change. Ces deux voies contournent le bloc médian du groupe épiscopal (d'où leur inflexion, encore bien visible aujourd'hui), et les terrains situés le long des chaussées se couvrent de constructions privées.

Le fait est d'une importance considérable, d'une part pour l'histoire du groupe cathédral, d'autre part pour la connaissance de la topographie du centre urbain à cette époque. Il signifie d'abord que le clos des chanoines et l'Hôtel-Dieu ne sont plus désormais liés de façon organique à la cathédrale. Il semble d'autre part que l'enceinte primitive des *claustra* (entre la rue Saint-Nicolas et la rue Saint-Romain) a cessé d'être l'espace réservé des chanoines pour laisser place à des activités artisanales réparties dans des secteurs spécialisés. Côté rue Saint-Romain, en face de la rue Croix-de-Fer, les fouilles ont fait apparaître dans les niveaux du Xe siècle tout un matériel de fondeur, ce que l'on peut rapprocher du fait que ce tronçon de rue s'appelait au Moyen Age la 'rue-aux-Férons'. Près de la rue du Change, sur le côté regardant le parvis de la cathédrale, les mêmes niveaux du Xe siècle ont livré la fosse d'un silo à grains de grande capacité qu'il faut sans doute mettre en rapport avec le droit de boulangerie qu'avait le chapitre de Rouen dans l'enceinte du parvis de la cathédrale, en vertu d'un privilège remontant à la première moitié du Xe siècle, sous le règne de Guillaume Longue Epée (927–42). Tout ceci semble indiquer d'une part que les maisons canoniales, précédemment contenues dans l'enceinte des *claustra* autour de la rue Croix-de-Fer, commencent alors à se disperser dans la ville. D'autre part, l'installation des artisans dans les lieux précédemment habités par les clercs du chapitre paraît s'être effectuée selon une répartition géographique des activités, par rues ou par quartiers.

Les transformations considérables auxquelles on assiste ainsi autour de la cathédrale au début du Xe siècle semblent être la conséquence d'un plan général de reconstruction de la cité, destiné à faire de celle-ci une grande ville marchande. Un réseau de rues d'une grande régularité métrique, presque entièrement indépendant de l'infrastructure antique, se met alors en place sur toute la surface de l'ancien *castrum*.[29] Diverses données, que nous nous proposons de publier dans un prochain article,[30] nous incitent à placer cette grande opération d'urbanisme sous le règne de Guillaume-Longue-Epée (927–42). Le cas de Rouen offrirait dans cette hypothèse un parallèle remarquable avec celui de plusieurs autres établissements scandinaves comme York et Dublin, ces cités ayant aussi fait l'objet d'une reconstruction planifiée autour des années 930, date à laquelle, les chefs locaux étant désormais stabilisés dans leurs conquêtes, elles entrèrent dans le 'nouvel âge économique des Vikings'. Il est possible que le modèle pour Rouen ait été Winchester, ville que des liens particuliers, essentiellement de nature commerciale, unissaient à la basse Seine dès le VIIIe siècle, et dont la cité repeuplée par le roi Alfred le Grand avait été dotée à la fin du IXe siècle d'un système de rues identique à celui que l'on retrouve un peu plus tard à Rouen. Il est remarquable, enfin, que la transformation de la ville en cité marchande coïncide chronologiquement avec la reprise de l'atelier monétaire de Rouen vers les années 930.

REFERENCES

1. J. Le Maho, 'Fouilles de la cour d'Albane (campagne de 1986), découverte d'une maison urbaine du IIIe siècle', *Bulletin des Amis des monuments rouennais* (1987–8), 85–90; *idem*, 'Rouen (Seine-Maritime), cour d'Albane, habitation urbaine du IIIe siècle', *De la Gaule à la Normandie: 2000 ans d'histoire, 30 ans d'archéologie* (catalogue de l'exposition du Musée des Antiquités de la Seine-Marime) (Rouen 1990), 184–5, 197.

2.   J. Le Maho, 'Cathédrale primitive (IVᵉ–XIᵉ siècle)', *De la Gaule à la Normandie*, 186, 197.

3.   Victricius de Rouen, *De Laude Sanctorum, Patrologia Latina*, xx, éd. J. P. Migne (Paris 1845), cols 443–58; G. Lanfry, Ch. Derivière et M. Morisset, *La cathédrale depuis quinze siècles au coeur de la cité* (Rouen 1963).

4.   N. Duval, *Naissance des arts chrétiens. Atlas des monuments paléochrétiens de la France* (Atlas archéologiques de la France, Paris 1991).

5.   Cf. n. 3.

6.   Lanfry, Derivière et Morisset, 74–5.

7.   L. Pietri, *La Ville de Tours du IVᵉ au VIᵉ siècle — naissance d'une cité chrétienne* (Collection de l'Ecole française de Rome, 69) (Rome 1983), 488.

8.   N. Gauthier, *Province ecclésiastique de Trèves (Belgica Prima) (Topographie chrétienne des Cités de la Gaule des origines au milieu du VIIIᵉ siècle*, I) (Paris 1986), 22–5.

9.   *Vita . . . Audoeni, Acta Sanctorum*, Aug., IV (Antwerp 1739), 815.

10.   R. Chevallier *et al.*, 'Trouvailles récentes de monnaies mérovingiennes dans le département de l'Aube', *Bulletin de la Société française de numismatique*, XLIII (1988), 385.

11.   Cf. n. 9.

12.   'S. Ansbertus', *Provincia Rotomagensis*, II, *Gallia Christiana*, XI, éd. Dom D. Sammarthan et Dom P. Piolin (Paris 1874), cols 16–19.

13.   G. Tessier, *Recueil des actes de Charles II le Chauve, roi de France*, 3 vols (Paris 1943–55), II, no. 399, 386.

14.   Lettre du pape Paul I à Pépin, *Epistolae Merowingici et Karolini aevi*, I, éd. W. Grundlach, E. Dümmler *et al.* (*Monumenta Germaniae Historica: Epistolae*, III) (Berlin 1892), no. 41, 553–4.

15.   *Vita Ansberti episcopi Rotomagensis . . ., Passiones vitaeque sanctorum aevi Meronvingici* III, éd. B. Krusch et W. Levison (*Monumenta Germaniae Historica: Scriptores rerum Merovingicarum*, V) (Hanovre et Leipzig 1910), 618–41.

16.   J. Van der Straeten, 'Vie inédite de S. Hughes, évêque de Rouen', *Analecta Bollandiana*, LXXXVII (1969), 252.

17.   *Gesta sanctorum patrum Fontanellensis coenobii . . .* (Rouen et Paris 1936), 107.

18.   Cf. n. 17.

19.   C. Heitz, *L'architecture religieuse Carolingienne* (Paris 1980), 51–2.

20.   A. Erlande-Brandenburg, *La cathédrale* (Paris 1990), 88.

21.   *Gesta sanctorum patrum Fontanellenis coenobii*, 105.

22.   BN, MS lat. 2718.

23.   Cf. n. 17.

24.   A. Cerné, *Les anciennes sources et fontaines de Rouen* (Rouen 1930), 180, fig. 20.

25.   Cf. les sources réunies par N. Gauthier, 'Rouen pendant le haut Moyen Age', *La Neustrie: les pays au nord de la Loire de 650 à 850. Colloque historique international, Rouen, 1985*, 2 vols (Sigmaringen 1989), II, 19.

26.   B. Florin, 'Cambrai (Nord)-Saint-Géry-du-Mont-des-Boeufs', *Le paysage monumental de la France autour de l'an Mil*, éd. X. Barral I Altet (Paris 1987), 545, 552, fig. 1.

27.   ADSM, 14 H 156.

28.   Nous nous proposons d'etudier de façon plus détaillée ces données inédites dans un article en préparation sur 'Rouen et les Vikings'.

29.   Voir à ce sujet la contribution de B. Gauthiez dans le présent volume. D'abord partisan d'une datation haute pour cette voierie (VIIIᵉ siècle), B. Gauthiez s'est rangé depuis à nos arguments en faveur d'une datation du Xᵉ siècle.

30.   Cf. n. 28.

Les vestiges romans de l'ancienne priorale Saint-Gervais de Rouen

Par Maylis Baylé

Monument rebâti à plusieurs reprises, l'ancienne priorale Saint-Gervais de Rouen est surtout connue des archéologues pour sa crypte et pour les sarcophages dégagés à proximité au XIXe siècle.[1] Le site fut en effet occupé très tôt par un sanctuaire funéraire hors-les-murs et la tradition fait de la crypte le lieu d'inhumation de saint Mellon et de saint Avitien; mais la structure actuelle de la chapelle souterraine peut difficilement remonter à une aussi haute époque. Un prieuré fut établi au XIe siècle. Son histoire est mal connue. On sait qu'entre 1023 et 1025 le duc Richard II donne à Arnoul, abbé de Saint-Père de Chartres, l'église Saint-Gervais à Rouen.[2] Mais en 1025 Saint-Gervais passe dans le domaine de l'abbaye de Fécamp et y demeure jusqu'à la Révolution Française.[3] En 1087 Guillaume le Conquérant, malade, se fait transporter à Rouen et meurt à Saint-Gervais le 9 Septembre.[4] Il ne semble pas que la vie monastique ait été très durable en ce lieu et l'église est surtout connue pour son rôle de paroisse.

LA PRIORALE ROMANE

Les témoignages sur l'église avant 1846

Il est difficile de tenter de reconstituer la priorale romane. Elle a été partiellement reconstruite en 1846, puis intégralement rebâtie en 1869, seule l'ancienne abside étant conservée. Elle avait subi en outre de multiples remaniements au cours des siècles comme l'attestent à la fois les archives et les divers dessins antérieurs à sa reconstruction. Les plans indiquent au sol une nef donnant directement sur le chœur hémicirculaire, sans transept.[5] Les documents plus précis comme le plan publié par Farin montrent la présence de collatéraux et d'un clocher-porche. Les archives de Fécamp et le fonds de la Fabrique de l'église paroissiale donnent des précisions sur les remaniements intervenus: réfection de la charpente et adjonction d'un porche au devant de la tour de façade en 1434, restauration du chœur en 1551;[6] enfin, après le pillage de 1562 par les protestants, intervint en 1595 une importante reconstruction d'ensemble.[7] La tour, rebâtie alors, sera en partie détruite par un ouragan en 1613 et devra à nouveau être refaite.[8] Un dessin au lavis antérieur à 1846 confirme ces données et atteste que, dans son dernier état, l'église n'était que très partiellement romane (Pl. IA). Les contreforts gothiques du mur sud, le porche à pignon ajouté en 1434 et restauré plus tard, sont effectivement visibles sur ce document. La première travée du mur sud, entre les contreforts, semble montrer un mur plus ancien avec une baie romane, mais cela sous toutes réserves. Le plan lui-même — clocher-porche, nef, chevet semicirculaire — semble correspondre à l'implantation première de l'édifice du XIe siècle. Compte tenu de la fréquence des clochers-porches dans la Normandie romane, il est probable que le parti d'une tour de façade exista dès le XIe siècle. Un doute subsiste en revanche sur la présence dès cette époque de collatéraux dans la nef romane. L'enquête de 1545 sur les trésoriers de la paroisse insiste sur la petitesse de l'église et sur la nécessité de l'agrandir. Comme les bas-côtés ne sont pas mentionnés dans le devis de 1434 et ne sont indiqués que sur un plan tardif (XVIIe siècle), Charles de Beaurepaire, supposant un agrandissement à la fin du XVIe, concluait à l'existence première d'une nef unique. Si notre interprétation du dessin au lavis du XIXe est exacte, la trace d'un mur roman au collatéral sud infirmerait cette opinion; mais il est évident que l'argument reste incertain en l'absence de preuves plus précises. La question reste donc ouverte et seules des fouilles permettraient de la trancher. Des substructions antérieures à cette nef furent retrouvées du côté nord lors de premiers travaux en vue de la reconstruction en 1836. Dix ans plus tard une muraille en petit appareil joignant le portail au mur extérieur du bas-côté sud fut visible sur une profondeur de trois mètres.[9]

Les vestiges en place

Les seuls vestiges actuellement en place restent la crypte et le mur extérieur de l'abside, lui-même restauré à de nombreuses reprises et dont le décor sculpté atteint maintenant un état de dégradation alarmant.

La crypte a fait l'objet de quelques courtes études et d'une fouille archéologique inachevée (1988) dont le rapport n'a pas été publié. Elle se compose d'une travée droite voûtée en berceau et séparée de l'abside en cul-de-four par un arc triomphal fourré en plein cintre qui retombe sur des pilastres à impostes. Il convient de distinguer deux époques dans la construction: l'une du haut Moyen Age, la seconde correspondant à une reprise sans doute antérieure de peu à la construction de l'abside du XIe siècle. Une baie largement ébrasée vers l'intérieur éclaire à l'est cette crypte; elle a été restaurée à plusieurs reprises, mais il convient de préciser que l'aspect d'ouverture entaillée dans le roc et sans parement appareillé, visible dans les 'Voyages romantiques' de Taylor et Nodier, est une fantaisie gratuite et n'a jamais été conforme à son état en 1818, comme le prouvent d'autres gravures de cette époque, et en particulier celle de T. de Jolimont (Pl. IB). Plusieurs temps sont discernables dans l'appareil mural à l'intérieur de la crypte. Nous laisserons ici les problèmes propres à la période du haut Moyen Age. Dans la partie droite de la crypte, la construction primitive en petit appareil peut remonter à l'époque carolingienne. Il reste qu'un remaniement est intervenu dans la construction avec rhabillage des parois et renforcement par un arc en plein cintre retombant sur des pilastres à impostes en moyen appareil. Cela comporta également réfection de la voûte (elle-même refaite à plusieurs reprises dans les siècles ultérieurs) et construction ou renforcement de la partie absidale à proximité de la baie orientale. Ce renforcement a été diversement daté. L'aspect des supports, de même que le petit appareil très régulier, proche de celui de la construction première, et encore très usité en Normandie au début du XIe siècle et vers la même époque dans d'autres régions (citons Ouilly-le-Vicomte, Vieux-Pont-en-Auge, Saint-Jean-le-Thomas, et, hors de Normandie, le reprise de Civaux au Xe siècle et la Basse-Œuvre de Beauvais) plaident en faveur d'une reprise de la crypte sans doute au temps de Richard II, alors que l'on s'apprêtait à rebâtir l'église haute et notamment l'abside. Des fragments sculptés d'entrelacs qui paraissent carolingiens ont d'ailleurs été remployés dans l'appareil de ce remaniement. L'arc et ses supports à impostes, manifestement ajoutés, correspondent à une même volonté d'asseoir l'église supérieure et se placent dans la foulée de cette campagne, sans doute dans le premier quart du XIe siècle. Le tout, et notamment les banquettes, fut restauré en 1618, 1675 et au XIXe. Extérieurement, l'abside était bâtie en moyen appareil mais dont les éléments sont maintenant pour la plupart le résultat de réfections ultérieures.

L'accès vers la crypte a été modifié au cours des siècles. Nous savons par les comptes de fabrique que l'on descendait directement vers la crypte par un escalier ménagé jadis 'devant le Crucifix', c'est-à-dire devant l'autel de la croix, selon toute vraisemblance, à l'extrémité de la nef et dans l'axe de celle-ci. Les mêmes archives mentionnent 'l'estrappe de saint Mellon',[10] trappe qui fut dégagée et remise en état à la fin du XVIe siècle.[11] C'est seulement en 1676–8 que l'entrée fut déplacée et qu'un escalier fut établi par Maître Antoine Millets, maître maçon, depuis le bas-côté sud.[12] Compte tenu de ces indications et des restitutions de niveaux, on peut envisager, avant cette date, à la limite de la nef et d'un chœur surélevé une fenestella comparable à celles dont la présence est attestée jusqu'en pleine époque romane dans des édifices ayant un long passé préroman et la nécessité de préserver des reliques et des vestiges d'une crypte plus ancienne: Saint-Benoît-sur-Loire, Yzeure, Saint-Aignan-sur-Cher, Wing (Bucks.) pour ne citer que quelques exemples.[13] Un vestige de transenne a d'ailleurs été découvert par J. Le Maho en remploi dans la voûte de la crypte et peut avoir appartenu soit à un premier état de la baie extérieure soit plutôt à une fenestella de séparation entre un chœur surhaussé et la crypte. Celle-ci est désormais accessible depuis l'intérieur de l'église moderne.

Au dessus de la crypte s'élève une abside dont les parements sont en majeure partie refaits. De plan polygonal à cinq pans, elle comporte à chaque angle une colonne engagée surmontée d'un chapiteau. Avant même que l'on remplace la toiture ruinée encore visible en 1823 sur une gravure de Villeneuve (Pl. Ic), le faîte de l'édifice avait été restauré et comportait des éléments du XVIe et du XVIIIe siècle. Cela est encore plus visible depuis qu'une couverture utilitaire et sans style a remplacé l'ancienne vers 1830. Telle qu'elle se présente maintenant cette abside qui jouxte la sacristie est un 'patchwork' de pierres d'appareil romanes remployées (en très petit nombre) et de restaurations des XVIe, XVIIe et XIXe siècle. La corniche, refaite en 1551, a été remaniée au XVIIe puis consolidée au XIXe. Seuls peuvent être pris en considération le parti d'ensemble, trois chapiteaux et quelques bases en partie bûchées.

La plan, relevé par Hyacinthe Langlois (Pl. IIA) avant que les parements soient partiellement masqués par l'église du XIXe, mérite attention car il est inusité dans la Normandie romane. La présence attestée d'un édifice antérieur suggère que ce parti rappelle les dispositions de la construction du haut Moyen Age établie jadis au dessus de la crypte. Ce plan est en effet fréquent du IVe au Xe siècle. Citons le cas de Civaux (Vienne), de Reculver (Kent), Wing (Bucks.), Brixworth (Northampton), Deerhurst (Glos.), de Saint-Maurice d'Agaune, S. Michele d'Arcevoli, entre autres exemples.[14] Cette abside à cinq pans reprendrait en fait un parti plus ancien et témoignerait du caractère sacré de celui-ci aux yeux des religieux du XIe siècle. Il n'est pas rare que le plan polygonal au dessus du sol soit assis sur une crypte à terminaison semicirculaire (Pl. IIB).

Seuls les chapiteaux (Pl. IIB, C, D) et quelques bases restent parfaitement authentiques. Attribués jadis par l'abbé Cochet à l'époque mérovingienne,[15] ils sont manifestement romans. D'autres subsistaient au XIXe siècle à l'intérieur mais ont disparu lors de la reconstruction.[16] Thieury affirme qu'ils avaient été déposés au Musée des Antiquités de Rouen mais nous n'avons pu en retrouver la trace. L'état de dégradation des corbeilles encore en place s'est considérablement accru depuis quelques décennies. L'une d'elles est réduite à un bloc bûché et dépourvu de décor et, pour les trois autres, l'on doit faire appel aux dessins du XIXe siècle effectués par Hyacinthe Langlois afin d'identifier certains détails.[17] L'un des chapiteaux comportait à l'origine des volutes d'angle, une collerette végétale associant un motif de feuille alternant avec un fruit stylisé, et de grandes palmettes retournées sous la volute. Les motifs de la collerette ne sont pas inconnus en Normandie et se voient dans la nef de Bernay.[18] Une seconde corbeille fait alterner palmettes et fleurons dans la couronne de feuilles qui constitue le registre inférieur, et illustre un principe de recomposition bien connu des composantes de la collerette corinthienne. Il faut insister immédiatement sur la souplesse de ces ces feuilles, leur traitement qui évoque encore de loin celui du chapiteau corinthien. Ces œuvres, encore éloignées de l'art très stylisé de la sculpture normande des années 1050 à 1060, confirment l'existence à Rouen d'un style de chapiteaux dérivés du corinthien aux feuillages riches et souples. On connait en effet l'existence d'une sculpture comparable dans la crypte de la cathédrale, achevée avant 1037, et cet unique vestige, joint à une base ornée d'acanthes, suggère qu'un tel style était beaucoup plus usité dans le milieu rouennais. C'est d'ailleurs ce que confirment les chapiteaux, également résiduels et datables vers 1040, de Fontaine-le-Bourg (anciennement Sainte-Marie-du-Vast et dépendance de Fécamp), tout proche de Rouen.[19] Un dernier chapiteau est orné d'aigles qui occupent les deux angles de la corbeille et dont les ailes se déploient sur les faces. Presque totalement bûché et difficilement identifiable, il nous est restitué par Langlois qui cependant donna trop de relief et de modelé à sa représentation, l'œuvre étant manifestement très stylisée et sommaire dans son traitement. Le thème est d'origine antique et bien connu dans la sculpture romane, avec de nombreuses séries en Italie, Auvergne, Nivernais. Les exemples en sont plus rares en Normandie; citons ceux de Secqueville-en-Bessin et surtout de Mont-Saint-Aignan, plus tardifs mais plus proches géographiquement. On ne peut affirmer que cette corbeille soit du même atelier que les deux autres, mais par son caractère également dérivé de prototypes antiques et par le traitement schématique des aigles, cela reste plausible.

Pour les chapiteaux végétaux, les comparaisons suggèrent une date antérieure à 1050 que confirment les profils de bases malgré leur mauvais état de conservation. L'un était de type attique, comme ceux que l'on voit dans la crypte de la cathédrale, à Bernay et sur une base provenant de Saint-Pierre de Jumièges, sans compter les bases refaites, mais sans doute à l'identique, de Saint-Marie-du-Vast; l'autre, plus complexe, a des équivalents dans la crypte de l'abside occidentale de la cathédrale Saint-Cyr de Nevers, bâtie dans le second tiers du XIe siècle.[20]

Les vestiges encore en place de Saint-Gervais de Rouen ont ainsi, malgré leur caractère résiduel, une importance primordiale pour l'histoire de l'art normand dans le second quart du XIe siècle. Ils constituent un jalon supplémentaire attestant la présence d'un courant de sculpture de corbeilles dérivées du corinthien aux feuilles encore souples. Outre leurs liens avec la première campagne de la cathédrale de Rouen, édifice majeur et sans doute atelier-pilote, il est remarquable que, comme Saint-Gervais, les autres édifices mentionnés pour des comparaisons sont liés à Fécamp dont le rôle dut être primordial. L'ensemble devait constituer, par la souplesse des corbeilles végétales dérivées du corinthien, un courant parallèle à celui de la Loire, peut-être non dépourvu de liens avec les grands ateliers de la France moyenne, mais développant très tôt un style similaire. Cette tendance, qui a également marqué quelques ateliers de Basse-Normandie (Bayeux, le Mont-Saint-Michel) dans les années 1050 à 1060, s'efface à partir de 1060, avec l'affirmation d'un art plus sec et plus sommaire, bien illustré par le décor des abbayes caennaises.[21]

REFERENCES

1. D. Fossard, 'Répartition des sarcophages mérovingiens à décor en France', *Etudes mérovingiennes: Actes des journées de Poitiers* (Paris 1953), 117–26 (avec bibliographie antérieure).
2. *AA SS OSB*, Saec. VI, pars I, 318.
3. Fauroux, *Recueil*, no. 34, 124.
4. *Ordericus Vitalis*, ed. L. Delisle, 5 vols (SHF, Paris 1838–55), III, 226–7; *The Ecclesiastical History of Orderic Vitalis*, ed. et trad. M. Chibnall, 6 vols (Oxford 1969–80), IV, 100–3. Sur l'histoire de Saint-Gervais, voir également F. Farin, *Histoire de la ville de Rouen*, 3e ed., 2 vols (Rouen 1731), II, 1 et suiv.; *idem*, *Normandie chrestienne* (Rouen 1659), 138; H. Gally-Knight, 'Excursion monumentale en Normandie', *Bull. mon*, IV (1838), 62–3; J. Thieury, *Saint-Gervais de Rouen* (Paris, Rouen et Dieppe 1859), G. Lanfry, Chanoine Derivière et M. Morisset, *La cathédrale depuis quinze siècles au cœur de la cité* (Cahiers de Notre-Dame de Rouen, Rouen 1963), 105–13.

5. Plan de Rouen, 1581, Plan de Gomboust (1655), Plan aquarellé (1750), tous consultables à la Bibliothèque
    Nationale, Estampes, Va 76, vol. 14.

6. ADSM, G 6583 (fonds de la Fabrique de Saint-Gervais). Voir également G 6593, Enquête de 1545 sur les
    droits des trésoriers de la paroisse.

7. ADSM, G 6584.

8. ADSM, G 6585.

9. C. de Beaurepaire, *Derniers mélanges historiques et archéologiques* (Rouen 1909), 209–13, et sur la crypte,
    idem, *Mélanges historiques et archéologiques* (Rouen 1887), 186–91. Sur les substructions retrouvées,
    Bulletin de la Commission des Antiquités de la Seine-Inférieure (1871), 312 (rapport de l'abbé Cochet);
    J. Thieury, *Saint-Gervais*, 75.

10. ADSM, G 6584.

11. ADSM, G 6584, à la date de 1585.

12. ADSM, G 6585.

13. Sur Civaux, F. Eygun, 'Civaux', *CA* (1951), 179–91; C. Heitz, *La France pré-romane, archéologie et
    architecture religieuse du haut Moyen Age, du IVe siècle à l'an mil* (Paris 1987), 87; R. Oursel, *Haut-Poitou
    roman* (La Pierre-Qui-Vire 1975), 72–7. Les exemples anglais sont répertoriés in H. M. Taylor et M. Taylor,
    Anglo-Saxon Architecture, 3 vols (Cambridge 1965–7); bibliographie plus récente in *The Cambridge Guide
    to the Arts in Britain: I, Prehistoric, Roman and early Medieval*, ed. B. Ford (Cambridge 1988). Sur
    Saint-Maurice, L. Blondel, 'Les anciennes basiliques d'Agaune', *Vallesia*, III (1948), 9–57.

14. Sur le maintien de cette disposition dans des édifices du XIe siècle afin de ménager un ancien mur de
    confession, E. Vergnolle, *Saint-Benoit-sur-Loire et la sculpture du XIe siècle* (Paris 1985), 218–19, M. Baylé,
    'Saint-Aignan-sur-Cher', *CA* (1981), 310–33, 'Yzeure, église Saint-Pierre', *CA* (1988), 477–93.

15. Abbé Cochet, 'Fouilles dans la crypte Saint-Gervais', *Bulletin de la Commission des Antiquités de la
    Seine-inférieure*, II (1871), 388–90.

16. V. Ruprich-Robert, *L'architecture normande aux XIe et XIIe siècles*, 2 vols (Paris 1883 et 1889), I, 117.

17. *Recueil de la Commission des Antiquités de la Seine-Maritime*, ASDM, 6 FI Rouen (8 et 9). Les chapiteaux
    sont également reproduits mais de manière très approximative in Ruprich-Robert, *L'architecture normande*,
    pl. XLVII, 1 et 2.

18. Sur Bernay et la sculpture rouennaise du XIe siècle, M. Baylé, *Les origines et les premiers développements de
    la sculpture romane en Normandie* (Art de Basse-Normandie No. 100 bis, Caen 1992), ch. VI, 107–24.

19. Reproduction des chapiteaux de Sainte-Marie-du-Vast in Baylé, ibid., 344, figs 365–8.

20. On sait qu'en Normandie les bases attiques disparaissent pour plusieurs décennies à partir de 1050: cf. Baylé,
    ibid., 419–21, relevés de bases (dont Saint-Gervais et Nevers), et figs 701 à 712 (Saint-Gervais, figs 711–12).

21. Baylé, ibid., 124 et suiv.

The Romanesque Sculpted Arch at Montivilliers: Episodes from the Story of David

By Jill A. Franklin

The sculpted arch in the east wall of the south transept of the abbey church at Montivilliers (Seine-Maritime) has been the subject of close scrutiny only in the last two or three decades (Pl. IIIA). There are several questions that have still to be raised in connection with the arch. Why, for example, did it alone in the building bear sculptural decoration of such a distinctive kind? What meaning can be drawn from the arch as a whole, rather than from the individual carved voussoirs?

The Abbey Church

The immediate context of the arch, the building itself, is a somewhat undervalued monument.[1] In the 1920s and 1930s, it was customary to stress its affiliation with the group of buildings comprising two of the parish churches of Falaise and the priory of Graville-Sainte-Honorine.[2] There are certainly points of comparison, especially between Monti-villiers and Graville — the two-storey elevation, the asymmetrical plan of the nave piers and the pair of western towers, each probably with an orientated apse in its lowest stage. Such similarities have a regional and chronological basis; Graville and Montivilliers are only a few kilometres apart and are probably comparable in date. But to dwell on them is to deny Montivilliers its proper place in the wider scheme of Norman architecture.

John Bilson, writing in 1911, located Montivilliers in the context of the major 11th-century buildings of 'the school of St Etienne at Caen': Saint-Etienne, Saint-Nicolas, Cerisy and Lessay.[3] Despite its geographical separation, Montivilliers does indeed belong with mainstream Norman and Anglo-Norman architecture, as a member — albeit a modest one — of the Caen group. Graville and Montivilliers may be roughly contemporary, but they are very different in status; while the origins of the Priory of Graville are obscure, the abbey church of Montivilliers has an impressive pedigree and a rich and intermittently well-documented history.

St Philibert founded the first convent for women at Montivilliers, c. 684.[4] It apparently suffered a decline during the period of the Viking incursions,[5] but may have recovered by c. 990, when the nuns of Fécamp are said to have been transferred there by Richard I.[6] Judith, wife of Richard II, is credited with restoring the abbey before her death in 1017.[7] Richard subsequently gave Montivilliers, and all its considerable possessions, to Fécamp in 1025.[8] In the early 1030s, however, Richard's son, Robert the Magnificent, initiated the withdrawal of Montivilliers from Fécamp.[9] In a charter of 1035, he confirmed his decision to restore the ancient abbey to its former greatness.[10] Prime mover in the revival of Montivilliers was Duke Robert's aunt, Beatrice. Having already entered the community, Beatrice became the first abbess of the reconstituted foundation. One of the witnesses to the charter was Robert, archbishop of Rouen, uncle to Duke Robert and possibly brother of Beatrice. Abbess Beatrice remained in office for 30 years, until 1065. The present building is, however, usually attributed to her successor, abbess Elizabeth.

Despite much modification and restoration, the Romanesque building survives, or is retrievable, in plan and elevation (Fig. 1). It consisted of a nave of eight bays with a pair of towers projecting to the west, a three-bay arcaded choir, a crossing with a lantern above,

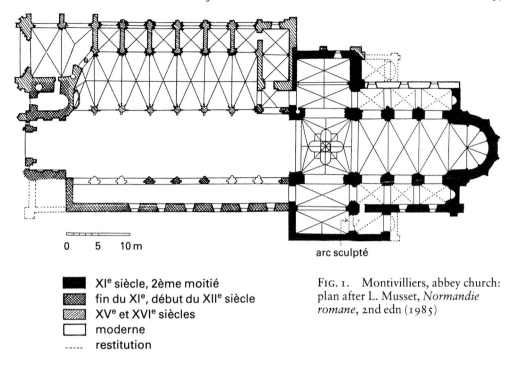

0   5   10 m

arc sculpté

XIᵉ siècle, 2ème moitié
fin du XIᵉ, début du XIIᵉ siècle
XVᵉ et XVIᵉ siècles
moderne
----- restitution

FIG. 1.   Montivilliers, abbey church:
plan after L. Musset, *Normandie
romane*, 2nd edn (1985)

and a transept of two bays with a single, apsidal chapel off the outer bay of each arm. The construction of the church is generally placed largely within abbess Elizabeth's term of office (1065–1116), an assumption for which there is some documentary support.[11] The consensus is that there were two campaigns of construction, the earlier of which, comprising the entire eastern arm, occurred in the second half of the 11th century.[12] A date bracket for the eastern arm of *c.* 1060 to 1090 is plausible. This first campaign would coincide with the building period of the Caen abbeys, the early years of Saint-Nicolas at Caen, and Cerisy. Montivilliers shares with these buildings a triapsidal east end. The length of its nave, at about 40 m is comparable to that of Saint-Nicolas, the smallest member of the group. Although Montivilliers lacks alternation of supports and a three-storey elevation, so, effectively, did La Trinité, the nuns' abbey, and Saint-Nicolas, the parish church. Montivilliers was, in status and function, almost a combination of these two: a ducal abbey for women, like La Trinité, but with the nuns' church occupying only the eastern arm. The nave was in effect the parish church of Montivilliers. This division of function is not documented until the middle of the 13th century, but was surely in operation when the present building was conceived.[13] Otherwise, one of the most remarkable aspects of the plan is difficult to explain, in Normandy in the second half of the 11th century, namely the length of the choir. It is 15 m long and consists of three bays rather than two as in all the other large churches of its generation in the duchy. Its equal could be found in post-Conquest England, of course, at Lincoln Cathedral, but even there, the three-bay Norman choir was over 2 m shorter than at Montivilliers. The nearby priory of Graville-Sainte-Honorine, with which Montivilliers has in the past been discussed, has a total length of 50 m. The entire building would fit quite snugly into the nave and crossing of Montivilliers.[14] Whether the 'superchoir' at

Montivilliers reflects liturgical requirements or is, rather, the linchpin connecting conservative post-Conquest Normandy with the dazzling experiments of Anglo-Norman architecture of the 1070s to 1090s, it is clear that this was a considerable building, with a well-endowed community and powerful friends and patrons.

The Arch

A comprehensive iconographic theme for the sculpted voussoirs of the arch in the south transept has never previously been proposed, but then the subject matter of Romanesque architectural sculpture is notoriously resistant to programmatic interpretation, portals apart. At Montivilliers, however, the organisation of the design is unusually considered, so that it seems calculated to convey a specific theme. To begin with, the opening is slightly, but appreciably, taller than that of the adjacent south choir aisle (Pl. IIIB). The arch is of two orders, both square in section. The topmost segment of the outer order contains seven decorated voussoirs which alternate with uncarved ones. On the inner order, the alternating system extends around the full semicircle. The only irregularity (a perfectly orderly one) is the pairing of two carved voussoirs at the top. In terms of subject matter, there is a hierarchical distinction between man and beast; each of the carved voussoirs of the lower order bears a bird or animal, mythical or natural, often beautifully executed and in an attitude suggestive of suffering or submission. The upper order is reserved for a range of human characters whose identity has yet to be established. As will be seen, the design is even more logical than is at first apparent. But undoubtedly the most striking quality, given its decoration, is the location of the arch. It is unique (or a unique survivor), not for its alternating pattern, but in being an internal arch bearing an elaborate scheme of historiated sculpture.[15]

Antiquarian sources before the early 1900s make no mention of the arch. The first reference seems to be that in Abbé Voiment's guide of 1913.[16] Voiment wrote of the recent discovery of the arch, the sculpture having previously been filled with mortar and whitewashed. He surmised that the decoration of the carved voussoirs — seven in the outer order, thirteen below — was inspired by the exploits of the Norman dukes.[17] More recently, three writers have discussed the sculpture. Georges Priem, writing in 1967, thought that the carved voussoirs were reused from an earlier building. He subsequently decided in 1979 that they were contemporary with the present church, which they surely are. They and their contiguous, uncarved voussoirs appear to be of the same stone; the same diagonal tooling can be seen on the carved voussoirs, the plain ones, and the surrounding wall. Priem was the first to suggest a detailed identification of the themes and characters depicted on the seven carved voussoirs of the outer order.[18] Lucien Musset dated the eastern arm, and thus the sculpture, to c. 1060–80; he proposed a rather different interpretation for some of the seven voussoirs.[19] More recently, the stylistic affiliations of the sculpture have been studied by Maylis Baylé. She has placed the sculpture in its regional context and proposed a date towards the end of the 11th century.[20]

The top of the arch is about 5 m from the ground and the sculpture is not easily deciphered. Reading from left to right, the outer order of carved voussoirs (Pl. IVA, B), is decorated as follows: (1) a badly damaged scene in which a man raises a sword to strike a kneeling figure; (2) a scene of armed combat; (3) a kneeling male figure with a knot of interlace; (4) a tonsured and nimbed ecclesiastic with chasuble, stole and crozier, raising his right hand in blessing; (5) a veiled woman looking out toward the spectator together with a smaller figure; (6) an armed man holding aloft a severed head; (7) a man with a crown and a flowering sceptre seated on a throne with a griffon- or bird-headed terminal.

The key to all existing interpretations is voussoir (6) the man holding the large severed head; this is universally read as David holding the Head of Goliath.[21] Reading again from left to right, the episodes and characters were deciphered as follows by the late Georges Priem: (1) Abraham's Sacrifice; (2) David felling Goliath; (3) David in the Sanctuary; (4) An Abbess; (5) The Virgin and Child; (6) David holding Goliath's head; (7) St Philibert.[22] Musset was cautious about the identification of the scenes in voussoirs (1) and (2). The tonsured figure in voussoir (4) was, he suggested, an abbot. He rejected the Virgin and Child as the interpretation of voussoir (5) but agreed that (6) may show David holding Goliath's head, on the grounds that the figure enthroned on the last voussoir may be David as king, rather than Philibert. In addition, moreover, he pointed out that the three voussoirs at the top of the arch form a discrete composition. In Musset's view, the central character, St Philibert, is thus flanked by figures turning towards him in attitudes of veneration.[23] Maylis Baylé agrees that the most likely theme for the outermost four voussoirs is the story of David and Goliath. She supports Musset's interpretations, rather than Priem's, but is uncertain about Philibert.[24]

There appears in fact to be one other sub-group, in addition to the set of three voussoirs at the top. The two outermost voussoirs on the right form a pair, if the enthroned figure is identified not as King David but as King Saul, extending his hand toward David, who presents him with Goliath's severed head (Pl. IVc). This episode comes from 1 Samuel 17:57. It occurs in Western manuscript illustration from the 9th century (Pl. Va).[25] The same incident can be identified in stone sculpture at a much earlier date, however, on an Early Christian sarcophagus from Marseille, now lost, but recorded in the 17th century (Pl. Vb).[26] On the right of the frieze are David, Saul and Goliath's head and on the left, the battle between David and Goliath. In manuscript illumination, the scene is found most commonly in psalter decoration, in conjunction with various of the psalms.[27] In sculpture, it sometimes occurs in a specifically memorial context.[28]

At least one of the remaining two scenes on the left of the outer order may represent another incident from the same story. The weapon carried by the aggressor in voussoir (2) has been read by Musset as an axe.[29] Georges Priem suggested that it was a sling.[30] A sling, rather than an axe, is what it should be, if this is David felling Goliath. The head of the weapon is certainly not the same as the wedge-shaped axes in the roughly contemporary Bayeux Tapestry. At Montivilliers, the weapon-head is curved and curls under itself. Equally, it is unlike any of the slings to be seen in the hand of various Davids, which are invariably little stringed pouches. In the battle with Goliath, David is quite frequently depicted brandishing a curved-headed stick (his shepherd's crook), sometimes in addition to his sling. He occurs thus, confronting Goliath, on a small number of Early Christian sarcophagi: on the lost sarcophagus from Marseille, on another, also lost, from Reims (Pl. Vc), and on two fragments, both from Vienne.[31] If the sculptor at Montivilliers had a visual model before him, perhaps it was one that he only imperfectly understood.

The David on these sarcophagus friezes is not the king and psalmist, but the shepherd, who triumphs over the indomitable foe. Like so much else in Early Christian funerary iconography, he comes from the *Commendatio animae*, the prayer for the dying: 'Deliver, O Lord, this soul, just as you delivered David from the hand of King Saul and from the hand of Goliath'.[32] Together with one other from Ancona, the four examples just cited are the only known depictions of the David and Goliath theme on Early Christian sarcophagi. These four have a French provenance. They were probably all produced in the first half of the 4th century in Arles. There are in fact no known examples from Rome.[33]

The outermost voussoir on the left side of the outer order at Montivilliers is damaged, but an upright figure swinging a large sword above a kneeling man is still legible. This could be

Abraham and Isaac, but if so, where is the ram? Or it could be David again, killing Goliath with his own sword (1 Samuel 17:51), as depicted in the 11th-century Werden Psalter (Pl. VA). Either of these Old Testament themes would be consistent with the apparently funerary character of the iconography of the arch. Abraham's sacrafice was likewise a metaphor for Christian deliverance in the early church and is a theme which occurs commonly on sarcophagi.[34]

This series of comparisons with sarcophagus reliefs suggests that the voussoirs of the outer order at Montivilliers might themselves be read as a frieze. Without the gaps, this is a fairly symmetrical composition with the nimbed ecclesiastic at its centre, slightly off axis (Fig. 2). Could this be an 11th-century representation of an Early Christian sarcophagus,

FIG. 2.   Montivilliers, abbey church: outer order of sculpted arch, represented as a
frieze

one that had perhaps been colonised for an early medieval saint? The reuse of antique sarcophagi was standard practice in the Early Middle Ages.[35] When the lost 'David and Goliath' sarcophagus from Reims was recorded in the 17th century, it stood in the nave of Saint-Nicaise. According to tradition, it held the remains of Nicasius, 5th-century bishop of Reims (Pl. VC).[36]

The Identity of the Saint

Who, then, might be commemorated by the arch at Montivilliers? The obvious candidate would seem to be St Philibert, the late 7th-century founder of the abbey.[37] He, however, appears to be excluded, principally because he was an abbot, whereas the saint at Montivilliers was evidently a bishop; this is indicated by his gesture of blessing.[38]

Another contender emerges from the meagre internal evidence furnished by the abbey itself, one which has, moreover, intriguing political implications. The earliest surviving account of the liturgical arrangements within the building dates from 1612.[39] It was written by Jean Bain who, as parish priest, also performed the offices of the nuns' church. In Bain's day there were four chapels 'in the choir'.[40] He gave the dedication of their respective altars and the relics contained in each, but not their precise whereabouts. From Bain's account, it appears that two of these chapels were in the vicinity of the Gothic extension to the nave and so lay on the north side of the church. They can, therefore, be excluded from consideration in relation to the arch.[41] The remaining two may well have been located on the south side. The altar of one was dedicated to St Barbara, the other to Sts Cosmas, Damian, Lawrence and Nicaise. Four of these five saints, can be discounted for reasons of gender, or status, none having been a bishop. The fifth, Nicaise, seems at first sight promising. Moreover, an altar dedicated to him was discarded by the abbey in 1605, being considered 'trop antique'.

The saint's name is, however, rendered by Jean Bain as 'Nigaise'.[42] Bain thus identified not the fifth-century bishop of Reims but the earlier decapitated saint with whom Bishop Nicasius has at times been confounded, namely Nigasius of Rouen.[43]

Nigasius, missionary and martyr of uncertain date, was never actually a bishop. However, in the last decades of the 11th century — precisely when the arch at Montivilliers was produced — Nigasius was officially designated first Bishop of Rouen.[44] The timeliness of Nigasius's inclusion in the episcopal list, spurious as it was and based only on recent tradition, is worthy of comment.[45] It occurred during the archiepiscopate of William Bonne Ame (1078/80–1110).[46] At the beginning of this period, the authority of the metropolitan diocese of Rouen was seriously impugned by Rome.[47] William himself faced recurrent problems with the reformed papacy for much of his term of office.[48] Legend had made Nigasius a follower of St Denis, likewise sent to Gaul by St Clement. The presence of Nigasius's name at the head of Rouen's episcopal list thus invested the diocese with apostolic credibility.[49] His 'elevation' to the episcopate at a critical period for the diocese was probably not fortuitous.[50]

Nigasius's history is obscure. According to legend, he and his companions Quirinus and Scubiculus were martyred in the Vexin and buried by their follower, Pientia. The suggestion that Nigasius is represented on the arch at Montivilliers places him at the centre of the frieze-like composition, flanked by the priest, Quirinus, and by the deacon, Scubiculus with the matron Pientia.[51] These figures are accompanied by episodes of a redemptive character from the Old Testament, wholly or partly from the story of David, much as on the lost sarcophagus of Nigasius's near-namesake at Reims (Pl. Vc). The creatures depicted beneath, on the inner order of the arch, may be purely ornamental. Equally, given their subordinate location and sometimes tormented postures, they could, to borrow Panofsky's phrase, represent 'the conquered monsters of the nether world'.[52] At all events, they bring to mind the aftermath of the murder of Nigasius and his companions as recounted by Orderic Vitalis; the bodies of the martyrs, although 'left by their persecutors to be devoured by carrion birds, dogs and wild beasts', were nevertheless preserved whole.[53]

Whether or not the identification of Nigasius is accepted, it can be stated that the saint depicted on the arch is a bishop who, by the second half of the 11th century, was closely associated with Montivilliers. Given the apparently funerary character of the sculptural ensemble of which he is the focus, his body (or some relic of it) appears to have lain in the south transept chapel to which the sculpted arch gave access.[54] The chapel would, moreover, have been designed from the start to accommodate him and its entrance decorated accordingly.

The Chapel

Romanesque architectural ornament, such as arch mouldings, is sometimes used to announce to spectators that they are about to enter a more important space than the one in which they are situated.[55] According to this view, the south transept chapel at Montivilliers is of key significance to our understanding of the arch. The chapel has never been discussed in connection with the sculpted arch, doubtless because nothing is known of its function, altar or relics, if any. However, something of its original character can still be recaptured.

The room which now lies to the east of the sculpted arch is a sacristy, as it has been since at least 1863, when the south transept chapel was extended.[56] In plan, the chapel consisted of an apse, now lost, preceded by a small, groin-vaulted bay which still survives (Pl. IIIc).[57] The semicircular window in the modern sacristy is effectively the top of the apse arch, the opening having been glazed once the apse had been dismantled. Existing reconstructions of the plan of the chapel are deceptive; it was really quite small. The springing of the apse was just to the east of the modern doorway connecting the chapel and the choir aisle, not aligned with the first pier of the south choir arcade, as is incorrectly shown on all published plans, including that reproduced here.

The chapel preserves one other feature, in addition to the arch, which suggests that it was liturgically distinctive or had a special function. It is entered today through the doorway in the westernmost bay of the south choir aisle. That doorway is evidently post-medieval, but the tall, deep arch, the imposts and capitals framing it on the inside, within the chapel, are all Romanesque (Pl. IIIc). From the aisle, it can be seen that the present stone doorway stands within a larger, partly blocked opening. The vertical joint of the blocking is discernible in the aisle wall, on either side of the doorway. The remains of two iron hinges in the eastern jamb of the blocked opening presumably indicate the presence of a grille. The Romanesque chapel and choir aisle were therefore interconnected, an arrangement that is far from common.[58]

The identification of the nimbed bishop at Montivilliers as St Nigasius hangs by the slenderest of threads, but one piece of architectural evidence within the chapel lends its support. Inside the vestigial chapel, the leading edge of the arch of the original entrance to the choir aisle bears an angle roll, albeit damaged (Pl. IIIc). This detail, hallmark of mature Romanesque, makes its first appearance in Normandy in the 1080s.[59] A date for the sculpted arch in the 1080s to 1090s is consistent with this evidence and with current dating of the eastern arm of the building.

The Design of the Arch

The influence of Muslim Spain has been detected in the Romanesque architectural sculpture of Normandy.[60] The form of decoration chosen for the arch at Montivilliers has been explained in this context.[61] An 'Islamic' source for Montivilliers holds good only if the arch is thought of primarily for its combination of plain and decorated voussoirs. But parallels in Islamic Andalusia for the historiated voussoirs, or for this partial or selective combination of plain and figural stones are not forthcoming. Moreover, since its recent very thorough cleaning, the arch now looks less Islamicising, minus its (presumably post-medieval) polychromy.[62]

It is possible to see the alternating pattern at Montivilliers as a device, chosen for its aesthetic or communicative properties, rather than as an example of stylistic borrowing. There are examples in other media of figural panels alternating with a plain or uniform ground. On some Byzantine icons, for example, there are marginal scenes, sometimes with captions, generally relating to the central image, as on the 14th-century frame of the icon of the Holy Face at Genoa.[63] The 'captions' on the Icon of the Virgin at Freising Cathedral in Bavaria alternate with busts of archangels and saints around the 13th-century border.[64] Such objects demonstrate that craftsmen and patrons might choose to space out images to enhance legibility or impact. An alternating rhythm might equally be adopted in order to combine picture and text, or two different media. The uncarved voussoirs at Montivilliers, which now simply serve as a foil for the decorated ones, could originally have borne painted motifs, or a painted inscription referring to the saint at the apex of the arch. An example of an 'interrupted' inscription, carved rather than painted, occurs on the arch on the 12th-century relief of the Virgin and Child at Saint-Aventin (Haute-Garonne), where the verse celebrating the virgin birth is interspersed with rosettes at regular intervals.[65] Maybe the odd pair of decorated voussoirs at the top of the inner order at Montivilliers served as a visual divider, separating two words, or punctuating a phrase, rather like the incised cross at the top of the arch surmounting the reliefs of the apostles of *c.* 1100 in the cloister at Moissac.[66]

There seems to be no parallel in Western architecture inside a building for the arch at Montivilliers. The closest comparisons occur on external entrances and are slightly later in date. At Verona, both at the cathedral and at San Zeno, on the arches of the western porch, carved motifs alternate with plain panels.[67] No source or reason seems to have been suggested for the alternating motif here. Wart Arslan's proposition that this group of north Italian porches of the 1130s derives from free-standing Byzantine ciboria suggests, however, a final observation.[68] It is as a built-in ciborium that the south transept arch and chapel at Montivilliers might be perceived, with its commemorative frieze and, perhaps, inscription, and small groin-vaulted 'baldacchino' sheltering an altar or shrine within. There are several parallels for the location of a significant tomb or shrine in a bespoke transept chapel. The closest to Montivilliers in concept and date is at Airvault (Deux-Sèvres).[69] If the identity of the dedicatee of the chapel at Montivilliers remains elusive, a good case for his existence can nevertheless be made.

ACKNOWLEDGEMENTS

I thank Prof. C. M. Kauffman, Prof. E. C. Fernie, Dr M. Baylé, T. A. Heslop and D. Hibler for information and advice and Timothy Makower for drawing Figure 2. I am grateful to Bob Allies and Stephen Heywood for their assistance during visits to Montivilliers. Dedicated to the memory of Hilary Hallpike (1943–90).

REFERENCES

1. See L. Musset, *Normandie romane*, II, 2nd edn (La Pierre-qui-Vire 1985), 129–38. See also A.-M. Carment-Lanfry, 'Les églises romanes dans les anciens archidiaconés du Grand-Caux et du Petit-Caux au diocèse de Rouen: Montivilliers', *Revue des Sociétés savantes de Haute-Normandie*, XLIV (1966), 5–19; J. Vallery-Radot, 'Montivilliers: église abbatiale', *CA*, LXXXIX (1926), 476–504; M. Anfray, *L'architecture normande* (Paris 1939), 181–5; G. Priem, 'L'abbaye royale de Montivilliers', *La Normandie bénédictine au temps de Guillaume le Conquérant* (Lille 1967), 153–77.

2. Vallery-Radot, 'Montivilliers', 489; Anfray, *L'architecture normande*, 181–5.

3. J. Bilson, 'The Plan of the First Cathedral Church of Lincoln', *Archaeologia*, LXII (1911), 554.

4. For the history of the foundation, see Vallery-Radot, 'Montivilliers', 476; see also E. Hall and J. R. Sweeney, 'An Unpublished Privilege of Innocent III in Favor of Montivilliers', *Speculum*, XLIX (1974), 662–79.

5. Inferred from Duke Robert's Charter of 1035. See n. 10.

6. *Les Chroniques de Normandie*, ed. F. Michel (Rouen 1839), 33.

7. *Chronique de Robert de Torigni*, ed. L. Delisle, II (SHN, Rouen 1873), 195.

8. Fauroux, *Recueil*, no. 34.

9. Ibid., nos 70 and 87.

10. Ibid., no. 90. See also, J.-M. Bouvris, 'La renaissance de l'abbaye de Montivilliers et son développement jusqu'à la fin du XIe siècle' and J. Le Maho, 'L'abbaye de Montivilliers et l'aristocratie locale au XIe et XIIe siècles', both in *L'abbaye de Montivilliers à travers les âges* [Actes du Colloque organisé à Montivilliers le 8 mars 1986], *Recueil de l'Association des amis du vieux Havre*, XLVI (1988).

11. In the mortuary roll of Mathilda, abbess of La Trinité, Caen (d. 1113), Elizabeth is referred to as 'fundatrix' of the church of Montivilliers, see *Rouleaux des morts du IXe au XVe siècles*, ed. L. Delisle (SHF, Paris 1866), 210.

12. Musset, *Normandie romane*, 131; Carment-Lanfry, 'Montivilliers', 9, 18; Vallery-Radot, 'Montivilliers', 489.

13. Vallery-Radot, 'Montivilliers', 477 n. 2, and n. 1, cites a document of 1766, claiming that the parish was established in the 11th century. Musset, *Normandie romane*, 129, suggests that the dual function of the church may have been pre-Norman in origin.

14. M. Deshoulières, 'L'église de Graville-Sainte-Honorine', *CA*, LXXXIX (1926), 508–30; Musset, *Normandie romane*. 194–201.

15. Noted by Deborah Kahn in 'Romanesque Architectural Sculpture in Kent' (Ph.D. thesis, University of London, 1982), 48–9.

16. Abbé Voiment, *Eglise de Montivilliers. Guide des visiteurs* (Montivilliers 1913), 37–8.

D

17. Ibid.

18. G. Priem, 'La sculpture de l'arc d'entrée de la chapelle orientée du croisillon sud à Montivilliers', *Recueil des publications de la Société havraise d'études diverses*, 1966 (Le Havre 1967), 5–14, *Abbaye royale de Montivilliers. Année des abbayes Normandes*, XIV (Rouen 1979).

19. Musset, *Normandie romane*, 131, 135–7.

20. M. Baylé, *Les origines et les premiers développements de la sculpture romane en Normandie* (Art de Basse-Normandie, C bis, Caen 1992), 99–100.

21. Voiment suggested this in 1913, see *Guide*, 38.

22. Priem, 'La sculpture', 9–12; and *Abbaye royale*, 20.

23. Musset, *Normandie romane*, 136.

24. Baylé, *Les origines*, 99–100, 220 n. 307.

25. K. E. Haney, *The Winchester Psalter, an Iconographic Study* (Leicester 1986), 88.

26. E. Le Blant, *Les sarcophages chrétiens de la Gaule* (Paris 1886), 35 no. 49.

27. E.g. in the 9th-century Utrecht Psalter, f. 91^v: Psalm 151, see Haney, *Winchester Psalter*, fig. 78; in the 11th-century Werden Psalter, f. 74^r: Psalm 109 (illustrated here, Pl. VA) and Odbert Psalter, Boulogne, BM, MS 20, f. 11^r: Psalm 1, see R. Kahsnitz, *Der Werdener Psalter in Berlin, Ms. theol. lat. fol. 358* (Düsseldorf 1979), figs 22 and 157; *c.* 1200, the Ingeborg Psalter, f. 97^r: Psalm 58, see F. Deuchler, *Der Ingeborgpsalter* (Berlin 1967), fig. 46.

28. Other examples with a memorial or funerary connotation include Irish high crosses at Monasterboice (Co. Louth): West Cross, east face, see F. Henry, *Irish Art during the Viking Invasions* (London 1967), 188, and at Seirkieran (Co. Offaly): base, see H. Roe, 'The David cycle in early Irish Art', *Journal of the Royal Society of Antiquaries of Ireland*, LXIX (1949), 39–59, 51, fig. 28. At Saint-Aubin, Angers: façade of the chapter house (as much burial chamber as place of assembly), P. d'Herbécourt and J. Porcher, *Anjou roman* (La Pierre-qui-Vire 1959), 152, pl. 7.

29. Musset, *Normandie romane*, 136.

30. Priem; 'La sculpture' (1967), 9.

31. For the sarcophagus from Reims (also recorded in the 17th century) and the Vienne fragments, see Le Blant, *Les sarcophages*, nos 17, 22, 24.

32. F. Cabrol and H. Leclercq, *Dictionnaire d'archéologie chrétienne et de liturgie*, IV (Paris 1920), 435–40.

33. G. Wilpert, *I sarcofagi cristiani antichi*, II (Rome 1932), 264.

34. R. Garrucci, *Storia dell'arte cristiana*, V (Prato 1879), illustrates some forty examples.

35. *The History of the Franks by Gregory of Tours*, ed. O. M. Dalton (Oxford 1927), I, 330–1, II, 124; *Bede's Ecclesiastical History of the English People*, eds B. Colgrave and R. A. B. Mynors (Oxford 1969), 395; Le Blant, *Les sarcophages chrétiens*, 34–55.

36. Ibid., 17.

37. R. de Lasteyrie, 'L'église de Saint-Philibert de Grandlieu', *Mémoires de l'Institut national de France. Académie des inscriptions et belles-lettres*, XXXVIII/ii (1911), 1–82, 9.

38. I thank Sandy Heslop for this. He has found no examples of figures blessing certainly identifiable as abbots, rather than bishops, see T. A. Heslop, *Image and Authority: English Seals of the 11th and 12th centuries* (forthcoming).

39. The relevant extracts from Jean Bain's autograph manuscript, 'L'histoire et description de l'abbaye de Monstiervillier . . . en l'an 1612', Montivilliers, Bibl. mun. MS 2, are published in E. Dumont, *L'abbaye de Montivilliers* (Havre 1876), 29 ff.

40. Dumont, *Montivilliers*, 31.

41. According to Bain, the altar of the first of the four chapels was dedicated to the Holy Sacrament and bore the tabernacle housing 'le precieux corps de Notre-Seigneur Jesus Christ'. The second chapel was that of St Michael. Bain said that the Gothic parish church — essentially an extension of the north aisle of the Romanesque nave — lay 'au-dessus de la chapelle Saint Michel, en tirant vers le sépulcre de Notre-Seigneur . . .', see Dumont *Montivilliers*, 29.

42. Ibid., 32.

43. *Acta Sanctorum*, Oct. v (Brussels 1786), 510–59; *Bibliotheca Sanctorum*, IX (Rome 1961), 858–60; *Lexicon für Theologie und Kirche*, VII (Freiburg im B. 1962), 940.

44. L. Duchesne, *Fastes épiscopaux de l'ancienne Gaule*, II (Paris 1910), 202–3.

45. Part of the Nigasius legend dates from the 9th century, but the tradition designating him first bishop of Rouen goes back only to the late 11th-century account of his martyrdom and translation, by a monk of Saint-Ouen, see E. Martène and U. Durand, *Thesaurus Novus Anecdotorum*, III (Paris 1717), 1677–82.

46. Duchesne, *Fastes épiscopaux*, 203.

47. D. C. Douglas, *William the Conqueror* (London 1964), 338–9.

48. G. H. Williams, *The Norman Anonymous of 1100 AD* (Cambridge Mass. 1951), 111–15. William was suspended from office by the papacy in 1081, 1093 and 1100; ibid., 119 n. 399.

49. Noted, without comment, in *The Ecclesiastical History of Orderic Vitalis*, ed. M. Chibnall, III (Oxford 1972), 36 n. 4.

50. The author of the late 11th-century account of Nigasius's martyrdom was a monk of Saint-Ouen, possibly the deacon, Jean, active *c.* 1042–92, see F. Pommeraye, *Histoire de l'abbaye royale de Saint-Ouen* (Rouen 1662), 339. The Saint-Ouen monk may have known the ? 10th-century 'Acts' of St Nigasius (passages cited in F. Pommeraye, *Histoire des archevesques de Rouen* (Rouen 1667), 30, 32, 34 and *passim*; see also *Histoire littéraire de la France*, VI (Paris 1865–75), 420, 701). For the view that the monk invented a *curriculum vitae* for Nigasius, as well as his episcopate, see *Bibliotheca Sanctorum*, 859. Nigasius's name was inserted in the episcopal list between 1079/80–1110. The monk may have produced both 'evidence' and 'forgery'.

51. Pientia is mentioned with Nigasius in the 9th-century martyrology of Usuardus, *Bibliotheca Sanctorum*, 858–9. She is represented in the 15th-century Salisbury Breviary (Paris, BN, MS lat., 17294, f. 604), with the bodies of Nigasius and his two companions, see V. Leroquais, *Les bréviaires manuscrits des bibliothèques publiques de France*, III (Paris 1934), 342.

52. E. Panofsky, *Tomb Sculpture* (London 1964), 49, where the phrase refers to the 'Reiterstein' from Hornhausen, Saxony.

53. *Orderic*, III, 36. Orderic acknowledged Nigasius as first bishop of Rouen, and apparently drew on the 11th-century *passio* of St Nigasius; see above n. 45.

54. Nigasius's translation to Saint-Ouen, Rouen, occurred in 1032, attended by Duke Robert the Magnificent and Robert, archbishop of Rouen. Duke Robert initiated the withdrawal of Montivilliers from Fécamp in the early 1030s. Conceivably, he conferred some relic of Nigasius on the abbey he was then promoting. Sandy Heslop kindly pointed this out. Fécamp was an earlier recipient of relics of Nigasius, F. Pommeraye, *Histoire des archevesques*, 37. Possibly some reached Montivilliers with the transfer of the Fécamp community *c.* 990.

55. E. C. Fernie, *The Architecture of the Anglo-Saxons* (London 1983), 141–2, 148.

56. Vallery-Radot, 'Montivilliers', 482.

57. The northern springing of the apse is still discernible within the sacristy. The north transept chapel no longer exists. Its foundations were exposed, but not recorded, in 1903, ibid., 495. The blocked entrance arch in the east wall of the north transept bears no sign of having been carved.

58. Interconnecting transept chapels and choir aisle occur in the second half of the 11th–12th centuries at: Sta Maria im Kapitol, Cologne, see K. J. Conant, *Carolingian and Romanesque Architecture 800–1200* (Harmondsworth 1959), fig. 67; La Charité-sur-Loire, see R. de Lasteyrie, *L'architecture religieuse à l'epoque roman* (Paris 1912), fig. 452; Hereford Cathedral, see RCHM *Herefordshire*, I (London 1931), 96; probably Worcester Cathedral, see R. Gem, 'Bishop Wulfstan II and the Romanesque Cathedral Church of Worcester', *Medieval Art and Architecture at Worcester Cathedral, BAA CT* I (1978), 28; Airvault (Deux-Sèvres), see A. de la Bouvalière, 'Abbaye d'Airvault', *CA*, LXX (1903), 75–8.

59. E. C. Fernie, *An Architectural History of Norwich Cathedral* (Oxford 1992), 142.

60. Most recently, see K. Watson, 'French Romanesque and Islam: Andalusian Elements on French Architectural Decoration *c.* 1030–1180', *British Archaeological Reports International Series*, I (Oxford 1989), 191–4.

61. See G. Zarnecki, '1066 and Architectural Sculpture', *Proceedings of the British Academy*, LII (1966), 87–104, 95, Pls XIII a and b, for the suggestion that the alternating pattern on the arch at Montivilliers originated in Islamic Spain, e.g. Cordoba. See also Watson, 'French Romanesque and Islam', 193, 261. For the possible French precedent for this alternation at Evrecy, *c.* 1000, see Baylé, *Les origines*, 100; Watson, 'French Romanesque and Islam', 193.

62. Earlier photographs show the carved voussoirs painted, Zarnecki, '1066' Pl. XIII. This polychromy presumably post-dated the modern rediscovery of the arch, see Voiment, *Guide*, 37–8.

63. A. Grabar, *Les revêtements en or et argent des icones byzantines du Moyen Age* (Venice 1975), no. 35, fig. 74, pl. C.

64. Ibid., no. 16, fig. 39, pl. XXIV.

65. R. Favreau, J. Michaud and B. Leplant, eds, *Corpus des inscriptions de la France mediévale*, VIII (Paris 1982), 49, no. 13, pl. XIX, fig. 34.

66. M. Schapiro, *The Sculpture of Moissac* (London 1985), e.g. figs 14–16.

67. A. M. Romagnini, *Nicholaus e l'arte del suo tempo*, III (Ferrara 1985), 234, fig. 4 and 265, fig. 11.

68. W. Arslan, *L'Architettura Romanica Veronese* (Verona 1939), 109.

69. At Airvault (late 11th-century), the north transept chapel consists of an apse preceded by a small, groin-vaulted bay, with the cenotaph of the first abbot and builder of the church, Peter, d. 1110, in a purpose-built niche, see de la Bouvalière, 'Airvault', 75–8. For La Trinité, Caen, see M. Baylé, *La Trinité de Caen, sa place dans l'histoire de l'architecture et du décor romans* (Geneva and Paris 1979), 14–15. At Lincoln in the late 12th century, see D. Stocker, 'Form and Function at Either End of Lincoln Minster', paper delivered at the Oxford Cathedral Archaeology Conference, 1989 (forthcoming). At York in the 13th century, see L. Hoey, 'The 13th-Century Transepts of York Minster', *Gesta*, XXV/2 (1986), 227–44, 229.

The Figural Capitals of the Chapterhouse of Saint-Georges-de-Boscherville

By Kathryn A. Morrison

The three surviving column-statues and one of the capitals adorning the entrance to the chapterhouse of the abbey of Saint-Georges de-Boscherville are well known. The column-statues represent Life, Death and an Abbot, while the capital depicts an act which would have taken place in the chapterhouse, an abbot administering corporal punishment to two monks. In 1973, Léon Pressouyre demonstrated that these four sculptures present a commentary on the duties of the abbot as outlined in the Rule of St Benedict.[1] They seem, however, to be the only chapterhouse images which would have conveyed ideas of particular relevance to the Benedictines who transacted their daily business there. The study of the remaining figural capitals has been seriously hampered by their poor state of preservation: the limestone has flaked badly over the last century, in some cases completely removing the carved surface. Their condition renders stylistic analysis extemely difficult, but their subject matter can be established from 19th-century representations. Fortunately, around the time the département acquired the chapterhouse in 1822, the full series of figural capitals was drawn by E.-H. Langlois and selected capitals were drawn by A. Deville, J. S. Cotman and others. This paper presents evidence for the appearance of the capitals and offers their enigmatic iconography for wider consideration.

The façade of the Boscherville chapterhouse is pierced by three round-headed apertures of equal width: a central doorway flanked by lateral bays with high sills (Pl. VI). The broad soffits of all three arches display imitation sexpartite vaulting, with ribs descending onto columns which stand against piers and responds of rectangular plan. On the front and back of the piers are twinned columns. Out of a total of 30 capitals, 13 were figural and 17 foliate. The numbering system applied to the capitals throughout this paper is shown in Figure 1.

The carving on capital 1, on the west face of the north respond, has worn away leaving an uneven surface but the scene which it carried, the Sacrifice of Isaac (Genesis, 22:1–14), was drawn by Langlois c. 1822 (Pl. VIIA).[2] Abraham stands in the centre of the composition, one hand resting on the head of his son Isaac, who kneels in prayer on an altar to the right. Meanwhile, an angel descends from the left and seizes Abraham's raised sword, while

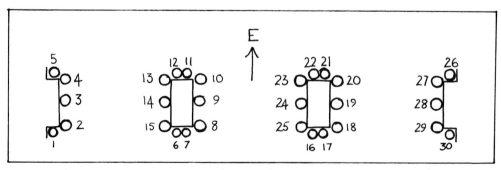

FIG. 1.   Plan of chapterhouse arcade showing numbering system for capitals
(not to scale)

beneath him is the ram caught in the thicket. Langlois depicted this two-sided capital in frieze format, but Abraham probably stood on the angle with the angel and ram on the broad west face and Isaac on the shallower south side. It is still just possible to discern the outline of the figures of Abraham and Isaac in these positions on the eroded capital, but the entire west face is lost.

The figures on the following capital, capital 2, have survived in a damaged condition, and cannot be identified with certainty (Pl. VIIA). On the west face are two figures, that on the left reaching out to the right-hand figure with one hand whilst pointing upwards with the other. Langlois' drawing of the scene gives the figure on the left a cross-halo, indicating the Deity, while that on the right is bearded and carries a staff.[3] Langlois thought that this represented God promising Abraham a numerous progeny: '. . . I will multiply thy seed as the stars of the heaven . . .' (Genesis, 22:17).[4] If this interpretation is correct, the remainder of the capital does not continue the biblical narrative. A second bearded figure with a staff stands on the angle of the capital. On the south face, the bust of an angel swoops down towards a bearded figure lying obliquely on a bed of foliage and stones. To the right, a standing bearded figure with a staff looks down: in Langlois' drawing he holds a spherical object in his left hand. The carving on the third face has been destroyed, but Langlois depicted two quadrupeds facing left, one above the other. The upper creature has a spiky spine and long snout, while the lower seems to be horned.

The remaining capitals on the north respond, capitals 3–5, were carved with foliage but are now heavily eroded.[5]

There are a number of figural capitals on the north pier. Capitals 15, 6, 7 and 8 are carved with scenes from the Book of Joshua, which survive in a better condition than any of the other figural scenes on the arcade (Pl. VIIB, C).[6] Capital 15 is carved on all three faces with soldiers in chain-mail. On the east side are two soldiers on horseback wielding swords; a third mounted soldier on the north face tramples a fallen soldier beneath the hoofs of the horse, while a kneeling soldier pleads for mercy. The sun is depicted on the angle as a face in profile surrounded by rays, and two foot soldiers carrying spears are carved on the west side. This scene has been identified as Joshua commanding the sun to stand still (Joshua, 10:12–14).[7] The Joshua cycle continues, if not in narrative sequence, on capitals 6–8. According to Joshua, 3:6–17, priests carried the Ark of the Covenant into the Jordan, causing the waters to part, thus enabling the Israelites to cross. Later, as recounted in Joshua, 6:4–16, seven priests blowing rams' horns encircled the besieged Jericho seven times. Capitals 6–8 present a strange conflation of these events. Six priests blowing trumpets as they cross the Jordan are followed by two priests bearing the Ark of the Covenant before Jericho, which is represented as a building occupied by soliders. If there is an iconographic reason for the Boscherville sculptor to have changed the biblical version of the story, it is not evident. Indeed, the changes may simply have resulted from a poor knowledge of the Bible, and in this may lie the reason why several ostensibly Old Testament scenes here remain unidentified.

On the east face of capital 8 is the flagellation scene referred to above (Pl. VIIc).[8] The reason for the juxtaposition of this scene with Jericho is not apparent.

The capital preceding the Joshua scenes, 14, presents a formal parallel for Joshua on horseback (Pl. VIIIB). The east face is carved with foliage, but on the main north face is an equestrian figure in civilian costume, possibly carrying a falcon. The forelegs of the horse trample a small figure. On the west face is a standing, crowned female figure who one held stylised plants in her raised hand: Langlois and Cotman depicted them as a type of fleur-de-lys and surviving traces bear this out.[9] This capital belongs to the series of so-called 'Constantine' figures, widespread in western France throughout the 12th century and thought to be modelled on the statue of Marcus Aurelius in Rome, then believed to represent the first Christian emperor.[10] The figures are generally thought to symbolise Christianity, vanquished Paganism and triumphant Ecclesia. The scene was not common on capitals and does not occur elsewhere in Normandy, although a lost Rider at Saint-Etienne, Caen (identified as William the Conqueror by Cotman, who published an engraving of the figure in 1822), can be regarded as a variation on the 'Constantine' type.[11]

Capital 9 is foliate and 10 appears to stand alone.[12] When Langlois drew capital 10, the east face was concealed by plaster (Pl. VIIc).[13] On the west face are two horses; on the south and east faces three praying figures, the foremost kneeling before a stag which displays a cross between its antlers. This must represent the vision and conversion of St Eustace rather than St Hubert who was popular at a later date. The inclusion of this scene is a warning that not all of the unidentified scenes must have a source in the Old Testament.

The south half of the damaged double capital on the east side of the north pier, capital 11, is carved with Corinthianesque foliage while the north half, capital 12, carries a formal scene which was drawn by Langlois and Cotman (Pl. VIIIA).[14] A figure wearing a fronded skirt, and with a fox's head, according to A. Besnard in his monograph of 1899, reaches out both hands towards a horned beast (goat?) which is slung over the back of a second, fully draped male figure who turns round.[15] The following capital, 13, is carved with a nude figure (demon?) with a short tail and two confrontational figures ostensibly on the verge of fighting. The nude figure was covered with plaster in 1822 and was consequently concealed from Langlois and Cotman.[16] The other figures were identified as female gossips by Besnard, and as fighting women in the presence of the devil by Musset, but from their short tunics, diapered leggings and short haircuts they are clearly male.[17] The north face of the capital is carved with two wrestling figures, again wearing short tunics and diapered leggings. They tumble over a strange object, depicted by Langlois as U-shaped with a diapered central panel and by Cotman as a standard. The scene on the third face of this capital shows Samson clasping a pillar in the house of the Philistines (Judges, 16:26–31). He wears a 'belt of strength', an attribute widely used to indicate the strength of the wearer and frequently employed to identify Samson.[18] The previous scene may therefore depict the cutting of Samson's hair (Judges, 16:17–20). In the absence of a female figure this must remain tentative, but according to biblical tradition if not always in medieval iconography, Delilah called in a man to do the evil deed. Another possibility is Samson setting about him with the jawbone of an ass.

Of the capitals on the south pier, 16 (effaced), 17, 18, 20 (effaced), 21 (effaced), 22 (effaced) 23 (effaced) and 25 were carved with foliage.[19] Enough survives on the face of 19 for it to be identified with a capital drawn by Langlois (Pl. VIIIc).[20] Several scenes are surmounted by a turreted arcade, clearly once supported by columns. Seated beneath the first arch is a crowned figure, possibly King David, playing a harp. Under the narrower second arch two goat-like creatures prance on their hind legs, one possibly beating a tambour. On the main face of the capital the drawing shows a headless knight, armed with sword and shield, confronting a quadruped balancing a fluted bowl on its right forepaw. Under the fourth arch a standing figure holds a crown over the head of a kneeling figure: the kneeling figure embraces and vomits over an object resembling two superimposed chalices. This scene encroaches onto the otherwise uncarved area beneath the fifth arch, which was not separated from the last scene by a column. Langlois identified the vomiting figure as Ezekiel, whom God instructed to eat a scroll (Ezekiel, 3:1–3), but this is doubtful.[21] Another capital drawn by Langlois represented Moses and the Brazen Serpent (Pl. VIIID).[22] When fiery serpents bit the people of Israel, killing them, God instructed Moses to make a serpent of brass and erect it on a pole. Those who had been bitten looked upon the serpent and lived

(Numbers, 21:6–9). The location of the Moses capital, not supplied by Langlois, is revealed by an undated drawing of the entrance arcade by Deville which clearly depicts Moses' horns on capital 24.[23] Langlois drew, from left to right, a standing woman facing left, her head veiled and her hand thrust into the mouth of a disembodied serpent's head; she faces a second human figure, again reduced to a head. Right of this the brazen serpent is raised upon a pole, with one worshipping figure on its left and three, accompanied by Moses, on its right. Behind these figures are three other serpents, and a large building. The building, not mentioned in the biblical episode, remains unidentified.

The capitals on the south respond are all badly damaged. Twenty-nine and 30 were carved with acanthus, and 26 and 27 with waterleaf, but 28 was figural. Now worn, it too was drawn by Langlois (Pl. VIIIE).[24] On the east side of the capital was a seated ass facing right and playing the lyre, and it may have been significant that this was located opposite the harp-playing king on capital 19.[25] On the north face a standing, headless figure thrust both hands into the jaws of rampant lions whose tails issued foliage. Besnard published this scene, which he identified as Justice plagued by Vices.[26] As the figure wore a *bliaut* and was therefore female, it cannot have represented Daniel in the Lions' Den. On the west face of the capital a headless knight with a split skirt (cf. 'Constantine') and a tall shield raised his sword against a rampant goat. Two heads served as volutes on the upper angles of the capital: these, together with the scene on the main face, are clearly visible in a photograph published in 1931 but probably taken in 1913.[27]

And so the identifiable capitals on the chapterhouse entrance are as follows: the Sacrifice of Isaac, Samson pulling down the house of the Philistines, a 'Constantine' figure, Joshua stopping the Sun, the Passage to Jordan, the Fall of Jericho, an abbot administering punishment to two monks, the Vision of St Eustace and the Brazen Serpent. It is difficult to read a coherent iconographic theme into those subjects, mostly drawn from the Old Testament, but including one scene from a saint's life. Only the Punishment capital relates specifically to the function of the chapterhouse. Some may have served as antitypes for New Testament scenes which decorated the cloister arcades. In the Musée des Antiquités de la Seine-Maritime are three cloister capitals found *c*. 1822, reportedly near the chapterhouse. One, which would have surmounted a pier composed of four columnar shafts, is carved with six Incarnation scenes. Another, which would have crowned double columns, is carved with ten musicians and a dancer/acrobat figure and the third capital is foliate. Two more historiated capitals from the cloister were illustrated in 1827 by Deville but are now lost. One bore the Entry into Jerusalem and the other an unidentified scene including Christ.[28] Without information about the location of the cloister capitals, it is impossible to infer that they enhanced the significance of the chapterhouse decoration.

Finally, a few words about the style of the chapterhouse carvings. The column-statues, capitals and accompanying decorative elements of the façade display a stylistic cohesion which extends to the purely ornamental decoration of the interior, namely the corbelled sill-band, window capitals and vault ribs. One workshop was active here, and close parallels for the foliage capitals are found in two other buildings within the region: the chapel of Saint-Julien at the Petit-Quevilly, built 1160–1, and the Tour Saint-Romain of Rouen Cathedral erected in the 1150s.[29] It seems likely that the Boscherville chapterhouse, known to have been erected in the time of Abbot Victor (1157–1210), was built during the early 1160s. Almost every scholar to comment on the Boscherville style has suggested that the workshop came from the Ile-de-France, often specifying Chartres or Paris,[30] but as no close stylistic or iconographic connections can be made with sculpture in these areas it is reasonable to propose that at Boscherville we are dealing with a workshop based in Normandy, most probably in or around Rouen.

ACKNOWLEDGEMENTS

I am grateful to the Archives départementales de la Seine-Maritime, Rouen, for permission to publish the Langlois drawings in their collection.

REFERENCES

1. L. Pressouyre, 'St Bernard to St Francis: Monastic Ideals and Iconographic Programs in the Cloister', *Gesta*, XII (1973), 71–92, especially 78–81.
2. ADSM, Albums de la Commission départementale des Antiquités de la Seine-Inférieure, t.1, pt 2, f. 58, no. 8. Two of Langlois' chapterhouse drawings are dated 1822, but the majority are undated. For other depictions of the Sacrifice of Isaac capital, see C. Nodier, J. Taylor and A. de Cailleux, *Voyages pittoresques et romantiques dans l'ancienne France. Ancienne Normandie*, II (Paris 1825), pl. 116, no. 4; A. Deville, *Essai historique et descriptif sur l'église et l'abbaye de Saint-Georges-de-Boscherville, près Rouen* (Rouen 1827), pl. V, 2.
3. ADSM, Albums, t. 1, pt 2, f. 58, no. 8.
4. Langlois' identification of this scene is found in ADSM, 2-Fi (photographs of Langlois manuscript, f. 12).
5. A drawing by Deville (ADSM, Albums, t. 3, pt 1, f. 33), shows capital 5 with upright oak-like leaves and capital 4 with three tiers of pointed leaves.
6. ADSM, Albums, t. 1, pt 2, f. 58, no. 7. For illustrations of this series of capitals, see also J. S. Cotman and D. Turner, *Architectural Antiquities of Normandy*, I (London 1822), pl. 11. The engraving in Nodier *et al.*, *Ancienne Normandie*, II, pl. 116, no. 1, has been reversed and is shown with column-statues below. There are numerous inaccuracies in this plate.
7. The scene was identified by Langlois. See also Deville, *Essai historique*, 34 and pl. V, 1.
8. Deville, *Essai historique*, pl. V, 3.
9. ADSM, Albums, t. 1, pt 2, f. 57, no. 6; Cotman and Turner, *Architectural Antiquities*, I, pl. 11.
10. See R. Crozet, 'Nouvelles remarques sur les cavaliers sculptés ou peints dans les églises romanes', *Cahiers de civilization mediévale*, 1 (1958), 27.
11. Cotman and Turner, *Architectural Antiquities*, I, 20 and pl. 20.
12. In a sketchy drawing by Deville, which is accurate in all other respects, capital 9 appears to carry figures (ADSM, Albums, t. 3, pt 1, f. 33).
13. ADSM, Albums, t. 1, pt 2, f. 58, no. 7.
14. ADSM, Albums, t. 1, pt 2, f. 58, no. 8; Cotman and Turner, *Architectural Antiquities*, I, pl. 11.
15. A. Besnard, *Monographie de l'église et de l'abbaye Saint-Georges-de-Boscherville* (Paris 1899), 144.
16. ADSM, 2-Fi (photographs of Langlois manuscript, f. 12). See: ADSM, Albums, t. 1, pt 2, f. 58, no. 8; Cotman and Turner, *Architectural Antiquities*, I, pl. 11.
17. Besnard, *Monographie*, 144; Musset, *Normandie romane*, 2nd edn, II (1985), 156.
18. G. Zarnecki, 'A Romanesque Bronze Candlestick in Oslo and the Problem of the "Belts of Strength"', *Arbok Kunstindustrimuseet i Oslo* (1963–4), 45–67, reprinted in *Studies in Romanesque Sculpture* (London 1979), VII, 45–67.
19. An undated pencil drawing by Deville showing the chapterhouse arcade from the east, depicts capitals 20, 21, 22 and 23 with broad leaved foliage (ADSM, Albums, t. 3, pt 1, f. 33).
20. ADSM, Albums, t. 1, pt 2, f. 58, no. 9.
21. ADSM, 2-Fi (photographs of Langlois manuscript, f. 14).
22. ADSM, Albums, t. 1, pt 2, f. 57, no. 6.
23. ADSM, Albums, t. 3, pt 2, f. 33.
24. ADSM, Albums, t. 1, pt 2, f. 58, no. 9. An engraving in Nodier *et al.*, *Ancienne Normandie*, II, pl. 116, no. 8 is reversed.
25. The east side of capital 28 can be seen in an undated drawing by A. Deville (ADSM, Albums, t. 3, pt 1, f. 33).
26. Besnard, *Monographie*, 144, and drawing, 133.
27. A. Gardner, *Medieval Sculpture in France* (Cambridge 1931), fig. 226, 224.
28. ADSM, Albums, f. 59, no. 10 (Entry into Jerusalem) and nos 11–13 (unidentified scene including Christ). There is a photograph of a second twin foliage capital from the cloister in ADSM, 2-Fi. Its present location is not noted.
29. For the dating of the Tour Saint-Romain and Saint-Julien, Petit-Quevilly, see L. M. Grant, 'Gothic Architecture in Normandy, *c.* 1150–*c.* 1250' (unpublished Ph.D., Courtauld Institute of Art, University of London 1987), 55–9.
30. Cotman and Turner, *Architectural Antiquities*, 7; Deville, *Essai historique*, 37; Besnard, *Monographie*, 156; L. A. Michon, 'L'abbaye de Saint-Georges-de-Boscherville', *CA* (Rouen 1926), LXXXIX, 548; Musset, *Normandie romane*, II, 156.

The Wall-Paintings of the Petit-Quevilly

By Neil Stratford

In the Middle Ages, the Petit-Quevilly was a settlement on the edge of the forest of Rouvray, on the left bank of the Seine, facing Rouen. The church of Saint-Julien du Petit-Quevilly (Pl. IXA) is a simple building, with a rib-vaulted apse, a rectangular choir bay covered by a sexpartite rib-vault decorated with the famous cycle of paintings which is the subject of this article (Pl. IXB), an aisleless nave slightly wider than the choir and now protected by a post-medieval wooden roof, and a severe west façade with a portal of several round-headed orders enriched with angle-rolls. The elevation is two-storey, with broadly splayed round-headed windows above blank arcading with outward-pointing chevron. In the nave, cut-back wall-shafts suggest that originally a sexpartite rib-vault covered the double bay at the east, and a quadripartite rib-vault the narrow western bay; these vaults were actually built, since traces of them are still visible where they were cut back to make way for the present wooden roof. The mouldings combine fat torus rolls (with or without fillets) and keeled rolls, with keeled or semicircular angle-rolls, while the Attic bases have a projecting lower torus. This vocabulary of profiles, the well-cut masonry and above all the capital sculpture of the wall-arcading, suggest comparisons with local buildings: the chapterhouse of Saint-Georges-de-Boscherville, the door of Ivry-la-Bataille and the Tour Saint-Romain of Rouen Cathedral.[1] Everything conspires to suggest that these buildings date from *c.* 1160, a chronology confirmed by the earliest known documentary reference to construction works at the Petit-Quevilly.

A number of documentary sources refer to the Petit-Quevilly and its buildings during the Middle-Ages. First, Robert of Torigny in his Chronicle writes ... *Anglorum Henricus 7.* [19 Dec. 1160–18 Dec. 1161] *Henricus rex ... parcum et mansionem regiam fecit circa fustes plantatos apud Chivilleium, juxta Rothomagum ...;*[2] abbot Robert was particularly well-informed about his hero, Henry II's, activities in Normandy. It is with these building works by Henry II for his manor-house that the construction of the present church can very probably be associated. Secondly, a charter of Henry II, datable between 1185 and 31 January 1188, confirms his gift *foeminis leprosis de Quevilli clausum meum domorum mearum de Quevilli, ubi mansionem suam construxi ...;* the charter provides a *terminus ante quem* for the establishment of a leper-house for women. Farin and Duplessis were the first to date Henry II's gift to 1183, although evidence for this date is not given. They also cite a charter of Walter, archbishop of Rouen from 1184 to 1207, in which *nos vero praedictarum mulierum leprosarum religionem commendantes et earum paupertati consentientes.* That is, the leper-house existed at that date with the women having taken vows.[3] Henry II's gift of *c.* 1185–8 has often been taken to be the date after which the choir vaults were decorated, but it will be shown that this assumption is probably wrong. Thirdly, a Fécamp document is said to mention that in May 1243 the church was already dedicated to St Julien, whereas it had previously been dedicated to Notre-Dame.[4] Fourthly, a charter witnessed at Rouen in November, 1366, records the gift by Charles V to the Maison-Dieu de Sainte-Madeleine at Rouen of his rights of patronage *in ecclesia Sancti Juliani ac in domo vocata Aula Puellarum in foresta nostra de Rovereto, prope Rothomagum situatis;* this is one of a series of gifts made by Charles to the Rouen Hôtel-Dieu, and the gift was subsequently confirmed by papal bulls in 1377 and 1384.[5] Throughout the two following centuries, the prior of La Madeleine was responsible for the inmates of the Quevilly leper-house.

In July 1600, as part of an exchange of property and lands with the Hôtel-Dieu, the Benedictine monks of the abbey of La Trinité from the Mont-Sainte-Catherine at Rouen took over the church, manor and lands at the Petit-Quevilly as their principal residence.[6] They gave way in 1667 to the Carthusians, whose major building works, including a new church, continued right up to the eve of the Revolution.[7] When in 1791-3 the Charterhouse was sold as a national asset, the old church was bought by a naval captain, Billaud (or Billard), who proceeded to whitewash over the biblical scenes painted on the choir vaults, apparently in order to save them from destruction by the iconoclasts. In 1818, the local historian, Auguste Leprévost, drew attention to the chapel and the whitewashing of its decorations.[8] Dawson Turner mentioned the building in 1820 and spoke of 'paintings of scriptural subjects' on the ceiling; he also published two views by Cotman in 1822.[9] It is clear that only the cross-ribs and transverse arches of the choir bay had escaped Billaud's whitewash, but Turner's reference proves that parts of the whitewash were already peeling off to reveal the vault paintings. The interior was again illustrated in 1825 in the Normandy volumes of the *Voyages pittoresques*.[10] However, during the 1820s, the building was turned into a stable, granary and dovecote; subdivided into two floors, it was undoubtedly in a terrible state. In 1831 the antiquary, Didron, gave an emotional account of how the pigeons were destroying the vault paintings, 'magnifiques d'or, de cinabre et d'azur'; the proprietor of the chapel had said to him: 'J'ai ramené Jésus-Christ à son premier état, et puisqu'il est né dans une étable, il faut bien vivre à l'écurie'.[11]

The first pictorial records of the paintings were made in 1833-4 for the Commission des Antiquités départementales by Eustache-Hyacinthe Langlois, assisted by his son Polyclès.[12] One watercolour of 1833 by Polyclès is particularly important (Pl. IXc): looking east, the chapel is subdivided into two storeys, and the choir vault is shown whitewashed, except for its ribs and the east apse arch. The geometric patterns of this arch are recorded in detail by Polyclès in a second watercolour, where he also refers to 'les peintures des douilles des voûtes qui représentaient des sujets religieux'.[13] Big spandrel figures on the east wall of the nave are also visible in Plate IXc (vestiges of the south one still survive). They were perhaps 14th century, while the sunflowers and sun-like bursts on the upper parts of the same wall continued onto the wooden roof, so that they were probably post-medieval.[14] By the 1840s, the chapel was attracting the attention of that pioneering generation in France who helped to found the Commission des Monuments Historiques; the minutes of the Commission for their meeting of the 24 February 1843 speak of the chapel as follows: 'L'édifice date de 1160. Il a été bâti par Henri II d'Angleterre, et est sans doute le dernier monument plein cintre construit en Normandie. Il renferme de curieuses peintures de plusieurs époques. La sculpture a été recouverte d'enduits pour les appliquer ...'.[15] An ambitious *devis* of restoration dated 9 December 1842, presented by the architect, Grégoire, was however rejected by the commissioners at the same meeting, one of the problems being that the owner of the chapel had other plans. These must have led to a partial restoration of the interior in 1843, since the building again became a church serving a community of young prisoners. Grégoire in his 1842 *devis* gave a brief description of the choir vault paintings, which were partially visible beneath the whitewash.[16] Another restoration project of 1853 came to nothing, and it was only in the 1860s that the owner finally handed the building over to the Commune, and that it was provisionally classed as a Monument Historique (on the list of 1862).[17]

Over the next few years, various proposals were made to put the the building in order and to uncover the choir vault paintings. Ruprich-Robert, for instance, reported in 1879 on their visibility beneath the whitewash and their need of conservation.[18] Interest was indeed growing. The influential book by Gélis-Didot and Laffillée which appeared in the 1880s illustrated for the first time a detail of the chapel's painted decoration, and old photographs show the interior with the vaults partially exposed.[19]

Finally in 1895–6, the full-scale campaign so long under discussion was executed, with Louis Charles Sauvageot (1842–1908) as architect, and under him the painter Louis Joseph Ypermann (1856–1935). Sauvageot's restoration of the building is fully documented.[20] As for Ypermann, he not only uncovered the paintings, but he repainted certain missing areas and outlines and he sealed the surface of the paintings with a layer of wax.[21] It is through his copies made in 1895,[22] and through his repainted and waxed vault surfaces that the paintings have become known to art historians. As we shall see, this fact has led to a misunderstanding of the true position of the Petit-Quevilly painter within the history of 12th-century art.

By 1929, water was penetrating the vaults and in 1932, the paintings were consolidated with gum. There was a further report on the poor state of the paintings in 1938 and this seems to have worsened by 1944, when an actual size copy was made by Paul-Albert Moras for the Musée des Monuments Français; this copy of the entire choir bay can still be seen *in situ* in the museum and preserves faithfully the state of the paintings as restored by Ypermann.[23] By the 1950s the paintings were not only badly discoloured (just as Tristram's waxed paintings so often were in England), they were also in serious condition, with humidity causing scaling and powdering of the surfaces (Pls XA, XIA). In 1958, scaffolding was erected and in 1959 a programme of photography and examination of the paintings was conducted by Marie-France de Christen under the direction of Jean Taralon, Inspecteur principal des Monuments Historiques.[24] A report of June 1959 by Taralon was a landmark in the history of the conservation of wall-paintings in France. It proposed a historical and technical approach to the damaged paintings, which was to be based on the most exacting analytical requirements.[25] De Christen was commissioned by Taralon to undertake the restoration, which turned out to be a long and delicate operation: a technical report in August 1959 led to the decision in February 1962 that one of the vault compartments (that with the Three Magi before Herod) should be taken down by the *a strappo* technique; a further report by Taralon in February 1963 resulted in the removal of the other vaults in 1965 and their transfer to the laboratory of the Monuments Historiques at the Château de Champs-sur-Marne, where they were remounted on portable frames with independent supports. From the late 1960s up to 1982, restoration of the building was also pursued in various stages, latterly under Georges Duval, so that the walls and their internal climate would be fit to receive the restored paintings suspended on their new frames. Finally, in 1983, the paintings were rehung on the vaults (compare Pls XA, XIA with Pls XB, XIB, XIIA, B). Techniques of restoration have evolved since the late 1950s and it may be that different decisions would now be taken as to how to deal with the acute problems of surface powdering and wax impregnation which the vaults presented. However, the fact remains that Taralon's intervention in 1958 almost certainly saved the paintings from extinction and that the twenty-five-year period of restoration has bequeathed to us the opportunity to study and appreciate them in something like their original form for the first time since the 1890s.

The ribs are boldly painted with a lozenge pattern in blue, yellow and white chequer-board, the main or transverse rib has a highly original key-pattern (Pl. IXB). The sequence of ten medallions devoted to the Infancy of Christ begins in the west compartment with the Annunciation, Visitation and Nativity, and proceeds anticlockwise, that is to the south, with the Journey of the Magi (Pls XA, B, XIA, XIVA), followed by the Magi before Herod (Pl. XIIA); the east compartment (Pls IXB, XIVB) houses three scenes, the adoring Magi (at bottom left) presenting their gifts to the enthroned Virgin and Child (above them), while (below right) is the dream of the Magi (Pl. XIIB); finally, the two northern compartments end the cycle with the Flight into Egypt (Pl. XIB) and the Baptism of Christ. Big blossoms (Pls IXB, XIIIB) fill the available spaces between the scenes, which are framed not by abstract medallions but by tendrils, forming a foliage scroll which develops into the blossoms in the corners of each vault compartment.

The iconography of the cycle does not call for extended comment, except to note that lack of space forced the painter to omit the Massacre of the Innocents (unless of course it was represented elsewhere in the chapel). The Baptism of Christ as usual closes the story of Christ's Infancy, just as it does in the Gospels. There is a heavy emphasis on the three Magi, which may or may not have a specific contemporary relevance to their emerging cult.[26] One thing is certain. The scheme is incomplete. Presumably the apse received an equally important set of paintings, perhaps a Coronation of the Virgin with the two protagonists painted singly in the two compartments on either side of the central rib and flanked by angels in the side compartments.[27] The later wall-paintings in other parts of the chapel have already been mentioned and it cannot be excluded that they cover an earlier painting scheme. It should also be noted that there is paint on some of the 12th-century capitals of the wall-arcading of the choir. Presumably at the least the entire east end was decorated in the 12th century.

There have been extensive losses to the surfaces of the vault paintings. De Christen's report on the restoration makes the following points:[28] the original free line-drawing in red ochre was executed in the wet plaster directly onto the vault; very few lines were incised, except that as usual a compass was used for haloes and medallions; after this stage, all painting was *a secco*, with a tempera or animal glue medium; the palette consisted of the standard earth colours (yellows, browns and reds) but a fine *terra verde* was also included (Pl. XIA) and *lapis lazuli* blue was lavished on the backgrounds (Pls XIB, XIIA) or sometimes laid over a brown ground to give a deeper hue; delicate highlights were added by hatchings in white, while brown hatchings were used in the shadows (Pl. XIA); some of the attributes, and particularly the crowns, may have been decorated with gold leaf (Pl. XIIA); vermilion may also have been used, but this is not certain. In sum, this was a lavish palette, with no expense spared. There is a miniature approach to details: for instance, two of the sleeping Magi (Pl. IXB) have draperies with elaborate and minutely rendered geometric patterns. The subtlety of the modelling is illustrated by a detail of the drapery of one of the Magi on horseback (Pl. XIA). On the other hand, de Christen was unable to remove all Ypermann's brown outlines, so that certain of the heads in the Journey of the Magi (Pl. XB) and the Baptism of Christ still have their late 19th-century contours.

What can be said about this painter? From the time of Dr Coutan onwards, the Petit-Quevilly has been compared with the glass of the Life of Christ lancet of the Chartres west façade. This, however, is an iconographic resemblance; Chartres is worlds apart in style. Indeed, none of the French monuments or illuminated manuscripts provides comparable points of reference. On the other hand, if we turn to England, we can easily find close parallels. Of course there can be no judgements about the nationality of the painter (Brown, Lebrun or Braun?), simply about the artistic milieu in which he was trained, for in spite of the fact that there is some documentary evidence to suggest that not only London but also the itinerant court was accustomed to employing foreign artists, there is nevertheless a distinctive insular production of wall-paintings, manuscripts and metalwork, which we can justifiably label 'English' in style. The various hypotheses which have been put forward towards the identification of an 'Angevin' or 'Plantagenet' style have helped to broaden the landscape in which the insular manuscripts are now studied; mutual contacts and influences across the Channel are generally accepted to have been the norm.[29] Yet the distinctively insular flavour of many of the manuscripts cannot be denied and it is to this stylistic milieu that the Rouen painter belonged.

It is in England that we find Romanesque wall-painting schemes with the layout used at the Petit-Quevilly: the triangular vault compartments are decorated with scenes either contained within medallions or surrounded by foliage tendrils, and with big flowers in the subsidiary spaces. It is possible that such a scheme with three scenes in roundels was painted in each vault compartment of the Worcester chapterhouse as early as the first half of the 12th century; the present vault is of late medieval date but the cycle is known from its inscriptions which were copied into a Worcester manuscript before the end of the 12th century. These same inscriptions, or at least some of them, reappear *c*. 1160–75 on the three famous *champlevé* enamel English ciboria, whose decorations with scenes surrounded by tendrils and with big flowers in the spandrels could well be a reflection of the layout of the lost Worcester chapterhouse paintings.[30] Be that as it may, fragments of vault scenes of this kind survive in the nave of the Saint Gabriel chapel of the Canterbury crypt *c*. 1160, and in the south aisle of Norwich Cathedral, where figured medallions with foliage spandrels decorate the intrados of a transverse arch.[31] Closest of all to the Petit-Quevilly are the fragmentary vault paintings in the south aisle of Ely Cathedral, *c*. 1150, where figured scenes are enclosed by leafy tendrils which develop into big blossoms in the spandrels (Pl. XIIIA).[32] To sum up, everything about the compositional layout at the Petit-Quevilly with the framing tendrils and big spandrel blossoms points to an English origin for this painter, and the Ely vaults are a most revealing parallel.

The great blossoms of the vault (Pl. XIIIB) are enough in themselves to point towards England. Denise Jalabert's discussion of these remarkable specimens does not draw the obvious conclusion, that the painter was 'English'.[33] If we accept the 'standard' chronology for the English illuminated manuscripts (and there are questionable assumptions currently in vogue for some of the most celebrated of them), then it is in the 1130s in the Bury Saint Edmunds' Bible that the earliest of these 'octopus' blossoms are to be found.[34] Around the middle of the 12th century, the forms of the flowers have become more various and more plastic in the Cotton MS Nero C.IV (the so-called Winchester Psalter).[35] A little later, *c*. 1170, they are even more elaborate and exotic in the copy of Zacharias of Besançon's treatise on the Concordance of the Gospels, which has a 15th-century *ex-libris* of Abbotsbury in Dorset (Pl. XIIIc),[36] or in metalwork, on a crosier from an anonymous bishop's tomb at Saint David's (Pl. XIIIF) and on the enamelled crosier from Whithorn (Co. Galloway, Scotland).[37] By the 1170s–80s, in the copy of the glossed Epistles at Durham and the 'last copy' of the Utrecht Psalter (Canterbury?) (Pl. XIIIE), the big flowers are regaining a certain symmetry, a tendency which we find at the Petit-Quevilly. In the Winchester Bible the tighter, stylised forms are framed by tendrils exactly as in Rouen (Pl. XIIID).[38]

The Rouen painter's style is harder to place. Once again, there seems to be nothing comparable in Normandy, in the Angevin lands further south or in Capetian France. However, the removal of Ypermann's 19th-century retouchings suggests that the paintings are earlier than was thought before. It was Ypermann (see Pls XA, XIA, XIVA, B), who was judged by Paul Deschamps and Marc Thibout when they wrote in 1963: 'ici, on ne peut guère parler d'un art de transition. Avec ces petits tableaux dont les personnages ont des attitudes si aisées, si naturelles, où les visages sont si calmes, nous voyons se révéler l'art gothique avec toute sa grâce et sa sérénité'.[39] One can only profoundly disagree. The sharply articulated 'damp-folds' of the mid-12th-century manuscript, Cotton Nero C.IV are here softened, although many substantial echoes of them survive. However, the approach to the narrative of the Magi is remarkably similar (cf. Pl. XIVA, C); the heads with long pointed beards (Pl. XIVB, C, D), the characterful horses, the repertoire of gesture, and the crowns still survive at the Petit-Quevilly (Pls XB, XIVA, B), as do the very distinctive female heads and angels' heads (Pls IXB, XIIB), while we also find the same grotesque profile heads (Pl. XIIA), which occur in the manuscript (Pl. XIVD). As so often, Francis Wormald's instinct was right; of the Petit-Quevilly, he wrote: 'In many ways the style looks like a further stage of that found in Nero C.IV'.[40] The Winchester provenance of Nero C.IV is highly debatable.[41] However, at Winchester, the wall-paintings in the Holy Sepulchre chapel, dated by David Park to *c.* 1175–85, show once again several of the characteristic head-types of the Petit-Quevilly, albeit with a more sophisticated modelling technique.[42] If we turn finally to the principle illuminated manuscript with a claim to a Winchester origin, the giant Bible so magnificently published by Oakeshott, the conclusion must be that at Rouen there are connections with the earliest artists of the Bible: for instance, the head of the angel in the Dream of the Magi (Pl. XIIB) belongs to the repertoire of Oakeshott's early 'Master of the Apocrypha drawings' (Pl. XIVE) and 'Master of the Leaping Figures' (Pl. XIVF); the draperies of the former are also reminiscent of Rouen.[43] Indeed, the more monumental figure style of the later artists of the Bible dated by Oakeshott to *c.* 1175–85, is no more than hinted at in the delicate, marionette-like figures of the Petit-Quevilly. As to the geometric patterns on the ribs of the Rouen vaults, the highly idiosyncratic variation on a 'Greek key' (Pl. IXB) is found in nearly the same form in a border of Nero C.IV.[44] Thus, if a Darwinian progress in the evolution of style in 12th-century England were to be constructed, the Petit-Quevilly painter would have to be placed closest to manuscripts produced in *c.* 1160–70; some of the figures in the Copenhagen Psalter, for instance, have draperies which present exactly the same undulating and looping contours (Pl. XIVB), so that they could well be of the same 'moment'.[45]

Therefore, with all due deference to the extremely imprecise laws which govern chronologies of style, it seems more likely that the Petit-Quevilly was painted for Henry II in the 1160s than for the leper-house in the 1180s, that is that the decoration of the choir vaults was contemporary with the building itself. This makes good sense. The king would hardly have wanted a barren little chapel next to his new manor house. Furthermore, Madame de Christen was certain that the preliminary drawings were made on the wet plaster, directly onto the masonry of the vaults; there was no earlier layer of paintings.[46]

The stylistic filiations suggest that Henry II brought to Rouen a major 'English' artist, whose links with the 'Winchester' monuments of the middle years and third quarter of the 12th century are clearly visible. Perhaps we should regard the 1160–1 date for the building of the manor at the Petit-Quevilly as a relatively solid point of departure when constructing a chronology of the English manuscripts?[47]

ACKNOWLEDGEMENTS

I thank the following for their help with the preparation of this article: David Bates, University of Wales, Cardiff; Françoise Bercé, Conservateur Général du Patrimoine; Marie-France de Christen, Peintre Restaurateur des Musées Nationaux; Marie-Laure de Contenson, Conservateur chargé des peintures murales au Musée National des Monuments Français; Lindy Grant, Courtauld Institute; Alexander Heslop, University of East Anglia; Claude Hohl, Conservateur en Chef des Archives de la Région Haute-Normandie; J. P. Marais, Conseiller Municpal chargé de la préservation du patrimoine, Ville de Petit-Quevilly; Patrick Périn, Conservateur en Chef du Patrimoine, Directeur des Musées départementaux de la Seine-Maritime; Jean Taralon, Inspecteur Général Honoraire des Monuments Historiques.

REFERENCES

1. Lindy Grant discussed these churches and their date in an introduction to my lecture at the Rouen conference in 1989. See also her article in this volume.

2. *Chronique de Robert de Torigni, abbé du Mont-Saint-Michel ...*, 2 vols, ed. L. Delisle (SHN, Rouen 1872–3), I, 331; *The Chronicle of Robert of Torigni: Chronicles of the Reigns of Stephen, Henry II, and Richard I*, 4 vols, ed. R. Howlett (RS, lxxxii, 1884–9), IV, 209.

3. *Monasticon Anglicanum*, ed. Dugdale (London 1661), II, 1013; *Recueil des actes de Henri II roi d'Angleterre et duc de Normandie*, ed. L. Delisle and E. Berger, 4 vols (Paris 1909–27), Intro. vol., 551; II, 296–7 (no. 486); F. Farin, *Histoire de la ville de Rouen* (Rouen 1668), III, 208–11; Dom T. Duplessis, *Description géographique et historique de la Haute-Normandie*, 2 vols (Paris 1740), II, 55.

4. Dr Coutan, 'La chapelle St-Julien du Petit-Quevilly', *Le Millénaire de la Normandie*, ed. abbé J. Touflet (Rouen 1913), 187–201, partic. 189; *id.*, 'La chapelle St-Julien du Petit-Quevilly', *CA* (1926), 238–49, partic. 239.

5. *Mandements et actes divers de Charles V (1364–1380)*, ed. L. Delisle (Paris 1874), 174 (no. 357): copy, 24 March 1385, of a charter witnessed at Rouen in November 1366; cf. Duplessis, II, 55–6.

6. *Histoire de l'abbaye de la Très-Sainte-Trinité dite depuis de la Sainte-Cathérine du Mont de Rouen, par un Religieux bénédictin de la Congrégation de Saint Maur* (Rouen 1662), 66–7: [18 July 1600] 'Eschange des Religieux de l'Abbaye de Sainte Cathérine, avec Messieurs les Administrateurs de l'Hostel-Dieu de Roüen, Au sujet de la Chapelle et des terres de S. Julian (*sic*) aux Bruyeres.'; cf. Duplessis, II, 68.

7. Duplessis, II, 68. See also *Entrée de Saint-Ouen, Chartreuse de Saint-Julien et église de Saint-Sauveur de Rouen. Quatre dessins inédits de Robert Pigeon, gravés à l'eau forte par E. Nicolle. Notices historiques par Paul Baudry* (Rouen 1878), 14–21, with an engraving of a 1790 view by Pigeon of the new buildings.

8. A. Leprévost, 'Notice sur les deux Quevilly et sur le prieuré de Saint-Julien près Rouen' [paper read 16 May 1818], published in full, *Revue de Normandie*, II (1863), 835–45, partic. 841.

9. D. Turner, *Account of a Tour in Normandy*, I (London 1820), 127–31; J. S. Cotman, D. Turner, *Architectural Antiquities of Normandy*, I (London 1822), 43–5, Pls XLII–XLIII (dated 1 April 1820).

10. *Voyages pittoresques et romantiques dans l'ancienne France*, by Ch. Nodier, J. Taylor, Alph. de Cailleux. *Ancienne Normandie*, 2 vols (Paris 1820–5), II, 66–7, 92–6, pl. 170.

11. Dr Coutan, 'Épisode d'un voyage de Didron en Normandie durant l'été de 1831 ...', *Précis analytique des travaux de l'Académie des sciences, belles-lettres et arts de Rouen, 1904–5* (Rouen 1905), 262–3.

12. For Eustache-Hyacinthe Langlois (1777–1837) and his son, Polyclès Langlois (1814–72), see P. Chirol, *Etude sur E.-H. Langlois, dessinateur* (Rouen 1922); exhibition catalogue *E.-H. Langlois (1777–1837)* (BM, Rouen 1977).

13. For the Langlois watercolours, see Albums de la Commission départementale des Antiquités de la Seine-Inférieure, Dessins et Gravures, t.I, pt II, nos 38–42 (ADSM, 6-Fi. Petit-Quevilly 1–8). Illustrated here as Pl. IXc is no. 41, signed 'Polyclès Langlois d'après nature del. 1833.' H. 33 cm; W. 40 cm.

14. In addition, in the nave there are the remains of a figure holding a cross (south wall) and other traces of nimbed heads. Like the east arch figure, they are executed in red and yellow ochres and probably of 14th-century date. In any case, they post-date the 12th-century wall-shafts, since in places they are found covering areas where the original wall-shafts have been cut back.

15. F. Bercé, *Les premiers travaux de la Commission des Monuments Historiques 1837–1848. Procès-verbaux et relevés d'architectes* (Paris 1979), 241.

16. Paris, Archives de la Bibliothèque du Patrimoine (hereafter Bibl. Pat.), Seine-Maritime, dossier no. 2687: *devis* for repairs, 9 December 1842, from H. Grégoire, Architecte du département de la Seine-Inférieure, to a total of 12,861 frs 26. Grégoire writes: 'Cette couche de chaux mise très épaisse et par une personne inexpérimentée qui a laissé des intervalles entre tous les coups de brosse permet de voir tout le dessin des personnages de grande proportion qui y sont peints au milieu de rinceaux dont le caractère rappelle les beaux enroulements du XIIᵉ siècle ...'. Views of the chapel by Alexis Drouin for Grégoire: Bibl. Pat., Seine-Maritime, plans 2963, 2965.

17. For the 1853 restoration project, Bibl. Pat., dossier no. 2687; plans by L. Desmaret, dated 1 June 1853, nos 4461–2, 4931.

18. Bibl. Pat., dossier no. 2687: report of Ruprich-Robert, 13 June 1879. He studied the church in his *L'architecture normande aux XIᵉ et XIIᵉ siècles en Normandie et en Angleterre*, 2 vols (Paris 1884–9), I, 39; II, 3, 9–10, Pls LIV, LXXXVIII. A letter of 31 January 1881 to Steinhlen, peintre-décorateur attaché à la Commission des Monuments Historiques, asking for copies of the paintings and a report on how to conserve them, seems to have come to nothing.

19. P. Gélis-Didot, H. Laffillée, *La peinture décorative en France du XIᵉ au XVIᵉ siècle* (Paris, in fasc., 1883–90), Pl. XXVII. Two photographs, undated, one signed 'Mieusement, photographe', show the interior with the disintegrating whitewash on the vaults (Bibl. Pat., photos pink box, Seine-Maritime).

20. Sauvageot's original report is dated 3 November 1893. His *devis* and studies were submitted in August 1894 and approved in March 1895. His watercolours and drawings of the building, dating from July 1894, are Bibl. Pat., plans, 10282–3, 62510, 62514. His plan, two cross-sections and two views of the exterior were published as an engraving by A. de Baudot, A. Perrault-Dabot, *Archives de la Commission des Monuments Historiques*, II (Paris 1900), pl. 31. The recent restoration dossiers are Bibl. Pat., Seine-Maritime, dossier no. 2687; Direction du Patrimoine, Bureau de la Documentation des Immeubles Protégées, dossier Le Petit-Quevilly. They cover not only the 20th but also the 19th century. It is to these dossiers that reference will be made in the following notes.

21. Bibl. Pat. (see n. 20): report by Sauvageot, 20 October 1895: 'Les peintures du XIIIᵉ siècle décorant la voûte du choeur . . . sont entièrement débarrassées du badigeon qui les cachaient, et l'enduit avarié, sur lequel elles sont peintes, est maintenant consolidé et solidement recollé dans toutes ses parties soufflées'. The payment to Ypermann made in April 1897 gives details of his work: 'Enlèvement des diverses couches de badigeon . . . 2. Lait de cire appliqué avec précaution sur les peintures mises à jour . . . 3. Peinture unie en raccord sur les parties d'enduit refaites dans les différents panneaux; tracés limitant le périmètre de la décoration et raccords de tons divers dans les panneaux'.

22. Ypermann's watercolour copies, paid for by the Administration des Beaux-Arts, are in the Musée National des Monuments Français, Inv. nos MH 10323–30.

23. (a) Bibl. Pat., dossier no. 2687: *devis* of October 1929 from the architect A. Collin; these works executed 1930 to prevent water penetrating the vaults. (b) Direction du Patrimoine, Bureau de la Documentation des Objets d'Art, dossier Petit-Quevilly: report of Jean Verrier, Inspecteur Général des MH, 23 July 1932: '. . . une détempre dont le liant (colle ou œuf) est devenu pulvérulent par suite de l'humidité et les pigments colorés se détachent par un simple frottement; le travail de consolidation consisterait à enlever la poussière superficielle et à fixer ensuite la peinture en projetant en surface une colle légère'. The work was carried out in 1932. (c) ibid., Baudot, Conservateur des Antiquités et Objets d'Art de la Seine-Inférieure, report of 1938. (d) The actual size copies on canvas by Paul-Albert Moras (1903–80) were executed in 1944–5, at which time he recorded that the paint surface was greatly altered (the copies are Paris, Musée National des Monuments Français, Inv. C98).

24. Dir. Patr., Immeubles Protegées (see n. 20): album of photographs submitted by M.-F. de Christen, 3 March 1959, taken by Photo Eilebé, Rouen; Dir. Patr., Bureau de la Documentation des Objets d'Art: photos Sorbets de Christen.

25. See n. 20 for the dossiers containing this report and other material relevant to the subsequent restorations. See also ADSM, V. 7.188 (Dossier administratif sur la restauration des fresques). A report by M.-F. de Christen, 'La conservation des peintures murales de la chapelle Saint-Julien du Petit-Quevilly', dated November 1986, was written for the administration of the town of the Petit-Quevilly, and kindly put at my disposal by J. P. Marais. Photographs of the paintings in the course of being removed from the vaults are Archives Photographiques, MH 62 P. 1362–4.

26. H. Kehrer, *Die Heiligen Drei Könige in Literatur und Kunst*, 2 vols (Leipzig 1908–9); B. Hamilton, 'Prester John and the Three Kings of Cologne', *Studies in Medieval History presented to R. H. C. Davis*, ed. H. Mayr-Harting and R. I. Moore (London and Ronceverte 1985), 177–91.

27. I am indebted to Alexander Heslop for pointing out to me that the capital carrying this central rib of the apse is carved with a dragon and a monstrous head, a highly suitable group to have been placed beneath the feet of Christ and the Virgin Mary, cf. Psalm XCI, 13.

28. De Christen (n. 25).

29. On the Worcester chapterhouse, M. R. James, 'On two series of paintings formerly at Worcester Priory', *Proceedings of the Cambridge Antiquarian Society*, x, ns, vol. IV (1898–1903), 99–115; Canon Wilson, 'On some twelfth-century paintings on the vaulted roof of the Chapter House of Worcester Cathedral', *Associated Architectural Societies' Reports and Papers*, XXXII (1913–14), pt 1, 132–48. On the enamelled ciboria and Worcester, see *English Romanesque Art, 1066–1200* (Hayward Gallery: London 1984), 263–6 (nos 278–81); N. Stratford, 'Three English Romanesque Enamelled Ciboria', *Burlington Magazine*, April 1984, 204–17.

30. L. M. Ayres, 'The role of an Angevin style in English Romanesque painting', *Zeitschrift für Kunstgeschichte*, XXXVII (1974), 193–223; *id.*, 'English painting and the Continent during the reign of Henry II and Eleanor', *Eleanor of Aquitaine. Patron and Politician*, ed. W. M. Kibler (Austin, Texas 1976), 115–46; see also, M.-M. Gauthier, 'Le goût Plantagenêt', *Stil und Uberlieferung in der Kunst des Abendlandes. Akten des 21. Internationalen Kongress für Kunstgeschichte, Bonn, 14–19 Sept. 1964* (Berlin 1967), Band I, 139–55.

31. E. W. Tristram, *English Medieval Wall Painting: The Twelfth Century* (Oxford 1944), 19–21, 104–5, pls 20–2, suppl. pls 2c, 3a–b (Canterbury, St Gabriel chapel nave); 55–7, 138–9, pls 84–5, suppl. pls 5b–c (Norwich, south aisle).

32. Tristram (n. 31), 55, 123, pls 82–3, suppl. pl. 5a.

33. D. Jalabert, 'Fleurs peintes à la voûte de la chapelle du Petit-Quevilly', *Gazette des Beaux-Arts*, XLIII (1954), 5–26.

34. C. M. Kauffmann, *Romanesque Manuscripts 1066–1190: A Survey of Manuscripts illuminated in the British Isles*, III (London 1975), 88–90 (no. 56), ills 148–53; *English Romanesque Art*, 108 (no. 44). In the following notes, references to MSS and metalwork will normally be restricted to these two publications, since they include previous bibliography, unless there is a more recent reference or a particular argument which needs to be cited.

35. F. Wormald, *The Winchester Psalter* (London 1973), pls 12, 95–7, 101 (ff. 9, 46, 98ʳ).

36. Kauffmann, *Romanesque Manuscripts*, 112–13 (no. 87), ills 246–9. Sold by the Doheny Library, Camarillo (California) at Christie's, 2 Dec. 1987, lot 143, for £1,320,000. Now Coll. J. Paul Getty Jr.

37. *English Romanesque Art*, 258 (no. 270), 269–70 (no. 285).

38. For the Durham epistles, Kauffmann, *Romanesque Manuscripts*, 122 (no. 99), ill. 286. For the 'Utrecht Psalter copy', BN, MS Lat. 8846, see now F. Avril, P. D. Stirnemann, *Manuscrits enluminés d'origine insulaire. VIIᵉ–XXᵉ siècle* (Paris 1987), 45–8 (no. 76), pls E, XXII–XXIV, partic. XXII (ff. 8, 15ᵛ) for blossoms similar to those of the Petit-Quevilly. For the Winchester Bible, see n. 43.

39. P. Deschamps, M. Thibout, *La peinture murale en France à l'époque gothique, de Philippe-Auguste à la fin du règne de Charles V (1180–1380)* (Paris 1963), 63–6, pl. opp. 70, pl. XXIV.

40. Wormald, *Winchester Psalter*, 84, pls 82–4 (Ypermann's copies).

41. For this claim, see most recently K. E. Haney, *The Winchester Psalter: an Iconographic Study* (Leicester 1986), 7–9.

42. D. Park, 'The Wall Paintings of the Holy Sepulchre Chapel', *BAA CT*, VI, *Winchester* (Leeds 1983), 38–62.

43. W. Oakeshott, *The Two Winchester Bibles* (Oxford 1982), and review by J. J. G. Alexander, *TLS*, 21 May 1982, 563–4. See also W. Oakeshott, *Artists of the Winchester Bible* (London 1945); L. M. Ayres, 'The Work of the Morgan Master at Winchester and English Painting of the Early Gothic Period', *Art Bulletin*, LVI, 1974, 201–23; *id.*, 'Collaborative enterprise in Romanesque manuscript illumination and the artists of the Winchester Bible', *BAA CT*, VI, *Winchester*, 20–7.

44. Wormald, *Winchester Psalter*, pl. 14 (f. 11).

45. Kauffmann, *Romanesque Manuscripts*, 118–20 (no. 96), ills 272–6; *English Romanesque Art*, 128 (no. 76), ill. p. 58.

46. De Christen (n. 25).

47. Since this paper was given in 1989, I have heard of two studies in preparation: by Dominique Poulain, Maître de Recherches, Université de Picardie, Amiens; and by Vincent Juhel as part of a thèse de Doctorat at the Sorbonne on the wall-paintings of Normandy from the 12th to the 16th centuries.

E

Rouen Cathedral, 1200–1237

By Lindy Grant

Rouen Cathedral has always been the Ugly Sister, the one aesthetic disaster, of French High Gothic design. As such, it has failed to attract much art-historical interest. It is also an archaeological nightmare. But Rouen Cathedral is the metropolitan church of Normandy. It was built during a key period in Norman history, begun in the last years of the Angevin Empire, and completed in the early 13th century, after Normandy had, in 1204, fallen to the French King Philip Augustus. It is a key building for any assessment of Norman Gothic architecture.

The Gothic rebuilding of the cathedral is unusually well documented. In 1200, it was damaged in a city fire.[1] The extent of the damage is difficult to assess. It stirred King John into activity, even personal generosity, on the cathedral's behalf. He donated 2,000 *livres angevins*, no mean gift given that the cost of the entire Château-Gaillard complex was around 45,000 *livres angevin*, though predictably 300 *livres* were still owing in 1204. John also issued two general appeals for gifts towards rebuilding.[2] But it is unlikely that destruction was total. In 1206, the new bishop of Bayeux was consecrated in the cathedral; in 1207, archbishop Walter of Coutances was buried in the ambulatory chapel of St Peter and St Paul.[3] Rebuilding began at the west end of the nave, so the choir was probably still serviceable after 1200.

Work continued throughout the early 13th century. Unusually, the names of architects and masons are recorded. Jean d'Andeli is called master of work at the cathedral in a charter of 1206.[4] In 1214, according to the Bec chronicle, the master of the work was Ingelran, who was called away from his task to rebuild the abbey church at Bec.[5] In 1233, a charter names Durandus as master mason. He was presumably responsible for the easternmost nave vault boss, which is signed *Durandus me fecit*.[6] This indicates that the eastern nave vaults date from the early 1230s.

1214 has become the accepted date for the beginning of work on the choir. But this is based on Aubert's misinterpretation of the Bec chronicle, which describes Ingelran as *magister operis Beatae Mariae Rothomagensis* before he was called to Bec. Aubert assumed that this meant master of the Virgin chapel, the axial choir chapel, conveniently forgetting that the whole cathedral was dedicated to the Virgin. Ingelran could have been working anywhere within it.[7]

Nevertheless, work was undoubtedly under way in the choir in the early 1220s. When archbishop Robert Poulain died in 1221, he was buried not in the choir, like most archbishops, but in the abbey of Mortemer. This suggests that the metropolitan choir was then unusable because of construction work.[8] In 1237, however, the consecration of Peter of Colmieu as archbishop took place in the cathedral. The occasion was an impressive one and the company distinguished and markedly French. All the major bishops and archbishops of the Ile-de-France, and many French magnates were there. It was a delicate political situation. Both previous archbishops of Rouen had clashed with the French crown over Norman rights and customs. The election had been disputed. Most of the chapter were in favour of an English candidate. But Peter of Colmieu was a Frenchman with powerful Roman connections. His election was something of a triumph for French influence in Normandy; he was the first in a line of French as opposed to Norman archbishops.[9] The ceremony is unlikely to have taken place in a choir that was not substantially complete. Indeed, it is possible that the building was finished by 1234, since in that year the cathedral

sold to the abbey of Le Tréport property in Rouen which had housed and supported two
generations of Rouen Cathedral architects, Jean d'Andeli and then Durandus.[10] Clearly, the
eastern bays of the nave and the choir, and presumably the crossing and transepts which link
them, were being built concurrently. There is evidence of haste in the eastern bays of the
nave; suddenly the dosserets separating the shafts on the main piers, which have hitherto
been carefully followed, or hidden behind extra shafts, appear in undisguised rectangular
nakedness.

The nave is very complicated (Pl. XV). Three separate early Gothic campaigns can be
distinguished, apart from later remodelling. The earliest campaign of which traces remain
predates the 1200 fire. It includes the north and south portals on the west front, which
derive from those at Mantes and Lisieux. This campaign can probably be dated around
1180. Its decorative plinth runs across the interior west wall, and along the north wall of the
west bay in the north aisle (Pl. XVIA, B). On the west wall, the masonry of this campaign
extends above the portals at least as far as the aisle vault line which can be traced in both
aisles. For reasons which will emerge later, this cannot possibly be part of a later campaign.

It is likely that this first nave campaign is all that is left of the 12th-century rebuilding of
the 11th-century cathedral, rather than all that was ever built in a late 12th-century
cosmetic remodelling of the west front. The evidence for a substantial mid- to late-
12th-century rebuilding includes archbishop Hugh's famous letter of 1145 describing a
local cart cult.[11] The cathedral crypt contains fragments which could have come from a
mid-12th-century campaign, though their exact provenance is unknown. They are rather
uncouth, but it is clear that the craftsmen who produced them also worked at the chapel at
the Petit-Quevilly, near Rouen, built in 1160-1.[12] Moreover, in 1179, the remains of St
Romain, the cathedral's tutelary saint, were transferred to a new feretory.[13] This does not
necessarily imply the completion of a new choir, but it does suggest it.

Presumably what remains of the first nave campaign was retained by the architect of the
second campaign in order to preserve the splendid and nearly new portals. Otherwise the
new design, which it seems reasonable to assume is the work begun after 1200, took no
account of the first campaign. The new western arcade responds were simply built over their
predecessors, cutting the earlier decorative plinth mouldings.

The second and third campaigns progressed from west to east. The third campaign
adheres to the general arrangement established in the second campaign, but differs in detail.
The break comes in the fifth bay, and is very clear, particularly in pier design, aisle respond
design and arcade mouldings (Pl. XV). In the second campaign, there are several minor
differences between north and south elevations — for instance, the north side has tentative
alternation between triple and quintuple shaft groupings at arcade level. These suggest that
the north side was slightly in advance of the south, where building is generally more
consistent. There are many inconsistencies and hesitations in this part of the building, for
instance indiscriminate use of rounded and rectangular abaci. The inconsistencies are too
frequent to indicate multiple campaigns; instead they suggest architects struggling with
unfamiliar design concepts.

The successive nave campaigns cannot be dated precisely. Aubert assumed, reasonably,
that the second campaign represents the building occasioned by the 1200 fire,[14] but there is
no evidence as to when work on this campaign was suspended, or how long the lapse before
the third campaign was begun. The siege of Rouen in 1204 was short and not necessarily
responsible for the break.[15]

It is always assumed that the architect of the second campaign intended a conventional
low aisle, surmounted by an equally conventional tribune, and that the present floorless
tribune and decorative catwalk are the result of a change of design implemented in the third

campaign (Pl. XVIc). The reasons advanced to support this interpretation are: first, the exceptional nature of the design, and the hesitation with which it was carried out; second, and more solidly, the existence of a communication passage leading from the first floor of the Tour Saint-Romain, which now forms the north-west tower of the cathedral, to the north wall of the western bay of the cathedral itself.[16]

But there is evidence that a floorless tribune was intended from the start. First, the west bay of the north aisle contains the single remaining original aisle window (Pl. XVIB). It extends into what would have been the tribune area, but there is no sign of masonry disturbance from heightening, and its considerable breadth would have been pretty disproportionate if it had been intended to be only half its present height. Second, the west wall arcade responds have no provision for aisle vault shafts. Moreover, on the south side, the masonry block which carries the catwalk corbelling was in place before the arcade arch, which is always ascribed to the second campaign, was built (Pl. XVIA). On this evidence alone, it is clear that the aisle elevation, bizarre though it is, was an integral part of the second, 1200, campaign. The vault lines visible on the west wall of the aisles must belong to a previous campaign.

The evidence of the link passage can also be disposed of. First, the link passage is clearly contemporary with the Tour Saint-Romain itself, dating from around 1160 (Pl. XVIIA, B). At this date, it did lead into the west end of the cathedral, through a large, now blocked opening. Access now is through a small passage and stairs which descend 2.9 m and emerge in the decorative passage running across the west wall of the cathedral at tribune level. In other words, the original opening from the Tour Saint-Romain entered the cathedral some 9 ft above the level of the present false tribune, probably opening into the upper chamber of a west tower. Liess doubted that the Romanesque cathedral had integral western towers, wondering why it was necessary to build the Tour Saint-Romain if it did.[17] But the Tour Saint-Romain was not originally integral with the cathedral. It stood some 15 ft apart and was the gatehouse to the canons' precincts, as is clear from two large aligned arched openings in the ground-floor chamber. It was always called the *Turra nova*, implying that there were other older towers.[18] A stretch of masonry on the reverse of the north bay of the west front, at triforium level, very different from either the 13th- or 14th-century masonry which surrounds it, may be all that remains of the Romanesque west towers. The stubs of long redundant towers on the upper parts of the west front may well have been the reason for the 14th-century screen façade, so unusual in a French context.

Finally, while it is true that a floorless tribune is unusual, it had always been an option from the Early Christian basilica on. The closest example to Rouen is the nave of Rochester Cathedral, although at Rochester the passage running along the extrados of the arcade arches goes right through the tribune piers, instead of being cantilevered round them.

This by no means exhausts the archaeological problems presented by the nave,[19] but the main design sources must now be briefly considered.

The main elevation reflects the staid architectural precepts of late 12th-century Normandy, as first established at Fécamp around 1170.[20] The design is tightly compartmentalised, with composite piers, four-part vaulting, and strong divisive shafts, which run the full height of the elevation virtually uninterrupted. There is no use of *en délit* shafting in the main elevation. Instead all shafting is coursed, and a typical Norman flat shaft and dosseret grouping is used for most responds. Rouen differs from this established building type in that it is four-level instead of three, and rises some 90 ft to the vault, while most of its Norman contemporaries are around 70 ft; and in being thin walled at clerestory level. The tentative alternation is not Norman; nor is the lavish use of *en délit* in the aisle elevations. Even if the names of the architects were unknown, one might have guessed that they were Normans, trained in a Norman tradition, but looking beyond Normandy for their design sources, because they were building on a scale quite new in the duchy. Rouen nave is doing its very best to be a High Gothic cathedral. Its contemporaries, Chartres, Soissons and Bourges, already gave new impressions of soaring height owing to the suppression of the tribune that had stabilised but also encumbered the buildings of an earlier generation. The architect of Rouen nave was not prepared to go quite that far. He retained the effect of a four-level main elevation, and produced a sadly compromised building; but he was still toying with the same set of ideas.

The way the architect of Rouen arranges his High Gothic design relates to Bourges rather than to the Chartrain solution. The triforium passage at Rouen is an unusual type, running beneath large viaduct arches. It also occurs at Bourges, and should be seen as a reduction of the original transverse-barrel vaulted tribunes of Notre-Dame in Paris. Another Paris/Bourges affiliation emerges in the unusual design of the north aisle responds in the western bays. Here the two *en délit* shafts which support the cross ribs are set flush with the wall against the sheered-off sloping shoulders of the coursed dosseret behind them. The closest comparison for this appears in the nave aisle responds at Notre-Dame in Paris, which differ only in that the central shaft is also *en délit*, and set back between two sheered-off dosserets. This Parisian form is rare, but appears in both the crypt and the choir responds at Bourges, while the Rouen and Paris/Bourges variants occur in conjunction in the small pilgrimage church of Larchant, which belonged to, and was built by masons from, Notre-Dame in Paris.

On the reverse of the main arcade, particularly in the south aisle, the projecting shaft clusters of the catwalk supports swell out beyond the plane of the elevation, and link the arcade and tribune piers into a giant order. The effect is of hollowed-out Bourges-type piers. If this seems fanciful, it is worth noting that the tribune piers at Eu (Pl. XVIIIA), which is an almost slavish reduction of the Rouen nave design, also resemble Bourges-type piers, having a round core, with slender coursed shafts disposed at broad intervals around them, though they do not swell out beyond the plane of the elevation.[21]

The Bourges-type pier in its full swelling form had recently been used for the nave arcade at Notre-Dame at Valenciennes. There are other suggestions that the architect of Rouen nave looked to Artois-Flanders for inspiration for building on a grand scale. It is clear that the clerestory and triforium were originally linked together by slender shafts rising from the triforium balustrade, much as in the simplified copy at Eu. This is not an indigenous Norman motif, but one associated with north-eastern France and Flanders, for instance Arras Cathedral. Another building in the north-east which may have influenced the Rouen architect was the destroyed cathedral at Cambrai, the only other large French Gothic building to combine composite piers with a four-storey elevation.[22]

So the two external sources of architectural influence informing Rouen nave seem to be Notre-Dame in Paris, and its derivative, Bourges, and the north-east. Parisian influence is not surprising. Rouen and Paris are linked by the great artery of the Seine, and Paris provides the standard consistent external influence behind Norman Gothic architecture. For the Normans, it seems to have been irresistible, and indigenous Gothic experiments were too tentative to counter it. But if an alternative was required, the north-east would have provided a Norman architect with tall, imaginative four-level elevations which would not have had Capetian undertones, and which might have been seen as expressing the wealth and prestige of an area which was often, until Bouvines, allied with the Angevins against the Capetians.

Political undertones are not to be underrated. Jean d'Andeli probably came, as his name implies, from the Château-Gaillard complex. The 1200 campaign at the cathedral has striking analogies with a group of buildings of the 1190s in the Seine Valley and the lower Eure which can be closely linked with Richard I and his immediate circle — Saint-Sauveur, the parish church of Richard's new town of Petit Andeli, his abbey of Bonport, and the first campaign at Saint-Aubin at Pacy-sur-Eure built when Robert Earl of Leicester held Pacy.[23] The analogies are particularly clear in the treatment of piers and responds. All these buildings use suppressed, concave dosserets, and single rounded socles below multiple shaft groups (Pl. XVIIc, D). And the nave of Rouen Cathedral was begun with substantial financial assistance, and considerable personal interest, from King John, who expressed his particular fondness for the cathedral as the mother church of Normandy, and, in an unlikely and belated display of fraternal affection, as a burial place of his brothers Richard and Henry.[24]

By the time the choir was begun, some twenty years, perhaps less, later, things had changed (Pl. XVIIIb). The nave was unfinished, but it looks as though the archbishop and chapter asked for something as unlike it as could be tolerated within a single building. Given the consistency of building design over long periods at Laon, Soissons or Reims, it is hard to avoid the conclusion that the choir at Rouen reflected a tacit acceptance that the nave was not a success. Nevertheless, the choir design cannot be seen in isolation from the nave, onto which it had to be tacked at the crossing.

The choir and transepts are archaeologically much less complex than the nave. Nevertheless, various elements receive different treatment according to whether they are in the ambulatory or the main vessel elevation. For instance, rounded abaci appear only in the ambulatory and related transept chapels; à bec abaci are used only in the main elevation. Norman shaft forms with flattened dosserets, like those in the nave, are used for ambulatory responds; tight bunched triangular shaft groups supported the high vault. These distinctions might suggest that the main vessel elevation belongs to a completely different and later campaign than the ambulatory. However, certain distinctive leaf and sun designs occur on both aisle and main vault bosses, suggesting that no great time lapse or new workforce was involved. Moreover, the design of the main elevation, with its small band triforium, is implicit in the height of the ambulatory vault and main arcade, which leaves no room for a middle storey of the tribune-like proportions usually associated with Norman Gothic building. The ambulatory has to be very high, because it has to correspond to the height of the nave aisles with their false tribunes. Unless the choir architect was prepared to set his main vault substantially higher than that in the nave — and obviously he was not — he was bound to be left with what in Norman Gothic terms was an unwontedly high arcade, and concomitantly cramped upper levels. In other words, in spite of differences of detailing, the main vessel and the ambulatory represent a single overall design. Two completely different design sources were, however, used to implement it.

The elevation of the main vessel invites immediate comparison with Chartres, or the Aisne valley tradition which is its source. It is of three levels, the upper wall is thin, and the apse wall is polygonal. The main arcade is high and columnar, the vault shafts are tight triangular bunches, and the triforium is a narrow band. Many of its features can rarely, and in some cases never, be found within an earlier Norman context. The à bec form of the apse abaci is virtually a hallmark of the Aisne Valley style. Here it makes its first and only appearance within the duchy, the telling detail which confirms that this is not a case of fortuitous resemblance, but that the architect was using an Aisne Valley or Chartrain design source.

The arcade piers are single columns with the vault shafts sprung from small heads projecting from the arcade capitals. They are not Chartrain piliers cantonnés, but have affinities with the pier forms at Soissons or the apse at Reims, where single slender colonettes run up the faces of the columnar arcade piers. The transept terminals at Rouen also point to Reims as a design source, in that they were designed from the start, independent of the later reworking, to be flanked by east and west aisles and twin towers with great open cages at clerestory level.

Most of the aisle, ambulatory and transept chapel responds belonged to the flattened type developed in Upper Normandy in the late 12th century and used extensively in the nave. The triple roll vault rib profiles are also consistent with work in the nave. This suggests that the architect of the choir had worked on the cathedral building site during the earlier stages of construction. However, many aspects of the ambulatory suggest that he was also very aware of a Lower Norman building tradition, established at Saint-Etienne at Caen in the 1180s. The *remois* passage at Rouen is the first full-blown application of this feature in the duchy (Pl. XVIIIc), but it is prefigured in the elaborate wall structure of the south transept chapel at Caen. The north transept chapel at Caen must be the source for opening the wall above the dado into the choir aisle. On the exterior, the decorative scaling on buttresses and roof cornices derives from the Caen tradition, and the architect has tried with predictable lack of success to adapt the distinctive Caen continuous chapel roof cornice to a spaced chapel plan for which it is completely unsuitable.[25] Again abacus forms are revealing. There is no *à bec* abacus in Rouen ambulatory, but instead a combination of rounded, rectangular, and new polygonal forms are used, often with different forms used on a single respond to differentiate the structural roles which the various shafts within the group play. This specific and sophisticated approach to abacus design, together with a lavish use of the faceted polygonal abacus, was one of the hallmarks of the Lower Norman group of Caen derivatives, the choirs of Lisieux, Bayeux and Le Mans. Of this group, the key monument in this case — because the only one to predate Rouen — is Lisieux (Pl. XVIIId), which was finished by 1215.[26]

In view of these Lower Norman resonances, it is worth considering the chequered career of the architect Ingelran, as narrated laconically by the author of the Bec chronicle. In 1214, he was master of the work at Rouen Cathedral. In that year, he was summoned to Bec to rebuild its abbey church. He worked with astonishing speed for a year, but then lost heart and slowed down. The abbot of Bec lost patience, and after a further eight months, dismissed Ingelran.[27] The chronicle does not indicate where Ingelran went after his summary dismissal. Perhaps he simply returned to his post at the cathedral. During his sojourn at Bec, he would have been well placed to absorb the architectural traditions of Lower Normandy. Bec had close historical ties with Saint-Etienne at Caen. Moreover, the choir at Lisieux would have been the nearest substantial piece of Gothic building; and in 1214–16 it would have been in its final stages of completion. This is no more than tempting speculation, but it does fit the architectural facts like a glove.

So neither nave nor choir at Rouen can be explained by local building traditions. It was not just a case of employing the best local architect and letting him get on with it. The inconsistencies and anomalies, pretensions and importations, at all stages of construction, suggest that there were strong, perhaps conflicting views as to what the metropolitan church, the mother church of Normandy, should be like. But who held, argued or enforced these views — King John, successive archbishops, interested members of the chapter, the architects? What exactly did they think they were trying to do, and what did they think of the result? This building cannot be divorced from its historical context. It was begun in a period of great instability and uncertainty, as the ecclesiastical symbol, the 'mother church' of a once-great political entity now in its death throes. The nave really does look like an attempt to beat the French at their own architectural game, and it was one of a series of royal building enterprises of the last decade of Angevin rule designed to put heart into the disenchanted barons, burghers and ecclesiastics of the Seine Valley.[28] In 1204, Normandy fell to Philip Augustus with embarrassing ease, but this did not mean that all Normans immediately embraced French food, reading habits, legal tenets, or attitudes to life or architecture. The Normans were very aware that they were not French, and the archbishops of Rouen were foremost among those who clashed openly with the French crown.[29] Rouen choir is deeply equivocal. The main elevation and the transept façades suggest a new and direct openness to French influences, from an area of France which had not influenced previous Norman building. The ambulatory draws heavily on the choir of Saint-Etienne at Caen, though there had not, in the past, been much architectural give and take between the Seine Valley and Lower Normandy.

Both external sources for Rouen choir are slightly surprising, but there is a context in which both make sense. Rouen Cathedral was the investiture church of the Norman dukes, and although the investiture ceremony seems to have been considered unnecessary by most of the Anglo-Norman duke-kings, it was revived at the end of the 12th century in a newly resplendent form for Richard and then for John.[30] John's investiture certainly, and thus presumably also Richard's, included crowning with the ducal coronet decorated with golden roses, so that by the end of the 12th-century Rouen Cathedral is in a sense a coronation church. This role was likely to be lost once Normandy had been absorbed into Capetian France, and it would not be surprising that the Rouennais clergy, in the early 13th century, should want to stress this aspect of their cathedral. Perhaps this is why the cathedral seems to be an uneasy compromise between Reims, the coronation church of the Capetian kings, which was begun in 1211, and Saint-Etienne at Caen, the house to which William the Conqueror bequeathed the ducal regalia.[31]

This may sound fanciful, but there is supporting evidence. The Norman coronation *ordo* for Richard and John was copied into the 11th-century Pontifical of archbishop Robert, which belonged to the cathedral. This copy has in the past been dated around 1300,[32] though it was unclear why anyone should have wasted their time copying it then. But it seems that a more reasonable date on palaeographical grounds would be between 1220 and 1230 — in other words, absolutely contemporary with the design of the choir.[33] So at this stage, the cathedral clergy were not only building a coronation church, but copying the ducal coronation *ordo* into the cathedral's grandest liturgical book.

At the same time, they remembered the cathedral's role as ducal mausoleum, as expressed by King John, and also by Henry I (who had once told his very sick daughter Mathilda that she should join her ancestors in Rouen Cathedral when she died),[34] and commissioned retrospective effigies of Richard the Lionheart and Henry the Young King.[35] The distinct architectural references to the design of the choir of Saint-Etienne at Caen, which was, of course, the mausoleum of William the Conqueror, take on a new meaning in this context.

It cannot have appeared a completely lost cause. Louis VIII was not popular, and after 1228, his widow, Blanche of Castile, faced serious magnate rebellion. Henry III of England was intriguing not only with Norman barons, but with many disaffected French magnates, too. A centrifugal, provincial reaction against the inexorable centralising tendencies of Philip Augustus occurred in other French provinces, as well as Normandy, and flickered into architectural form elsewhere, before the administrative and artistic homogeneity of St Louis put out the light. At all events the equivocal and dependent architecture of Rouen choir is scarcely more successful than that of the nave. Rouen Cathedral is the mother church of a people in the grip of a deep identity crisis.

REFERENCES

1. Recorded in, e.g. 'Chronicon Rotomagensis', in *Recueil des Historiens des Gaules et de la France*, ed. M. Bouquet *et al.*, 24 vols (Paris 1869–1904), XVIII, 358, and Roger of Howden, *Chronica*, ed. W. Stubbs (RS, London, 1871), IV, 116, and see M. Allinne and A. Loisel, *La cathédrale de Rouen avant l'incendie de 1200: la Tour Saint-Romain* (Rouen 1904), 66–7.

2. *Rotuli Normanniae*, ed. T. D. Hardy (Record Commission, London 1835), 86; *Rotuli Litterarum Patentium*, I, ed. T. D. Hardy (Record Commission, London 1835), 19. For the Château-Gaillard expenses see *Magni Rotuli Scaccarii Normanniae sub Regibus Angliae*, ed. T. Stapleton (London 1840), II, 309–10.

3. *Gallia Christiana*, XI, cols 57–8; and Allinne et Loisel, *La cathédrale*, 71.

4. C. de Beaurepaire, 'Notes sur les architectes de Rouen', *Les Amis des monuments rouennais* (1901), 77.

5. *Chronicon Beccense*, ed. A. Porée, (SHN, Rouen 1883), 28.

6. De Beaurepaire, 'Notes sur les architectes', 78–9; A. Deville, *Revue des Architectes de la cathédrale de Rouen* (Rouen 1848), 1–5.

7. *Chronicon Beccense*, 28; M. Aubert, 'Rouen: la cathédrale', *CA*, LXXXIX (1926), 44.

8. *Gallia Christiana*, XI, col. 60.

9. *Gallia Christiana*, XI, col. 63–4, and 'Chronicon Rotomagensis', in *Recueil des Historiens des Gaules et de la France*, XXIII, 337.

10. De Beaurepaire, 'Notes sur les architectes', 78–9.

11. Printed in e.g., F. Pommeraye, *Sanctae Rothomagensis Ecclesiae Concilia ac Synodalia Decreta* (Rouen 1677), 141.

12. L. M. Grant, 'Gothic Architecture in Normandy, c. 1150–1250' (unpublished Ph.D. thesis, London 1987), 55–9. See also the articles by K. Morrison and N. Stratford in this volume.

13. 'Translatio Corporis S. Romani in Augustiorem Thecam, ex Archivo Cathedralis Ecclesiae', in Pommeraye, *Sanctae Rothomagensis Ecclesiae Concilia*, 162–3.

14. Aubert, 'Rouen: la cathédrale', 16.

15. For the siege of 1204, see A. Chéruel, *Histoire de Rouen, 1150–1382* (Rouen 1843–4), I, 86–93, and F. M. Powicke, *The Loss of Normandy* (1st edn, Manchester 1913), 383–7.

16. Aubert, 'Rouen: la cathédrale', 31–4, 47; Allinne et Loisel, *La cathédrale*, 56–7.

17. R. Liess, *Der fruhromanische Kirchenbau des 11. Jahrhunderts in der Normandie* (Munich 1967), 163–4.

18. A. Deville, *Revue des Architectes*, 5.

19. See L. M. Grant, 'Gothic Architecture in Normandy', 125–39. E. Roth, 'Das Langhaus der Kathedrale von Rouen. Ein Wandaufbau im viergeschossigen AufrißSystem?', *Baukunst des Mittelalters in Europa, H. E. Kubach zum 75. Geburtstag*, ed. F. J. Much (Stuttgart 1988), 351–70, starts from the premise that the original intention at Rouen included a vaulted aisle and tribune; as a result his interpretation of the building is completely different from mine. I would like to thank Ute Engel for help in translating the article.

20. See Grant, 'Gothic Architecture in Normandy', 51–73.

21. Eu nave was finished in 1227, see the account of the translation of St Laurent into the new building, Pommeraye, *Sanctae Rothomagensis Ecclesiae Concilia*, 215.

22. See L. Serbat, 'Quelques églises anciennement détruites du nord de la France', *Bull. mon.*, LXXXVIII (1929), 365–435; J. Thiébaut, 'L'iconographie de la cathédrale disparue de Cambrai', *Revue du Nord*, LVIII (1976), 407–33; J. Thiébaut, 'Quelques observations sur l'église Notre-Dame-la-Grande de Valenciennes', *Revue du Nord*, LXII (1980), 331–4.

23. See Grant, 'Gothic Architecture in Normandy', 145–7, 158–60, 202–9. Robert of Leicester lost Pacy in 1194, see Powicke, *Loss of Normandy*, 161. To this group of buildings could be added the splendid Grandmontine church of Notre-Dame-du-Parc, which must date from the 1190s.

24. *Rot. Lit. Pat.*, 19, 'nos autem eanden ecclesiam tenere diligimus et sincere, tum quod fratrum et amicorum nostrorum sepultura nobis eam venerabilem in perpetuum commendat'.

25. See Grant, 'The choir of St-Etienne at Caen', in *Medieval Architecture and its Intellectual Context: Studies in Honour of Peter Kidson*, ed. E. Fernie and P. Crossley (London 1990), 113–25.

26. Grant, 'Gothic Architecture in Normandy', 234–7. The chevet at Lisieux is usually considered to be repair work after a fire in 1226, e.g. by L. Serbat, 'La cathédrale de Lisieux', *CA*, LXXV (1908), 301; J. Vallery-Radot, *La cathédrale de Bayeux* (Paris 1922), 68; and J. Bony, *French Gothic Architecture of the 12th and 13th Centuries* (Berkeley, Los Angeles 1983), 514 n. 24. But the clean, stepped nature of the break between the chevet and the western bays of the choir indicates that the chevet is not a new extension to a previously completed and then damaged building. There is thus no reason to date the eastern choir campaign after the 1226 fire. An obit of Jourdain du Hommet, bishop from 1201 to 1218, records that he much enlarged and enriched the church (see G. Huard, 'La cathédrale de Lisieux au XIe et XIIe siècle', *Études Lexoviennes*, II (1919), 35). In 1215, Jourdain gave 100 *livres tournois* to support the choir clerks (*Gallia Christiana*, XI, col. 781), suggesting the choir was then finished.

27. *Chronicon Beccense*, 28.

28. See above, n. 24.

29. 'Chronicon Rotomagensis', in *Recueil des Historiens des Gaules et de la France*, XXIII, 332–6, and see Grant, 'Gothic Architecture in Southern England and the French Connection in the Early Thirteenth Century', *Thirteenth Century England* III, ed. P. R. Coss and S. D. Lloyd (Woodbridge 1991), 119.

30. For Richard and John's investitures see Roger of Howden, *Chronica*, III, 3 and IV, 87. I would like to thank Dr David Crouch for help on ducal investiture.

31. B. English, 'William the Conqueror and the Anglo-Norman Succession', *Bulletin of the Institute of Historical Research*, LXIV (1991), 232–6.

32. *The Benedictional of Archbishop Robert of Rouen*, ed. H. A. Wilson (Henry Bradshaw Society, London 1903), 157.

33. I should like to thank Mlle Rose and the staff of the Bibliothèque Municipale at Rouen; Dr Sandy Heslop for suggesting that the ducal *ordo* ought to be much earlier than 1275–1300, and for photographing it, and Professor A. C. De la Mare for confirming that it should be dated *c.* 1220–30.

34. Robert of Torigny, 'Chronica', in *Chronicles of the Reigns of Stephen, Henry II and Richard I*, ed. R. Howlett (RS, London 1889), IV, 124.

35. J. Adhémar, 'Les tombeaux de la collection Gaignières', *Gazette des Beaux Arts*, LXXXIV (1974), 18, nos 43, 44, and A. Way, 'An Effigy of Richard Coeur de Lion, in the cathedral at Rouen', *Archaeologia*, XXIX (1842), 202–16.

Some Medieval Ironwork in North-East France

By Jane Geddes

Rouen is an appropriate venue for starting an examination of French medieval ironwork because a most extensive collection of decorative iron is housed in the city's Musée Le Secq des Tournelles. The collection, displayed in the church of Saint-Laurent, was given to the city of Rouen by two Norman benefactors, Louis and his son Henri, Le Secq des Tournelles. They accumulated all forms of decorative ironwork between the 1870s and 1917. Their purpose was both to provide an art-historical survey of the craft and to provide models for blacksmiths wanting to improve their skills by studying masterpieces. The bulk of the collection is post-Renaissance, but there is a sizeable amount of late 15th-century material, less from the central Middle Ages, and a few Carolingian and Roman keys.[1] The architectural pieces, grilles, locks, hinges, devoid of their context and often without secure provenance, are a melancholy warning of what happens to iron when it is carelessly removed from its original site. Without adequate documentation it becomes hard to date or to explain. The quantity of medieval iron at Rouen, in the Musée de Cluny, Paris, and the Victoria and Albert Museum, London, testifies to the wholesale clearances of medieval buildings, particularly in the 19th century.

Having said that, it is possible to suggest a context for certain museum pieces by relating them to iron which is still *in situ*. The remainder of this article falls into two parts: a brief discussion of the surviving or recorded door furniture from Rouen Cathedral, and then an examination of a group of iron ornaments centred on Beauvais.

The majority of decorative ironwork is hand wrought and subject to infinite individual variation, but one technique, that of die stamping, was a precise mechanical process which was used primarily in north France and England in the 13th and 14th centuries, though extensively revived in the 19th century. The same stamp was used over and over again, sometimes on one work, sometimes on several different pieces, until in broke and the smith made another in the same pattern to match. The designs of the stamps follow a basic vocabulary of trefoils, rosettes and asymmetrical leaves, but each smith, workshop or pattern book provided individual variations. These variations can be identified and compared closely by making plaster-cast moulds of the shapes. This technique, probably pioneered by goldsmiths in the early 13th century, first appears in a fully developed form on the west doors of Notre-Dame, Paris, *c.* 1240.[2]

At Rouen Cathedral, stamped hinges decorated with bunches of leaves on stalks were recorded on the Portrait des Libraires but are now lost. Another example, from an unnamed location in the cathedral, was recorded by Digby Wyatt in 1852 (Pl. XIXA, B, C).[3] Land for the north portal was acquired in 1280 and archbishop Guillaume de Flavacourt mentioned the Portail des Libraires in 1305, so the hinges must have been made around 1300.[4] A small shouldered door on the west side of the sacristy (in the south choir ambulatory) has also lost its stamped hinges (Pl. XXA).[5] These were decorated with pointed oak leaves and veined rosettes. The sacristy is separated from the ambulatory by a stone openwork screen. Its door, completely made of iron, is designed to mimic the stonework. The lower part consists of solid panels and the upper part of spiky openwork tracery panels centred on three-dimensional rosettes. There is also a fine openwork lock plate and door ring. The ironwork is 15th century, contemporary with the stone screen (Pl. XXB).[6] Massive decorated hinges are used on the west doors of the cathedral (Pl. XXC). They consist of straps ending in a bunch of scrolls and a central stamped leaf. The design is of medieval derivation but its coarse scale suggests a post-medieval date. The west doors have a delicate archway carved in wood around the wicket gate, decorated with a flat strapwork design of possibly 16th-century Renaissance date. The hinges appear to be contemporary with the doors. Lastly, panels from the 14th-century choir screen were presented to the Musée des Antiquités in 1835 and 1866 (Pl. XXIA). The choir screens, made in the 14th century, had been removed and broken up in 1480 because they were 'trop antiques'.[7] The grille is based on a lozenge grid filled with scrolls ending in a man's head. Two panels of looser scroll work were added to the bottom when the screens were remade as gates in the 17th century.

The metal-working guilds were well represented in Rouen in the Middle Ages, being settled particularly around the parish of Saint-Maclou. The locksmiths (*serruriers*) were the best paid and most highly skilled, but the usual nailmakers, farriers, and cutlers were also represented. In 1397 the locksmiths were put in charge of maintaining the city clock.[8]

Beauvais Group

A group of iron objects, now widely scattered, share a distinctive set of stamp designs which appear to be centred around Beauvais. The comparison of the stamps illustrated here is based on a survey of all the known stamp designs in northern France; this revealed several other distinctive groupings based on the use of totally different details in the rosettes and leaves.[9] The stamps used in the Beauvais group are a seven-lobed leaf, a single rosette with six concave petals decorated with a line and dot; a double six-petal rosette with a line in each petal; and a flat six-petal rosette with star-shaped surface pattern (Pl. XXIB). One or more of these stamps is used on grilles at Beauvais Cathedral, Saint-Germer-de-Fly, fragments in the Musée de Cluny and the Victoria and Albert Museum, a chest in the Musée de Cluny and posts at Troyes.

The grille and gates at Beauvais Cathedral are placed across one of the north ambulatory chapels, and a copy is across one of the south chapels. They are constructed of vertical panels containing back-to-back C scrolls. The frame is grooved and has an H section (Pl. XXIC). The grilles at Saint-Germer surround the choir (Pl. XXID). They are constructed in exactly the same way as those at Beauvais with grooved frame of H section, C scrolls and stalks. However, in detail they are not identical. The bars at Saint-Germer are flat with lines along them, while those at Beauvais are ridged, with a wavy surface. The stamps also show slight variations: the Saint-Germer seven-lobed leaf has a narrow, straight-sided top lobe while those at Beauvais have drop-shaped lobe. The grilles at Saint-Germer are altogether less skilfully wrought than those at Beauvais.

Some fragments incorporated into the Musee de Cluny screens, Cl. 19962, are now part of a composite grille with a new frame (Pl. XXIIC). The panels with back-to-back Cs and seven-lobed leaves are very close to those at Beauvais. The seven-lobed leaf is identical and the rosette with lines and dots is the same design, though not made from the same die. The bars covering the welds are identical, with the same pattern of dots and zigzag. The quality of these fragments is so close to that of the Beauvais grilles that they could be from the same workshop, if not from the cathedral itself.

The rosette with line and dot on its petals is also used extensively on a chest in the Musée de Cluny, Cl. 9323–6064 (Pl. XXIIA). Here it is found in combination with a rather amorphous leaf stamp and another, in high relief, of a man's face.

The grille fragment at the Victoria and Albert Museum 4830/1875 is slightly different from the preceding pieces (Pl. XXIID). It is composed of multiple scrolls ending in rosettes.

Stamps used are the double rosette found at Beauvais, and flat rosette with star patterns found at Saint-Germer. The third rosette is an outsider. It has eleven narrow petals with a line and dot on them.

On the periphery of this group are four posts in Troyes Cathedral (Pl. XXIIB). The screen which they held has been renewed. They are decorated with miniature castles supported by the same type of seven-lobed leaf as at Beauvais.

The grilles at Beauvais cannot have been made long before the completion of the choir in which they stand. This provides a *terminus post quem* for the whole group, assuming they are roughly contemporary. The apse chapels at Beauvais Cathedral were begun in 1227 and the choir constructed from 1247 to 1272.[10] At Saint-Germer, a need to protect the old choir probably arose when the new Lady Chapel was built. Its main access was around the 12th-century ambulatory. The Lady chapel was added to the east end by abbot Peter de Wesencourt (1257–72). Thus, architectural evidence at Beauvais and Saint-Germer suggests that this group of stamped ironwork was made after *c.* 1272.

The differences in quality between pieces in this group and the variety of stamps which supplement the four characteristic designs indicate that the work was made by several smiths. The grilles at Beauvais and Saint-Germer are very close in design and their stamps are related but not identical. Their quality is not comparable so it would seem that the Beauvais Cathedral smith merely provided the model for Saint-Germer. The Cluny screen fragments, 1B, appear to be by the Beauvais workshop itself, with near identical stamps and comparable quality. The Cluny chest, with one well-made Beauvais rosette and a collection of very inferior stamps, suggests that a less accomplished smith had access to one good stamp, perhaps passed on from a central workshop at Beauvais, and made the rest up himself without knowledge of the standard forms. The castellated posts of Troyes are of high quality and could come from the Beauvais workshop. Although they share one stamp with Beauvais, the comparison between grilles and a post is hard to make. Lastly, the Victoria and Albert Museum fragment, sharing designs if not quality or execution with both Saint-Germer and Beauvais, suggests the existence of a pattern book in which the eleven-petal rosette also featured.

The significance of this evidence is hard to assess from the historical point of view. In the Beauvais group, similar stamps found on works of widely varying technical accomplishment suggest a central source for the manufacture of high grade dies which were distributed to some provincial smiths. Insufficient evidence survives from the Rouen stamped ironwork to draw any conclusions on the nature of their manufacture.

REFERENCES

1. H. R. d'Allemagne, *Musée Le Secq des Tournelles à Rouen: ferronnerie ancienne* (Paris 1924); trans V. K. Ostoia, *Decorative Antique Ironwork* (New York 1968). C. Vaudour, *La ferronnerie architecturale, Musée Le Secq des Tournelles* (Rouen 1978); C. Vaudour, *Musée le Secq des Tournelles* (Rouen 1981).
2. The present decoration is a 19th-century reproduction.
3. H. R. d'Allemagne, *Les anciens maîtres serrurriers*, I (Paris 1943), 166. J. H. Parker, *Glossary of terms used in Architecture* (Oxford 1850), II, 97; M. Digby Wyatt, *Metalwork and its artistic design* (London 1852), pl. XIII, 6.
4. C. de Beaurepaire, *Derniers mélanges historiques et archéologiques* (Rouen 1909), 154.
5. L. Labarta, *Hierros Artisticos* (Barcelona 1902).
6. D'Allemagne (1943), II, XL.
7. *Corpus des objets domestiques et des armes en fer de Normandie*, eds P. Halbout, C. Pilet, C. Vaudour (Caen 1986), 202. Museum inventory no. 581–1835, 1836.

8. Délibérations capitulaires de Notre-Dame de Rouen, ADSM, G 2141, 1479–82.
9. J. Geddes, 'English Decorative Ironwork, 1100–1350' (University of London, unpublished Ph.D. thesis, 1978), 183–95.
10. M. Monteillard, 'Artisans et artisanat du métal à Rouen à la fin du Moyen Age', *Hommes et travail du métal dans les villes mediévales*, ed. P. Benoit, D. Cailleaux (Paris 1988), 109–26.
11. *Dictionnaire des églises de France*, ed. J. Brosse (Paris 1966–71), IV, D12.
12. L. Regnier, 'L'église de Saint-Germer', *CA* (1905), LXXII, 85.

Early Fourteenth-Century Canopywork in Rouen Stained Glass

By James Bugslag

In the early 14th century, a remarkable style of canopywork emerged in the stained glass of Rouen, which exercised a considerable influence in Normandy during the first half of the 14th century.[1] This article considers the design sources of that canopywork, outlines its salient characteristics and suggests some of its implications for the interpretation of contemporary French pictorial concerns.

The late 13th century witnessed considerable experimentation with new canopy forms in western French stained glass, for instance in the choirs of Sées Cathedral and La Trinité at Vendôme and in the Saint-Vincent Chapel of Beauvais Cathedral.[2] This stage of experimentation, in which the residual three-dimensional elements of an essentially Late Antique tradition were eliminated from canopies, culminated in a magnificent synthesis in Rouen, first in the Lady Chapel of the cathedral, then in the choir of the abbey church of Saint-Ouen. This canopy style developed in close association with masons' workshops. It reflects both architectural forms current in Rouen and the influence of architectural draughtsmanship, helping to produce a remarkable balance between stained glass and architecture. The prominence of these canopies in relation to the figures and scenes they shelter owes an initial debt to the Rhine Valley, but it is clear that the principles of an exceedingly complex canopy structure were mastered in Rouen and manipulated to create a rich variety of designs.

ROUEN CATHEDRAL: THE LADY CHAPEL

The surviving stained glass in the Rouen Cathedral Lady Chapel, dating from between 1310 and 1320, consists of sixteen figures of canonised archbishops of Rouen under magnificent canopies, in a band window format, now in windows 5, 6, 7 and 8 (Pl. XXIIIA–D, XXIVA).[3] The glass underwent some restoration in the 15th and 16th centuries but escaped major work in the 19th century. The canopies in windows 7 and 8 are for the most part complete, although a few are fragmentary close to the borders. Those in window 5 appear to be truncated at the top, and those in window 6, lights b and d (6-b-d), are either composite or the top panels have been shifted.

Grodecki suggested that this glass embodies a new style of painting, which appears here in a fully developed form.[4] The plasticity of the figures and developments in glazing technique, such as the increased use of smear shading and stickwork and the introduction of silver stain, are remarkable. The style of the canopywork is also new — at least in France. Sometimes towering more than three panels above the two-panel-high figures, these canopies set a new standard for the elaboration of canopywork. A new sense of architectural definition is also apparent. The only place where such features had been combined previously was in the Rhine Valley, where from the mid-13th century the design of canopies had been influenced by the techniques of architectural draughtsmanship. Rhenish examples seem to have provided models for these canopies, but the masons' workshops of Rouen Cathedral also exercised a strong influence on the glass.[5]

In windows 5 and 8, one cartoon was used for all four canopies, while in window 7, two canopy designs alternate. In window 6, one design was used in lights a and c; in lights b and d, the bottom and middle panels are identical in design, but neither of the top panels co-ordinates exactly with the panels below. The designs all have certain features in common. They have side-buttresses against the borders, composed of multiple members, with bases, string courses, drip-stop profiles and gabled tracery panels, which rise to slender pinnacles standing clear of the borders. Against the inside edges of the side-buttresses, attached shafts support the canopy arch and a tall crocketed gable filled with tracery. Above the gable is a tall superstructure, usually free-standing and connected by flyers to the side-buttresses; the superstructures present different designs, but all conform to the same basic scale and massing. The canopies in window 5 (Pl. XXIIIA) appear to be incomplete; it would seem that the superstructure continued into the panel above, probably in a central pinnacle, although it is not entirely clear what they looked like. One possibility is exemplified in the canopies in lights 7-a-c (Pl. XXIIIB), where the central spire continues into the grisaille panel above. No close precedents survive for this arrangement, with the possible exception of the canopies in the Annunciation Chapel of Troyes Cathedral nave, although these may well be later in date.[6]

The superstructures of these canopies find some close parallels in contemporary glazing in the Rhine Valley. The superstructure design used in window 5 is particularly close to Rhenish examples. A tall, narrow, two-light window flanked by thin vertical members rises from a base behind the canopy gable. It is joined to side-buttresses by flyers, which meet the central structure at the window head. One of the earliest similar examples is the canopy design for the west window of the Freiburg Dominican Church of c. 1300,[7] and this basic design continued to be used along the Rhine (Pl. XXIVc). Although of more solid and less vertical proportions than most Rhenish examples, the design in window 5 is otherwise comparable. In addition, the central window is defined by independent cutting and leading of the tracery compartment. This is a common element of Rhenish workshop practice (for example, the Cologne Cathedral choir glass), seldom encountered in France, where tracery patterns are more commonly defined in stickwork on a single piece of glass. Birds and figures perched on the top of pinnacles (Pl. XXIIID) were also common in Rhenish canopies (for example, the Strasbourg Cathedral nave glass), although similar angels can be found in the, again strongly Rhenish, hemicycle canopies in Saint-Père, Chartres, datable to c. 1295–1300.[8]

Although the debt owed to Rhenish glazing design and practice is evident, it cannot explain every aspect of these canopies. For example, where side-buttresses appear at all in the Rhine Valley, they are usually slender structures of a single order, their lower parts defined mostly in a plain, painted masonry pattern; there are few equivalents to the relatively more articulated and substantial side-buttresses found here. Previous examples in French glass can be found from the very end of the 13th century, and it seems clear that this feature was generally adopted from other media at about this time. Side-buttresses are elements of 'microarchitecture' which from the mid-13th century began to appear on ciborium tombs, metalwork and incised tomb slabs. Undoubtedly, architectural draughts-manship provided an important means by which such interchanges between craft traditions could take place.

The latter point is particularly relevant here, because the process whereby the Lady Chapel canopies were designed and drawn on the glazing table clearly involved aspects of architectural drafting. This is indicated by the two-dimensional quality and geometrical exactitude of the canopies, which form 'elevations' of comparable scale to the large architectural drawings preserved in Strasbourg and elsewhere.[9] It is also indicated by the knowledgeable use of architectural elements in the designs. In their complexity and variety, the tracery patterns represented in the Rouen canopies are unmatched even in the Rhine

Valley, and constitute one of the most distinctive features of the Rouen style. Moreover, these tracery patterns, and other elements of the canopies, are recognisably related to the masons' workshops at Rouen Cathedral.

The tracery filling the canopy gables, for instance, was inspired by the façades of the cathedral transepts, begun *c.* 1280.[10] Each gable features a large roundel, with the bottom corners filled either with subdivided mouchettes (Pl. XXIIID), as on the Portail de la Calende (south), or with a smaller mouchette and cusped roundel (Pl. XXIIIc), as on the Portail des Libraires (north). Some gable roundels (Pl. XXIII) contain figures represented behind pierced quatrefoil cusping, a common feature in the relief carving of both transept façades. Others contain complex tracery patterns. That in the window 8 canopies features eight trefoils in spherical triangles around a quatrefoil roundel,[11] the distinctive pattern in the portal gable of the Portail des Libraires. That used in lights 6-b-d (Pl. XXIIID), six two-light windows radiating from the centre of the roundel, is very close to the tracery of the south transept window at Meaux and is also a simplification of the rose pattern on the Portail de la Calende. Other close correspondences between the Lady Chapel canopies and the transept façades can be identified. And the background pattern used within the canopies of window 5 (Pl. XXIIIA), consisting of cusped quatrefoils in square panels, is close in form to the relief panels that decorate the dados of both transept façades.

The superstructures of the Lady Chapel canopies, however, contain a wider variety of tracery patterns than can be found in the Rouen workshops. Some are close to the tracery of the Lady Chapel apse windows themselves (Pl. XXIIIc); others are free but coherent extrapolations of tracery design. Moreover, the tracery depicted in the canopies is so complex and precisely laid out that the same techniques of draughtsmanship must have been used as in the masons' lodges (Pl. XXIVB). The designer of these canopies was not only familiar with the techniques of architectural draughtsmanship and methods of tracery design, but also with the actual tracery designs and architectural details then current in the cathedral lodges. It is, thus, difficult to escape the conclusion that masons participated directly in the design of these canopies. Certainly, the revolution in canopy style apparent here depends as much on the adoption of new approaches to design as on the abandonment of old ones. The new direction in canopy design initiated in the Lady Chapel of Rouen Cathedral was soon taken up in the glazing of the east end of nearby Saint-Ouen, where it seems that a continuing connection with masons contributed to the magnificent canopies there.

SAINT-OUEN: THE CHOIR CHAPELS

The abbey church of Saint-Ouen is the single most important building in northern France for the study of canopies in stained glass.[12] The complexity of the canopies and the sheer number of them make an analysis of their forms particularly instructive in determining design sources. Moreover, the stained glass comprises part of a complete rebuilding programme that encompassed the whole east end of the church, providing a rare opportunity to study the glass in relation to the masonry, with which it combines in a unified interior effect.[13] The canopies are particularly important in such an undertaking because, with their larger relative size, they predominate over the scenes they shelter and thus within the windows containing them (Pl. XXIVD); the contrast between the style of the scenes and that of the canopies is also instructive in arriving at an appreciation of the pictorial effects which were valued in the glass.

The east end of Saint-Ouen was rebuilt between 1318 and 1339, and Lafond has estimated that the glazing was begun *c.* 1325.[14] The glass was presumably in place by 1339,

F

and a high proportion survives *in situ*. The low windows are all band windows. Each light contains a figure or scene, generally two panels high, sheltered by a monumental canopy that towers three to five panels above the scene. Cartoons have consistently been used for more than one canopy, and designs were often modified slightly. Within each window, either one canopy design was used throughout, or two were used in a symmetrical arrangement. Nevertheless, great variety is evident, with about twenty-eight different designs used for approximately sixty surviving canopies.

In conception and scale, these canopies owe an indisputable debt to those in the Lady Chapel of Rouen Cathedral. The superstructures are all of the same dominant scale, unknown previously in Normandy, and the scale and technique of details are virtually identical. Each canopy presents an 'elevation', with panelled side-buttresses rising to a tapering series of pinnacles. Against these, attached shafts support a canopy arch, which takes a variety of forms. The one most often used, certainly amongst the earlier (eastern) canopies, is also that of the cathedral Lady Chapel: a cusped arch surmounted by a tall crocketed gable, filled with tracery. There are also similarities between some of the Saint-Ouen canopy designs and those of the Lady Chapel of the cathedral. For instance, the design of the superstructures in lights 30-a and 32-a (CVMA, pls 20, 21)[15] is related to a Rhenish model comparable to that in window 5 of the Lady Chapel (Pl. XXIIIA), and the design in lights 38-b and 34-b (CVMA, pls 8, 12) is very close to that of window 7-a-c in the Lady Chapel (Pl. XXIIIB). The practice of continuing a central spire into the grisaille panel above, which is found in some early windows here (CVMA, pls 3, 6), also finds a precedent in the Lady Chapel (Pl. XXIIIB).

Moreover, as with the cathedral Lady Chapel canopies, the degree of architectural expertise demonstrated by the Saint-Ouen canopies indicates a close relationship with masons. In fact, the Saint-Ouen canopies seem to exhibit a similar connection with the cathedral masons' workshop. For instance, a distinctive type of canopy arch (Pls XXIVD, XXVA), composed of superimposed arches with tracery between them, is found in the cathedral in both the inner transept doorways, and could formerly be seen on the ciborium wall tomb of Archbishop Guillaume de Flavacourt in the Lady Chapel.[16] In lights 36-a-c (Pl. XXVA) and some others, the central tracery roundel contains the figure of an angel behind pierced cusps. This is another prominent feature of the transept façades, which can also be found in the stained glass of the Lady Chapel (Pls XXIIIA–C). In lights 26-a-b-e-f (Pl. XXIVD), the gable above has three tracery-filled mouchettes meeting in the centre, the distinctive treatment of the gable above the rose window on the Portail des Libraires. In general, a common approach to design between these canopies and the cathedral transepts is apparent in the density and variety with which such tracery elements as trefoils in spherical triangles and mouchettes are used to create surface effects.

The tracery patterns and reflections of masonry used in the Saint-Ouen canopies are, however, more extensive than those to be found in the cathedral transepts. The pattern of the cathedral Lady Chapel windows, for instance, a cinquefoil roundel and two quatrefoil roundels over two or four cusped lights, occurs in a number of the Saint-Ouen canopies (Pl. XXVC; CVMA, pls III, 32). Other tracery patterns can only be found further afield. The pattern used in light 21-d, an octofoil roundel over three lights, the outer two having in addition hexafoil roundels over the lights, is close to that of the apse of Chambly, which dates from the late 1250s.[17] The principle of tracery units stacked up within lights, which is taken to such an extreme in some of the Saint-Ouen canopies (for instance, CVMA, pl. 26), has been traced by Branner to Beauvais and Saint-Germer-de-Fly, whence it spread to the Ile-de-France.[18] A pattern used in light 32-b (CVMA, pl. 20), a subcusped quatrefoil roundel, two smaller quatrefoil roundels and four impaled trefoils over four lights, is close to some of the Cologne Cathedral tracery. As well as the ubiquitous gargoyle water spouts, the flying buttresses represented in canopy 23-a (Pl. XXVB) feature arcaded flyers, as on the choir of Amiens Cathedral. Like so many of the features in these canopies which are specifically related to masonry design, this is extremely rare in stained glass, and indicates that the designer of these canopies had considerable experience of masonry design. A likely conclusion is that, as in the cathedral, masons participated directly in the design of these canopies, and architectural draughtsmanship provided the means whereby the two craft traditions could merge.

Further comparisons make clear that there are explicit resemblances between the Saint-Ouen canopies and those of a specialised branch of masonry practice, namely tomb-slab carving. Perhaps the most distinctive feature that links the Saint-Ouen glass with tomb-slab design is the incorporation of figurines in small niches within the canopies, both in the panelled side-buttresses and in superstructures (Pls XXIVD, XXVA–C). Although a few other examples are known in French stained glass, very few of them are earlier than at Saint-Ouen.[19] Figurines are used widely in the Saint-Ouen canopies, however, and the obvious source of this feature is tomb slabs. Although superstructures are not as common nor as developed in the canopies on tomb slabs as they are in stained glass, both superstructures and side-buttresses inhabited by figurines occur on tomb slabs from the late 13th century.[20] A telling feature, sometimes seen in inhabited tomb-slab canopies, and used to form niches for figurines, is also found in Saint-Ouen light 34-b (Pl. XXVC). The mullions of a traceried window are cut off by a second arch, below which stands the figurine. In stained glass, this is a unique occurrence, but the feature can be seen quite often in tomb-slab canopies (Pl. XXVD).[21] Other architectural and decorative elements in the Saint-Ouen canopies can be compared with features on tomb slabs, and it would thus appear that the designer(s) of the Saint-Ouen canopies had considerable knowledge of tomb-slab design.

Besides these strong connections with the workshop practice of the cathedral masons and *tombiers*, it would appear that, as in the canopies of the cathedral Lady Chapel, there was also some influence from the Rhine valley in the Saint-Ouen canopies. For instance, both double and triple canopy arches occur at Saint-Ouen (Pls XXIVD, XXVB). Both these forms can be found extensively in the Rhine Valley. Double canopy arches can be found occasionally in previous French stained glass, for example at Saint-Urbain, Troyes, but in the developed form in which they appear at Saint-Ouen, the closest similarities are with Rhenish examples.[22] Triple canopy arches appear to have only a couple of isolated precedents in France: one is in the axial window of Le Mans Cathedral, the other in the Saint-Vincent Chapel of Beauvais Cathedral, in window sVI; and these in turn have close links with the nave glass of Strasbourg Cathedral.[23] Another apparent link with Rhenish stained glass is the way in which canopies and their coloured fields often extend past the horizontal top of the upper coloured panel to impinge on the grisaille panel set above it (Pls XXIVD, XXVB). This occurs in nearly all the later (westernmost) windows. A somewhat comparable treatment can be seen in the choir chapel glass of Cologne Cathedral; the arrangement in the nave windows of Saint-Thomas in Strasbourg is also close to Saint-Ouen (Pl. XXIVC).

There are problems, however, in assessing the nature of Rhenish influence on the Saint-Ouen canopies. For one thing, many isolated details in the Saint-Ouen canopies which could derive from Rhenish models remain distinct in workshop practice. These include, for instance, the extensive use of stickwork and silver stain in the Saint-Ouen canopies, which is lacking in the Rhenish equivalents. For another, the dates of comparable Rhenish examples are often later than the Saint-Ouen glass. To some extent, this may simply reflect accidents of survival and destruction, but reflections from the Saint-Ouen glass have also been postulated in the Rhine Valley.[24] Further research may clarify the seemingly indisputable, but puzzling, connections between Rouen and the Rhine Valley.

ARCHITECTURAL PLANES AND PICTORIAL SPACE

All the Rouen canopies are defined in a systematically two-dimensional style derived from the techniques of architectural draughtsmanship. Only occasionally are tentative three-dimensional effects achieved. One means of suggesting planes at different depths is overlap (for example, vertical members seen through an openwork parapet), and oblique surfaces are occasionally suggested on vertical members by the depiction of drip-stops. Most of these effects are found in Saint-Ouen 23-a-b-e-f (Pl. XXVB), but even here, the predominant two-dimensional effect is hardly compromised. Lafond's claim of 'perspective' effects in the Saint-Ouen canopies is technically incorrect.[25] Nowhere do the few clear examples of orthogonals converge — or even diverge; they are all horizontal, as in a pure architectural elevation.

In contrast to the two-dimensional appearance of the canopies, the figures and scenes they shelter frequently display a determined and even sophisticated sense of three-dimensional space. The emphatically modelled figures in the cathedral Lady Chapel frequently overlap their side-buttresses, thus appearing to emerge from their niches (Pl. XXIIIA). The scenes within the Saint-Ouen canopies, however, are consistently set behind the plane defined by the canopy arches; figures and objects at the sides of scenes are cut off by the side-buttresses. Within scenes, objects are frequently depicted in foreshortened frontal settings, or combined in a depth created by overlap of structures or figures.

Some of the three-dimensional elements in these scenes are of Italian inspiration. In the scene of the Baptism of a King by St Matthew (CVMA, pl. 29), the undersides of the arches of the corbel table of the font are coffered, and discs in relief are set in the wall beneath. The use of jagged Italo-Byzantine rock formations, such as in light 23-e, also reflects Italian models. Perhaps the most pictorially sophisticated of the examples at Saint-Ouen is in the scene of the Beheading of St John the Baptist (CVMA, pls 15, 19). A castle is represented in the far distance, appropriately proportioned in diminutive scale. Italian paintings, such as the frescoes in the upper church of S. Francesco at Assisi, offer comparisons for all these features.

Comparison of the pictorial space found in these scenes with the two-dimensional quality of the canopies reveals highly contrasting pictorial concerns. An added contrast between them is provided by the purely Gothic definition of the canopies and the Italianate content of the three-dimensional architecture within the scenes, and in some of the pedestals of the Saint-Ouen clerestory figures (CVMA, pls 65, 75). Thus, it appears that the style of architecture being depicted and the mode of depiction were conceptually linked; Gothic architecture was depicted in a two-dimensional mode, and Italianate in a mode incorporating pictorial space. These different pictorial modes stem from two very different but equally sophisticated traditions, raising the possibility that more than one designer or design team was responsible for laying out designs on the glazing tables at Saint-Ouen.

It cannot be accepted that the canopies here merely frame the pictorial fields they shelter (Pls XXIVD, XXVB). The canopies occupy a much larger area of glass than their fields. In conjunction with the ornamental network of grisaille glass around them, they forcefully maintain a sense of the window plane. The predominance of the two-dimensional Gothic canopies over the Italianate pictorial space in the scenes within them suggests, in fact, a concern to augment the architectonic conception of the master who designed the masonry. Thus, while an awareness of pictorial space was present in the Saint-Ouen glazing workshop, it was not chosen for the leading effect of large-scale pictorial compositions. The two-dimensional effect of the canopies in Rouen can in fact be regarded as an integral part of a pictorial tradition which imposed limits on the use of Italianate pictorial space in French stained glass until the mid-14th century.

Large, two-dimensional canopies are a characteristic of French stained glass between the 1290s and the 1340s, and the Rouen canopies stand out as amongst the most accomplished formulations. The direct influence of the Saint-Ouen canopies can be seen in the Pentecost window in Rouen Cathedral, now in the south transept clerestory, c. 1340.[26] Elsewhere in Normandy, at Jumièges, Les Andelys and particularly Evreux, the influence of the Rouen canopies was felt, but with noticeably less detailed representations of masonry design than those surviving in Rouen.[27]

ACKNOWLEDGEMENTS

I am grateful for the help of my thesis supervisor, Professor Andrew Martindale, in researching this subject and for the help of Dr Jenny Stratford.

REFERENCES

1. This article is based on research undertaken for my dissertation, 'Antique Models, Architectural Drafting and Pictorial Space: Canopies in Northern French Stained Glass, 1200–1350' (University of East Anglia, Ph.D., 1991).

2. Bugslag, thesis, 218–74.

3. The Lady Chapel was begun in or shortly after 1302 and was probably completed c. 1311. Lafond believed it was glazed subsequent to that date, see G. Lanfry, 'La cathédrale après la conquête de la Normandie et jusqu'à l'occupation anglaise', Les cahiers de Notre-Dame de Rouen, IV (Rouèn 1960), 72; J. Lafond, 'Le vitrail du XIVᵉ siècle en France' in L. Lefrançois-Pillon, L'art du XIVᵉ siècle en France (Paris 1954), 191.

4. L. Grodecki and C. Brisac, Gothic Stained Glass 1200–1300 (London 1984), 178, 256–7.

5. The destruction of all contemporary Parisian stained glass creates serious difficulties. Comparable developments probably took place in Paris, but the many close connections between the Rouen canopies and Rouen masons' workshops suggest a distinctive synthesis in Rouen. Some of the canopies of c. 1330–40 in the choir clerestory of Evreux Cathedral, e.g. in the Raoul de Ferrières window, may reflect parallel Parisian formulations. See Bugslag, thesis, 385–400.

6. Bugslag, thesis, 254–6, 264–6. There is little dating evidence for this glass, see J. Roserot de Melin, Bibliographie commentée des sources d'une histoire de la cathédrale de Troyes, I: Construction (Troyes 1966), 109; J. Lafond, 'Les vitraux de la cathédrale Saint-Pierre de Troyes', CA, CXIII (1955), 48–51.

7. R. Becksmann, Die architektonische Rahmung des hochgotischen Bildfensters: Untersuchungen zur oberrheinischen Glasmalerei von 1250 bis 1350 (Berlin 1967), 77–80; idem, Deutsche Glasmalerei des Mittelalters: Eine exemplarische Auswahl (Stuttgart 1988), 47, 124–5.

8. M. Lillich, The Stained Glass of Saint-Père de Chartres (Middletown, Conn. 1978), 48; and Bugslag, thesis, 243–9.

9. For the Strasbourg drawings, see Les bâtisseurs des cathédrales gothiques, ed. R. Recht (Strasbourg 1989), 381–405.

10. L. Lefrançois-Pillion, 'Nouvelles études sur les portails du transept de la cathédrale de Rouen', Revue de l'art chrétien, LXIII (Sept.–Oct. 1913), 281–99, 361–75.

11. The tracery in the gables of these canopies is difficult to make out because it is largely defined in silver stain. This glass has also been awkwardly releaded in a restoration, perhaps of the 15th century.

12. For the state of the choir glass, restoration history, window numbering and illustrations, see J. Lafond, Les vitraux de l'église Saint-Ouen de Rouen, CVMA France, vol. IV–2/1 (Paris 1970).

13. For relations between the stained glass, masonry and wall paintings in the choir of Saint-Ouen, see Bugslag, thesis, 326–31.

14. Lafond, 'Le vitrail du XIVᵉ siècle en France', 195; Lafond, Les vitraux, 14–15.

15. This and subsequent references in this form refer to the plates in Lafond, Les vitraux.

16. J. Adhémar and G. Dordor, 'Les tombeaux de la collection Gaignières. Dessins d'archéologie du XVIIᵉ siècle', *Gazette des Beaux-Arts*, LXXXIV (1974), no. 542. The tomb dates from the second decade of the 14th century, when the Lady Chapel was finished, even though Guillaume de Flavacourt died in 1306. The tomb was destroyed in 1769.

17. R. Branner, *St Louis and the Court Style in Gothic Architecture* (London 1965), pl. 109. Chambly, in fact, has an octofoil roundel and two quatrefoil roundels over three lights.

18. Ibid., 96–7.

-19. One possibility is the Annunciation Chapel window in the nave of Troyes Cathedral, but this is not firmly dated, see n. 6 above.

20. See Adhémar and Dordor, 'Les tombeaux', nos 334, 449, 563, 622 and *passim*. A corpus of surviving French tomb slabs has yet to be completed, see F. A. Greenhill, *Incised Effigial Slabs* (London 1976), I, 35.

21. See also the tomb slab of the anonymous architect in Saint-Ouen. A similar feature, deriving from the Saint-Ouen glass, can be seen in the canopy in the axial clerestory window of Evreux Cathedral, *c.* 1335–40, see Bugslag, thesis, 369.

22. Bugslag, thesis, 320, 352 n. 134.

23. Bugslag, thesis, 277–81.

24. V. Beyer, C. Wild-Block and F. Zschokke, *Les vitraux de la cathédrale Notre-Dame de Strasbourg*, CVMA France, vol. IX–1 (Paris 1986), 507, 509 (for the Sainte-Catherine Chapel glass); and G. Schmidt, 'Die Chorschrankenmalereien des Kölner Domes und die Europäische Malerei', *Kölner Domblatt*, 44/45 (1979/80), 293–340. See also K. Gould, 'Jean Pucelle and Northern Gothic Art: New Evidence from Strasbourg Cathedral', *Art Bulletin*, LXXIV (1991), 51–74.

25. Lafond, *Les vitraux*, 33.

26. Lafond, *Les vitraux*, 44; and Bugslag, thesis, 359–62.

27. Bugslag, thesis, 362–82.

The Export of Decorated Floor Tiles from Normandy

By Christopher Norton

Normandy was one of the principal regions in Europe for the production of decorated tile pavements. Indeed, taken as a whole, floor tiles were manufactured in Normandy for a longer period, in larger numbers, in greater variety and, not least, to a higher artistic standard than probably anywhere else.[1] The high point came in the 13th and 14th centuries, when numerous workshops were active throughout Upper and Lower Normandy. This was also the period of greatest influence on other areas. The early English mosaic tile pavements, best known at sites such as Byland and Rievaulx, probably derive, directly or indirectly, from Norman antecedents.[2] The lower Seine valley has produced what appear to be some of the first experiments at making two-colour tiles, and the earliest inlaid tiles in both Anjou and southern England (most famously at Clarendon Palace) were inspired by Norman pavements;[3] they could well have been made by tilers trained in Normandy.

By the later 13th century, the new two-colour techniques were well established over much of France and England, and Normandy no longer appears as a source of ideas, in terms of either technique or style, for other regions. On the other hand, it became for the first time in a limited way an exporter of the finished products themselves. Most tile production in Normandy followed a pattern familiar throughout France and Britain; it was generally a fairly localised affair. The distribution pattern for a fixed workshop may typically extend to perhaps 50 km from the kiln site; anything above 80 km is unusual, since the costs of transport were liable to be prohibitive. Local geography however was an important factor, and the availability of river transport could enable the regular despatch of consignments over considerably greater distances.[4] Whereas Lower Normandy has no major river permitting the easy export of tiles to other regions, in Upper Normandy the Seine provides an excellent means of transport for heavy goods to Paris and the Ile-de-France. Extant material and documentary sources combine to prove that Norman tilers based somewhere in the lower Seine valley exported their products to customers in Paris and beyond in the late 13th and 14th centuries. Paris indeed is a classic example of the attractive power of a rich conurbation sited on a major river system; other floor tiles were transported considerable distances downstream to the capital along the Marne and Seine from the vicinity of Reims and Troyes. By contrast, there is no sign of importation from equivalent distances to the north and south, from Amiens or Orléans for instance, since there are no easy river connections.[5]

Long-distance river transport was always confined to a small minority of tile workshops, but it is a well-attested phenomenon. Quite exceptional is the maritime trade in decorated tiles produced by a Norman tilery in the late 14th century which is the main concern of this article. They have a very distinctive distribution (Fig. 1): a concentration of sites around Dieppe, a number of finds across the Channel along the Sussex coast, in eastern Kent and in and around London, plus one site in Humberside and a few examples in Ireland and along the south-west Atlantic coast of France around La Rochelle and Bordeaux. Over 60 designs can currently be identified (Figs 2–7). A few of them have long been known in this country as the 'Lewes Group', since they were first recorded at Lewes Priory in the 1840s. As long ago as 1937, J. B. Ward-Perkins suggested that two designs from London (which he did not in fact associate with the 'Lewes Group') might be Flemish imports.[6] More recently, Elizabeth

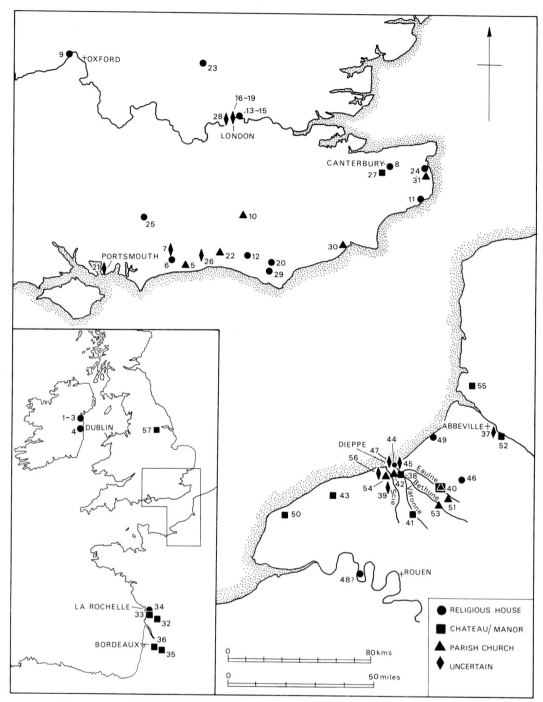

FIG. 1. Distribution map of the Dieppe Group of tiles. Site numbers refer to the list of sites in the Appendix

Eames suggested in her British Museum *Catalogue* that 'this trade may have been based on a tilery in Sussex, perhaps in Lewes itself . . . . A possible alternative source is northern France, although there is no evidence for this apart from the slightly unusual appearance of the tiles'.[7] By the time these words were published in 1980 it had become clear that the source of the tiles was indeed France.[8] It is a sobering reflection on the often slow progress of international scholarship that the publication of some of the most distinctive designs in the group by Léon de Vesly in his study of Norman tiles as long ago as 1912 had so long escaped attention;[9] and that it has taken some twelve years to assemble the material which follows from excavations, museums and libraries as far apart as Bordeaux and York.

The essential data are presented in the distribution map, the tile drawings and the list of sites at the end. The status of the evidence is variable. Few sites have produced more than ten designs; indeed the total number of specimens from any site is generally very small, often no more than a handful. Some of the tiles are lost and are known only from antiquarian sources or published drawings. Of those that do exist, the ones in old museum collections tend to be intact and reasonably well-preserved, but many are without provenance; the recent archaeological finds, by contrast, are well provenanced but often very fragmentary and worn. In England and Ireland many of the finds come from recent excavations; in Normandy, however, most were discovered in the 19th century. More intensive archaeological work in Normandy would doubtless turn up many more. Unfortunately, the Norman evidence is the least satisfactory, because the examples preserved in the two local archaeological museums, at Dieppe and Neufchâtel-en-Bray, were destroyed during the Second World War. There are Norman specimens at the Musée des Antiquités at Rouen and at the Musée de Sèvres in Paris, though in each case often unprovenanced. Some of the examples at the Musée de Sèvres were duplicates presented by M. Mathon of Neufchâtel, whose drawings in the Bibliothèque de la Manufacture Nationale de Sèvres include numerous tiles from that region. Although many of them are again unprovenanced and of poor quality (particularly when it comes to distinguishing close variants), the Mathon drawings are none the less the only evidence we have for the existence of a number of the designs in Normandy itself. The more recent destruction by fire of the museum at Jumièges also means that it is no longer possible to verify the presence there of one design in the group. There are doubts also about one or two provenances among the old collections in this country. My conclusions about all the known tiles in the group, whether provenanced, unprovenanced or doubtful, are given in the Appendix. I have excluded a few sites which have been cited in connection with this group but for which the evidence is insufficient.[10]

The tiles generally measure between 97 and 104 mm square and 17–23 mm thick. They have a fine, homogeneous fabric which generally fires a bright orange-brown colour, but with some paler streaks and spots of darker clay mixed in. In some cases there is a considerable tempering of very fine white sand. The clay is seldom reduced, though on overfired examples it takes on a darker brown tint. The tiles have vertical or very slightly bevelled sides; the bases are smooth or very finely sanded, and lack keys of any kind. The slip-decorated designs are in very thin white slip, often smudged. In some cases the patterns can be seen to have been applied by the less common stamp-on-slip technique, whereby the surface was covered with slip before being stamped.[11] Characteristic of this technique is the fact that on some examples, where the stamp was applied with greater pressure, the design is sunk below the surface of the tile and the slip has sharply defined edges within the impression. With the more common slip-over-impression technique, whereby the tile was first stamped and then covered with liquid slip, the slip usually runs up the edges of the impression and is far less sharply defined. The glaze imparts a pale yellow tint to the slip and a bright orange colour to the body clay; on more heavily fired specimens the background is darker, sometimes purplish. There are occasional green spots in the glaze. In principle, the tiles are easily identifiable by their small size and thickness, their fabric and decorative technique, and by the designs. Yellow and dark green plain tiles of the same group have been recorded from Drogheda and Cowick.

Most of the designs are recorded from more than one site in more than one of the separate regions where the group has been found; in these cases the attribution may be considered certain. The significant factor here is not mere geographical distance, but whether or not the sites in question are within the normal range of the local workshops. Thus La Rochelle and Bordeaux are quite distinct regions in terms of tile distribution, since they belong to different regional traditions. Likewise, London, eastern Kent and south Sussex are quite separate in terms of tile production. In south-western France, this group is so different from all local products that it is instantly recognisable. Designs 22 and 61, and the fragments 27, 63 and 65 have only single provenances in England or Ireland, but are close variants of otherwise well-attested designs. In Normandy there is some potential for confusion with other local products in the case of a few patterns unattested elsewhere. Designs 18 and 23 may be included as they are consistent with a larger assemblage of the same group at Cany-Barville. Designs 8, 10, and 30 from Abbeville, Saint-Nicolas-de-Caudecote at Dieppe and Rue respectively were also discovered with other known examples of the group. Designs 5 and 19, from unprovenanced examples in the Musée des Antiquités at Rouen, may be included on grounds of design and general appearance. I have omitted some patterns possibly of this group recorded in 19th-century drawings or publications on Normandy but of which no examples survive. The study of the variants has been particularly tricky. Given that some of the tiles are worn or fragmentary, some no longer exist, some have been studied through the medium of tracings or publication drawings from a number of different hands and of varying reliability, it has not always been clear how many variants of some patterns genuinely exist. Numbers 43–7 are the most difficult case; there may be more versions of no. 48 and nos 3–5 than I have allowed for. The illustrations represent my best estimate of the number of designs so far recorded. They have been taken from full-size tracings or drawings, where possible, or redrawn from publication drawings which appear reliable. A few patterns for which the sources are of uncertain reliability have not been inked in but given shaded backgrounds. I have rejected a few doubtful designs from England and Ireland recently attributed to the group,[12] while in Upper Normandy there are a number of tiles with very similar designs which have been excluded on account of differences in size or other characteristics which point to a different origin. In sum, the group as a whole is easily characterised and identified, though there are some uncertainties at the margins.

In the absence of a kiln site and of any documentary evidence, there are two pointers to a Norman origin: their distribution and their designs. The distribution is wide-ranging, yet surprisingly concentrated in particular areas, with large gaps in between. The Irish evidence is based on the recent corpus of Irish tiles by Elizabeth Eames and Tom Fanning.[13] In England, where there is already a very extensive literature, research in progress by various scholars on most of the coastal regions from Essex to Scotland, and from Hampshire right round to Cheshire has not produced any examples, to the best of my knowledge, apart from Cowick in Humberside. Mark Horton's work in Belgium and Holland failed to turn up a single example.[14] In France, all the literature and most of the major collections have been searched. The distribution pattern of the tiles (including the gaps) should therefore present an accurate picture in the present state of our knowledge. Simply in terms of numbers of finds, Normandy is well ahead of Sussex, Kent and London, even though there has been relatively little archaeological work in the relevant area in recent years. Apart from one case in Kent, Sussex and Normandy are the only areas where the tiles have been recorded in parish churches. Elsewhere, where the type of site is known, they have been found only in religious houses of one sort or another or in châteaux and manor houses. These are precisely the sorts of establishments which could afford the cost of transporting tiles from far afield; parish churches were generally supplied from nearby sources.[15] In England, the group has long been seen as something of an oddity. Although a few of the designs have parallels on English tiles, they are of the commonest type (e.g. nos 13–15) and there is no consistent relationship to local products in any one area. In Upper Normandy, by contrast, there are parallels for many of the designs (e.g. nos 12, 24–8, 36–8, 41–2, 51). Significantly, they can be found among the products of a number of different workshops, not just in the Dieppe area itself, but also in the Seine valley and further afield; and some of the parallels are almost certainly earlier in date.[16]

With the possible exception of Jumièges, on a bend in the Seine valley, all the Norman find-spots are concentrated in a coastal band within about 60 km to either side of Dieppe, reaching just over the border into Picardy at the mouth of the Somme and penetrating as far inland as Neufchâtel-en-Bray, about 35 km from the coast. The inland find-spots are situated in or near the valleys of the three small rivers which flow into the sea at Dieppe, namely the Varenne, the Béthune and the Eaulne. It is also noticeable that all the parish churches are grouped within this area or in the immediate vicinity of Dieppe itself; the more distant sites are all monasteries or châteaux. The clear inference is that the tiles were manufactured close to Dieppe, which must have been the port of departure for the overseas trade. It would therefore seem appropriate to replace the old, misleading term 'Lewes Group' by Dieppe Group.

Dating evidence is remarkably scanty for a group attested at so many places. In the absence of documentation, tiles can often be dated from *in situ* remains associated with datable structures. The château de Langoiran near Bordeaux produced a pavement in a 14th-century context. The floor contained heraldic tiles identified as the arms of Bernard d'Escoussan, who died in 1354 without a male heir. However, the square heraldic tiles and the rectangular border tiles which constituted the greater part of the floor do not belong to the Dieppe Group, while the designs illustrated as filling the edges of the panels and one of the borders seem to include 13th-century patterns as well as the Dieppe tiles. They could represent repairs, or simply a device to include more designs in the illustration.[17] No longer preserved *in situ*, the Langoiran tiles cannot be used as evidence for dating. Nowhere else do we have tiles of the group *in situ*; nor are the heraldic tiles (nos 1–6) of any help, since they are clearly intended merely to give the impression of heraldic devices without having any specific reference; they have been found throughout the range of sites. A firm *terminus post quem* is provided by Winchelsea. The town was moved to its present site in the 1280s; the chancel of the parish church, where some of the tiles were found, is of the early 14th century. The designs certainly suggest the 14th century, though stylistic dating of tile patterns is always hazardous.[18] A date towards the end of the century is indicated by two sites in Sussex — Poynings and Arundel. Poynings Church was rebuilt under the will of Michael of Poynings, who died in 1369. At Arundel, the Maison Dieu was conceived as an adjunct to the College of the Holy Trinity planned by Richard Fitzalan, 3rd earl of Arundel. Following his death in 1376, both foundations were carried out by Richard, the 4th earl, and the buildings of the Maison Dieu are said to have been completed by 1396.[19] On the evidence of these two sites alone, the Dieppe Group should probably be dated in the last quarter of the 14th century or the very beginning of the 15th. Production may have continued for some years, to judge by the number of variants of some of the designs. Although it is impossible to prove, generally speaking tilers do not seem to have employed many variants of a single pattern at any one time; they often seem to indicate replacements for stamps which had worn out.[20] Certainly with the Dieppe group it is seldom the case that more than one version of a particular motif has been found at any one site. A large establishment such as Saint Augustine's Canterbury, which has produced fragments of designs 44, 46 and 47, could well have been purchasing tiles over a number of years and so does not disprove the point. If the hypothesis is correct, it should be possible to produce a relative chronology by seriation of the designs, but unfortunately there is insufficient evidence to attempt this. In any case, there would at present be no way of knowing which were the earliest sites and which the latest; nor do we know how long a stamp might have remained in use — one year, or ten?

Examples of a maritime trade in decorated floor tiles are few in number and small in scale. By contrast, the importation of large quantities of plain Flemish or Netherlandish tiles into England from the late 14th century into the 16th is well known. It now also appears that Norman tiles captured some of the British market in plain tiles for a time in the early 16th century. The distinctive white or pale pink fabric tiles probably originate somewhere in the Seine valley.[21] But although the problems of transport are identical, plain tiles have one critical advantage over decorated ones; they require no special expertise to lay. With decorated tiles, each workshop had not only its own repertoire of individual patterns, but also its own preferred designs for the pavement as a whole. Laying a decorated pavement was often a skilled affair, requiring a paviour with some knowledge of the particular products in question. This must have been a powerful factor restricting the distribution of most tiles to a fairly small area around their kiln site. Overseas trade posed obvious problems, which must largely explain why instances of long-distance maritime trade are so rare. A mere handful of sites in Sussex have produced early 16th-century tiles from Brémontier-Massy, near Neufchâtel-en-Bray, presumably also shipped from Dieppe.[22] These are the only other decorated French tiles known to have been exported overseas, or even along the French coast, apart from the products of a workshop in Artois which relate more closely to some Flemish tiles. Some tiles from Artois seem to have been shipped round to La Rochelle at an uncertain date in the 13th or 14th century.[23] From the middle of the 14th century onwards there are sporadic examples of Flemish and Netherlandish decorated tiles turning up in England, Ireland and Scotland, but they are exceptionally few and far between compared to the plain tiles. The only ones found in any quantity, and the only real parallel to the Dieppe Group, are the so-called Dutch 'motto tiles' from the 1550s which have turned up in small numbers over much of the British Isles.[24] Though there is evidence for occasional trade in English tiles round the coasts of Britain or across the Irish Sea, exportation to the continent is to all intents and purposes non-existent. In fact, in terms of numbers of designs and numbers of finds, the Dieppe Group probably equals or even exceeds all the known examples of maritime export of decorated tiles across the North Sea, across the Channel and around the Atlantic coast of France in any direction.

One can only speculate as to how and why the Dieppe tilers managed to penetrate markets so far afield, and why the distribution of their products is so patchy. Were they responding to chance personal contacts, or gaps in the local markets? Were the tiles exported to middle-men in the various regions for sale locally, or were they only sent out in response to specific orders? Were the tiles in south-western France perhaps re-exported from England as part of the regular commercial contacts between the two regions? How did the tilers solve the problem of pavement design? If we were able to compare *in situ* floors from different regions, it would be interesting to see whether they all adopt a common layout. If so, it could indicate some means of transmitting the design of the floor along with the tiles. Or did they follow the types of arrangement current in the various localities where they were used? How exactly were the logistical problems overcome?[25] Why did this workshop, almost alone, succeed in exporting so many of its products so far afield? There is nothing exceptional about the tiles themselves or their designs; had they been restricted to Normandy, they would hardly merit a special study. It is their distribution which has earned them a chapter in the history of the European tile industry.

APPENDIX: LIST OF SITES

The sites are numbered in order; they may be located on the distribution map (Fig. 1). The information given is restricted to the type of site (where known) and the designs recorded, numbered according to the illustrations (Figs 2–7). Where the number is followed by a question mark, the identification is not certain; numbers listed as e.g. 32/33 indicate a pattern whose precise variant is not certain. References have had to be kept to a minimum: only the most recent literature, or older sources when not cited elsewhere; and museum inventory numbers, etc. (when they exist), only if not accessible in print. I have marked with an asterisk all the sites from which I have personally examined some if not all of the the tiles.

IRELAND

1. **Drogheda** (Co. Louth), Dominican Friary, site of.[26, 27]
Nos 14, 16, 20, 39, 41.
2. **Drogheda** (Co. Louth), Hospital of St James, site of.[26, 27]
Nos 14, 16, 20, 24, 33, 39.
3. **Drogheda** (Co. Louth), Carmelite Friary or St Mary's Church.[26, 27]
Nos 3, 24.
4. **Dublin** (Co. Dublin), Christ Church Cathedral.[26]
Nos 16, 27.

ENGLAND

5. **Angmering** (Sussex), church.[28]
Nos 32/33, 38, 41, 48, 49/50, 55.
6. **Arundel** (Sussex), Maison Dieu.[29]
Nos 16, 33, 44?
7. **Bury** (Sussex).[29, 30]
No. 44/45/46/47?
8. **Canterbury** (Kent), St Augustine's Abbey.[31]
Nos 13, 25?, 31, 32, 44, 46, 47, 53, 55.
*9. **Eynsham** (Oxon.), Abbey.[32]
No. 31 (possibly doubtful provenance).
10. **Horsted Keynes** (Sussex), church.[33, 34]
Nos 1, 2, 3, 6, 9, 21, 37, 56.
*11. **Langdon** (Kent), Abbey.[35]
Nos 32/33, 47, 52, 53, 55.
*12. **Lewes** (Sussex), Priory.[32, 33, 34, 36]
Nos 1, 2, 3, 6, 9, 28?, 32, 40.
*13. **London**, Crutched Friars.[37, 38, 39]
No. 20.
*14. **London**, Greyfriars, site of.[37, 38, 40]
Nos 17, 25, 34?, 43?
*15. **London**, St Mary Graces, site of.[41]
Nos 36, 50.
*16. **London**, Billingsgate Market Car Park.[41]
Nos 17, 20, 21, 37, 38/39, 49/50, 65.
*17. **London**, 282–96 Bishopsgate.[41]
No. 39.
*18. **London**, 50 Cornhill.[37]
No. 24.

*19. **London**, City of, no precise provenance.[32, 37]
Nos 7, 25, 32, 33, 46, 47, 61.
20. **Michelham** (Sussex), Priory.[42, 43]
Nos 12, 14/15, 16, 28?, 31, 32/33, 37, 43?, 53, 55.
*21. **Portsmouth** (Hants), found near Quay Gates 1868.[35]
No. 31.
*22. **Poynings** (Sussex), church.[32, 33, 34, 36, 43]
Nos 1, 2, 3, 6, 9, 12, 13, 17, 22, 25, 31, 33, 34, 37, 45, 52–5.
23. **St Albans** (Herts.), Abbey.[43]
Nos 15, 20, 38/39, 42, 56, 60.
24. **Sandwich** (Kent), Whitefriars.[43]
No. 13.
*25. **Shulbrede** (Sussex), Priory.[44]
Nos 17, 31, 34, 42, 47, 64.
26. **Steyning** (Sussex).[45]
Nos 32/33, 48?
27. **Tonford** (Kent), Manor.[43]
Nos 20, 21, 35, 42.
*28. **Westminster**.[35, 37, 39]
No. 53.
29. **Wilmington** (Sussex), Priory.[44]
Nos 33, 41/42.
*30. **Winchelsea** (Sussex), church.[32, 46]
Nos 25, 30, 32, 33, 37, 47, 63.

31. **Woodnesborough** (Kent), church.[43]
     Nos 13, 15, 20, 35, 36, 39, 44, 48, 57.

   UNPROVENANCED

*   British Museum: nos 21, 22, 25, 60.[32]
*   Cambridge, Museum of Archaeology and
     Ethnology: no. 55.

SOUTH-WEST FRANCE

32. **La Folatière** (Charente-Maritime),
     château.[49, 50]
     No. 29.
33. **La Rochelle** (Charente-Maritime),
     Château de Vaucler.[50, 51]
     Nos 9, 48.
34. **La Rochelle** (Charente-Maritime),
     Couvent des Cordeliers (Franciscans).[50, 52]

     Nos, 4, 17, 20, 24, 26, 33, 39, 40, 44, 48,
     49, 52, 55, 57, 59, 62.

Kettering Museum: nos 31, 46.[47]
Lewes Museum: nos 33, 55.[43]
*   York, Yorkshire Museum: no. 33.[48]

*35. **Langoiran** (Gironde), château.[17, 53, 54, 55, 56]

     Nos 12, 29, 32, 37, 44?, 49–51, 56,
     58/61.
*36. **Mérignac** (Gironde), tour de Veyrines.[54, 56, 57]

     Nos 49, 50, 51?

NORMANDY AND PICARDY

(All in Département de la Seine-Maritime, unless specified otherwise)

*37. **Abbeville** (Somme), found in ruins nearby
     in 1852 and 1865.[58]
     Nos 8, 11, 16, 43.
38. **Arques**, château?[59, 60]
     Nos 6, 11, 25?, 34, 54.
*39. **Auppegard**.[61]
     Nos 3, 7.
40. **Bailleul**, château and church.[59, 60, 62]
     Nos 17, 20, 21?, 29?, 32/33, 38/39, 41,
     44, 55/56, 57.
41. **Bellencombre**, château.[59, 60]
     Nos 6, 11, 14?, 37.
*42. **Bouteilles**, church.[59, 61, 62, 63]
     Nos 1, 2, 6, 32, 37.
*43. **Cany-Barville**, château.[64]
     Nos 12, 17, 18, 23, 25, 33, 45, 53, 55, 57.
44. **Dieppe**, priory church of St-Nicolas-de-
     Caudecote.[59, 65]
     Nos 6, 10.
*45. **Dieppe**.[59, 61]
     Nos 10, 13, 17, 37.
46. **Foucarmont**, Abbey.[59, 66, 67]
     Nos 13, 29?
47. **Janval**.[59]
     No. 25?
48. **?Jumièges**, Abbey.[59, 68]
     No. 32.
*49. **Le Tréport**, Abbey.[61, 63]
     Nos 58, 59.

*50. **Les Loges**, château.[58, 59, 62]
     Nos 17, 25, 60.
51. **Lucy**, church.[60, 66]
     No. 12.
*52. **Mareuil-sur-Somme** (Somme), château.[58]
     No. 33.
*53. **Quièvrecourt**, church.[58, 60, 66]
     Nos 3/4/5, 28.
54. **Rouxmesnil**, church.[59, 62]
     No. 25?
*55. **Rue** (Somme), château near.[58]
     Nos 30, 48.
56. **Varengeville**.[59]
     No. 13.

   UNPROVENANCED

*   Musée de Boulogne: no. 26?[69]
*   Musée de Dieppe: no. 20.[59]
*   Musée des Antiquités, Rouen: nos 5, 6,
     10, 15, 19, 26, 29, 56, 60.[61]
*   Musée national de la Céramique, Sèvres:
     nos 2, 5, 26, 32/33, 55.
     Mathon drawings: nos 1, 3, 13, 16, 17,
     20, 21, 24, 28?, 29?, 33–5, 38/39, 40, 41,
     44?, 48–50, 55/56, 57?

   ADDENDUM

57. **Cowick Manor** (Humberside).[70]
     Nos 25, 31, 46, 52–5, 66–8.

FIG. 2.   Dieppe Group tiles, designs 1–12. Scale 1:3

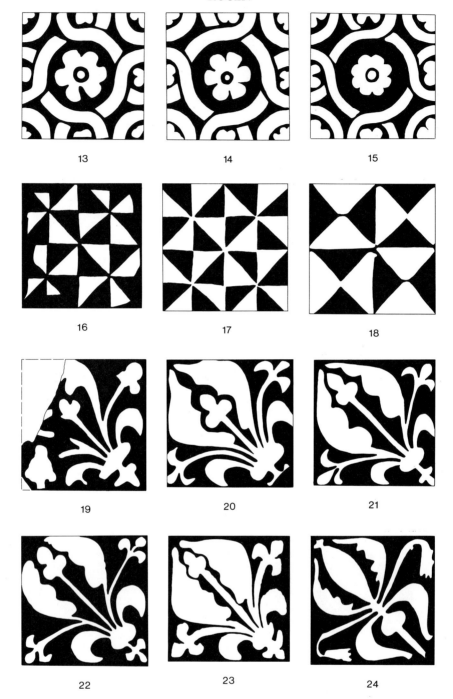

13   14   15

16   17   18

19   20   21

22   23   24

Fig. 3.   Dieppe Group tiles, designs 13–24. Scale 1:3

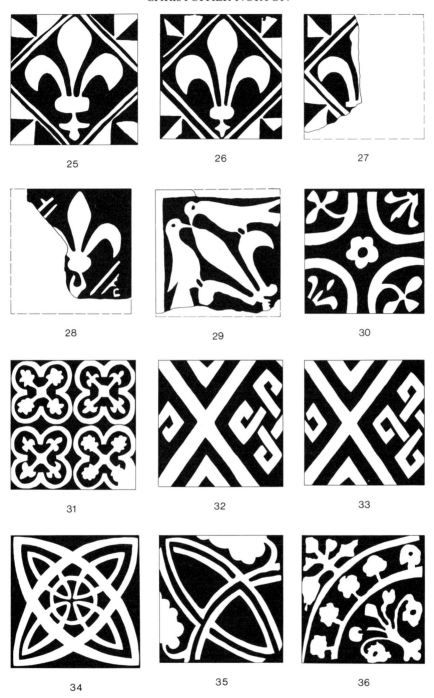

FIG. 4. Dieppe Group tiles, designs 25–36. Scale 1:3

FIG. 5. Dieppe Group tiles, designs 37–48. Scale 1:3

FIG. 6.   Dieppe Group tiles, designs 49–56, 66–7. Scale 1:3

FIG. 7.   Dieppe Group tiles, designs 57–65, 68. Scale 1:3

ACKNOWLEDGEMENTS

This article could not have been written without the help over a number of years of excavators, museum curators and librarians from many different institutions far too numerous to cite individually. A particular debt of gratitude is owed to Mark Horton for information on many sites in south-east England, and to Nathalie Roy, conservateur at the Musée des Antiquités, Rouen for facilitating the study of the Rouen collection over the years. I am also indebted to Claire Hanusse and Jacques Boucard for copies of their unpublished mémoires de maîtrise. The drawings are by Trevor Pearson.

REFERENCES

1. See principally L. de Vesly, 'La céramique ornementale en Haute-Normandie pendant le Moyen Age et la Renaissance', *Congrès du millénaire de la Normandie, 911–1911*, II (Rouen 1912), 189–263 (and reissued separately, Rouen 1913), and G. Lachasse and N. Roy, 'Les pavés de céramique médiévale', *Trésors des abbayes normandes* (Exhibition catalogue, Rouen-Caen 1979), 308–47. Full bibliography in C. Norton, 'Bibliographie des carreaux médiévaux français', *Terres cuites architecturales au Moyen Age*, ed. D. Deroeux (*Mémoires de la Commission départementale d'histoire et d'archéologie du Pas-de-Calais*, XXII.2, Arras 1986), 321–48.

2. C. Norton, 'Early Cistercian Tile Pavements', *Cistercian Art and Architecture in the British Isles*, ed. E. C. Norton and W. D. Park (Cambridge 1986), 228–55, pp. 247–50.

3. C. Norton, 'The Origins of Two-Colour Tiles in France and in England', in Deroeux, *Terres Cuites*, 256–93, pp. 271–9.

4. On these and other factors, see E. S. Eames, *Catalogue of Medieval Lead-glazed Earthenware Tiles in the Department of Medieval and Later Antiquities, British Museum* (London 1980), 278–84; P. J. Drury, 'The Production of Brick and Tile in Medieval England', in D. W. Crossley, *Medieval Industry* (Council for British Archaeology Research Report 40, 1981), 126–42; C. Norton, 'The Production and Distribution of Medieval Floor Tiles in France and England', *Artistes, Artisans et Production Artistique au Moyen Age*, ed. X. Barral i Altet (Actes du Colloque International de Rennes 1983), III (Paris 1990), 101–31.

5. Ibid., 107; C. Norton, *Carreaux de pavement du Moyen Age et de la Renaissance* (Musée Carnavalet, Paris 1992), 39–40, and Groupes IV–VI, VIII; see also the essay by D. Cailleaux, 'Paris, capitale des bâtisseurs au Moyen Age', ibid., 9–16 on building materials in general in Paris.

6. J. B. Ward-Perkins, 'Late Medieval Flemish Inlaid Tiles in England', *Antiq. J.*, XVII (1937), 442–4, nos 2 and 3.

7. Eames, *Catalogue*, 210.

8. E. C. Norton, 'The British Museum Collection of Medieval Tiles', *JBAA*, CXXXIV (1981), 107–19, p. 109. A Norman origin has been assumed in some of the more recent literature (see references cited in Appendix).

9. De Vesly, 'Céramique ornementale', esp. pl. V design 1. There appears not to be a copy in this country.

10. These are Muchelney Abbey and Stonar and Pivington in Kent, all cited by M. C. Horton, 'Medieval Floor-Tiles 1972–78 and earlier' in D. Sherlock and H. Woods, eds, *St Augustine's Abbey: Report on Excavations, 1960–78* (Kent Archaeological Society Monograph Series, Maidstone 1988), 144–76, p. 163. The single fragment from Pivington was published by S. E. Rigold, 'Excavation of a Moated Site at Pivington', *Archaeologia Cantiana*, LXXVII (1962), 27–47, fig. 8v. Drawings of fragments from Stonar communicated by Mark Horton do not belong to this group.

11. For the techniques, P. J. Drury and G. D. Pratt, 'A Late 13th- and Early 14th-century Tile Factory at Danbury, Essex', *Medieval Archaeology*, XIX (1975), 92–164, pp. 138–49.

12. Namely designs 104 and 110 (a small fragment) from St Augustine's Canterbury published by Horton, 'Medieval Floor-Tiles' — whereas his no. 35 *is* of this group; and design T90, a tiny fragment from James St, Drogheda (E. S. Eames and T. Fanning, *Irish Medieval Tiles* (Royal Irish Academy Monographs in Archaeology, 2, Dublin 1988).

13. See n. 12, and review by Laurence Keen in *JBAA*, CXLIV (1991), 139–42. A follow-up volume is promised.

14. Horton, 'Medieval Floor-Tiles', 163. The two designs illustrated in J. Helbig, 'Ancienne céramique de carrelage et de revêtement en Belgique', *Revue Belge d'archéologie et d'histoire de l'art*, XXII (1953), 219–40, nos 62–3 are copied from Ward-Perkins, 'Late Medieval Flemish Inlaid Tiles'.

15. Compare the distribution of the different categories of sites which have produced late 14th-century Bawsey tiles as shown in Norton, 'The Production and Distribution', 105–6, and fig. 5.

16. Compare e.g. de Vesly, 'Céramique ornementale', pl. IV no. 12, pl. VIII no. 5, pl. IX no. 6, pl. X no. 11, pl. XIV no. 9; there is not space here to cite other unpublished examples, except for a version of the very distinctive designs 32 and 33 in Dieppe Museum (unprovenanced).

17. L. Drouyn, *La Guienne Militaire*, 3 vols (Paris 1865), II, 1–28 and pl. 66; C. Hanusse, 'Les carreaux de pavage vernissés et historiés du Moyen-Age en Gironde' (Mémoire de maîtrise, Université de Bordeaux III 1977–8), 17–18. Some of the heraldic and border tiles are preserved in the Bordeaux museums.

18. One comparison worth citing is a distinctive fleur-de-lys very similar to no. 24 (and a parallel for no. 12) from the royal Château de Beauté, just east of Paris, dated *c.* 1375 (Norton, *Carreaux de Pavement*, Groupe XXXI, nos 185–6).

19. I. Nairn and N. Pevsner, *Sussex* (Buildings of England, Harmondsworth 1965), 586, 631–5; K. J. Evans, 'The Maison Dieu, Arundel', *Sussex Archaeological Collections*, CVII (1969), 65–77. M. A. Tierney, *The History and Antiquities of the Castle and Town of Arundel*, 2 vols (London 1834), II, 662–72.

20. Compare the roughly contemporary Bawsey tiles published by E. S. Eames, 'The Products of a Medieval Tile Kiln at Bawsey, King's Lynn', *Antiq. J.*, XXXV (1955), 162–81.

21. E. C. Norton, 'The Medieval Tile Pavements of Winchester Cathedral', in *BAACT Winchester*, VI (1983), 78–93, 90 and n. 36; J. P. Allan and L. Keen, 'The Medieval Floor Tiles', in J. P. Allan, ed., *Medieval and Post-Medieval Finds from Exeter, 1971–1980* (Exeter 1984), 232–47, 240–1; L. Keen, 'The Floor-Tiles' in I. P. Horsey, ed. K. S. Jarvis, *Excavations in Poole 1973–1983* (Dorset Natural History and Archaeological Society Monograph, 10, 1992), 133–4.

22. Eames, *Catalogue*, 97; Norton, 'The British Museum Collection', 114 and n. 39; bibliography of French examples in Norton, *Carreaux de pavement*, 147, Groupe XL, nos 210–11.

23. D. Deroeux and D. Dufournier, 'Les carreaux décorés du "groupe de l'Artois occidental", caractérisation et diffusion' in Deroeux, *Terres cuites*, 186–206.

24. M. C. Horton, 'Imported Motto Tiles: a Group of Sixteenth-Century Slip-Decorated Dutch Floor Tiles in England', *Collectanea Historica: Essays in Memory of Stuart Rigold*, ed. A. Detsicas (Maidstone 1981), 235–46.

25. On some of these questions, see the interesting speculations by J. M. Lewis, 'The Logistics of Transportation: a 15th-century Example from South Wales', Deroeux, *Terres cuites*, 234–40.

26. Eames and Fanning, *Irish Medieval Tiles*, 32, 62, 70–1, nos T88–90, T106, T110, T119, T123, T155, T210–11.

27. Kieran Campbell, pers. comm.

28. O. Bedwin, 'The Excavation of the Church of St Nicholas, Angmering, 1974', *Sussex Archaeological Collections*, CXIII (1975), 16–34, fig. 8. Note the drawing of n. 41 has been reconstructed with the corner of no. 49/50.

29. Evans, 'The Maison Dieu . . .', 75, fig. 2 nos 1–3.

30. K. J. Evans, 'Worthing Museum notes 1965 and 1966', *Sussex Archaeological Collections*, CVI (1968), 136.

31. Horton, 'Medieval Floor-Tiles', nos 35, 103, 105–9.

32. Eames, *Catalogue*, 210, designs 1401, 1621, 1962, 2060, 2165, 2180, 2387, 2514, 2597, 2844, 2961, 3043, 3044.

33. W. Figg, 'Sussex Tiles', *Sussex Archaeological Collections*, III (1850), 239 and pls.

34. Lord Alwyne Compton, Volume of tracings of medieval floor tiles in the library of the Society of Antiquaries of London.

35. V & A Department of Ceramics and Glass, nos 1419–22 and 1426. 1904 (Langdon) and 1274.92 (Portsmouth). No. 1327. 1892 from Westminster, cited by Ward-Perkins, 'Late Medieval', 443 as possibly belonging to this group, does not belong.

36. Lewes Museum (ex. inf. Mark Horton).

37. Museum of London, nos A302, A13737, M.XII.44.6830, MA 2229, 6810, 6817, 6872, 23938, 79.242/41, 85.59/43.

38. Ward-Perkins, 'Late Medieval', nos 2 and 3.

39. J. B. Ward-Perkins, *London Museum, Medieval Catalogue* (London 1940), fig. 79 no. 46 and fig. 81 no. 66.

40. L. Keen, 'Decorated Floor-Tiles', in T. Johnson, 'Excavations at Christ Church, Newgate St, 1973', *Transactions of the London and Middlesex Archaeological Society*, XXV (1974), 220–34, fig. 9 nos 8–9.

41. Museum of London Archaeology Service, BOS 87, BWB 83, MIN 86.

42. K. J. Barton and E. W. Holden, 'Excavations at Michelham Priory', *Sussex Archaeological Collections*, CV (1967), 1–12.

43. Mark Horton, pers. comm.

44. Lord Ponsonby and Hon. M. Ponsonby, 'Monastic Paving Tiles, with Special Reference to Tiles discovered at Shulbrede Priory, Lynchmere', *Sussex Archaeological Collections*, LXXV (1934), 19–64, nos 32–7 (no. 37 drawn with colours reversed). Note that Shulbrede no. 14, which is very similar to the Dieppe Group no. 33, is in fact a larger tile, 120–130 mm square. It goes with Shulbrede no. 10, a very odd design which finds a very close parallel in Upper Normandy (de Vesly, pl. V no. 6). Both designs are therefore probably part of another group of imported tiles, otherwise unattested.

45. K. J. Barton, 'Excavations at Cuthman's field, Church Street, Steyning, 1962', *Sussex Archaeological Collections*, CXXIV (1986), 97–108, nos 79–80.

46. W. D. Cooper, *The History of Winchelsea* (London 1850), 127.

47. Christine Orr, pers. comm.

48. No. 9 in the manuscript tile catalogue by W. H. Brooke, 1921– , attributed to St Mary's Abbey, York. However, many of the attributions to St Mary's are unreliable. There are no other examples of this group from St Mary's, and the tile appears, unprovenanced, in the drawings by G. Rowe, BL, Add. MS 41670, f. 204. It is almost certainly a stray antiquarian acquisition.

49. Musée de Saint-Jean-d'Angély.

50. J. Boucard, 'Carreaux de pavage médiévaux d'Aunis et Saintonge' (Mémoire de maîtrise, Ecole des Hautes Etudes, Paris 1977), nos 62, 92, 98, 99, 104, 107, 113, 124–33.

51. Musée d'Orbigny, La Rochelle.

52. J. Flouret, 'La crypte de l'église des Jésuites de La Rochelle, fouille à la salle du Moyen Age', *Bulletin de la Société des Antiquaires de l'Ouest*, 4ᵉ série, XIII (1976), 421–36, nos 46–62.

53. Bordeaux, Musée d'Aquitaine.

54. Bordeaux, Musée de la Société Archéologique.

55. A. Bardié, 'Les carrelages vernissés des XIIᵉ, XIIIᵉ et XIVᵉ siècles en Guienne', *Bulletin et mémoires de la Société archéologique de Bordeaux*, L (1933), 112–19 (unreliable).

56. Hanusse, 'Les carreaux de pavage', 17–18, 20, 51, 56–7.

57. G.-J. Durand, 'Notice archéologique sur la tour de Veyrines à Mérignac (Gironde)', *Bulletin archéologique publié par le Comité historique des arts et monuments*, II (1842–3), 297–8.

58. Musée national de la Céramique, Sèvres, nos 4552, 4557, 6359, and not inventoried.

59. De Vesly, 'Céramique ornementale', pls III.2, IV.5–6, V.1, 7–8, VI.5, VIII.2, IX.1, 5, XI.1, 3, XIV.6.

60. M. Mathon, 4 volumes of drawings and notes on medieval tiles, mostly from Normandy, Bibliothèque de la Manufacture nationale de Céramique de Sèvres, Q 510, *passim*.

61. Rouen, Musée des Antiquités, dons Cochet, Baudry, de Girancourt, and not inventoried.

62. J.-B. Cochet, *Répertoire archéologique du département de la Seine-Inférieure* (Paris 1871), *passim*.

63. Lachasse and Roy, 'Les pavés de céramique', nos 341, 361.

64. *De la Gaule à la Normandie, 2000 ans d'histoire, 30 ans d'archéologie* (Rouen 1990), 63–4; J.-M. Nicolle, pers. comm.

65. J.-B. Cochet, 'Exploration de la chapelle de Caudecote, près Dieppe, en 1861', *Revue de la Normandie* (1862), 65–70.

66. J.-E. Decorde, 'Pavage des églises dans le pays de Bray', *Revue de l'art chrétien*, I (1857), 481–92.

67. M. Louis Thiebert, pers. comm.

68. P. Oliver, 'Les carrelages céramiques de Jumièges', in *Jumièges. Congrès Scientifique du XIIIᵉ centenaire, 1954* (Rouen 1955), II, 537–51, fig. 17. There are no examples of this or any other design of the Dieppe group among the many extant fragments from Jumièges. Since it is notably outside the main distribution of the group in Normandy, the attribution must be considered dubious, though Jumièges was of course a major site.

69. Collection Camille Enlart no. 10595, part of a miscellaneous lot said (unconvincingly) to be from Lisieux — probably purchased there.

70. C. Hayfield and J. Greig, 'Excavation and salvage work on a moated site at Cowick, South Humberside, 1976', *Yorkshire Archaeological Journal*, LXII (1990), 111–24, fig. 4. I am grateful to Dr Jennie Stopford for this reference.

John, Duke of Bedford, as Patron in Lancastrian Rouen

By Jenny Stratford

John, duke of Bedford, brother of Henry V and regent of France for his nephew, Henry VI, was a major patron of the arts in Rouen. This paper concerns first the building works and religious foundations begun for or by Bedford in his lifetime and continued after his death by his executors, second the goldsmiths' work and other luxury goods he ordered from Rouen craftsmen. The English occupation of Rouen lasted for thirty years from 1419 to 1449; Bedford's regency, from 1422 to his death in 1435, coincided with a partial economic recovery in Rouen. As the historic capital of the duchy of Normandy, and the second city of Anglo-Burgundian France, Rouen was a key centre of English rule.[1] Bedford's works were a manifestation of English power and presence in the Norman capital, when this presence looked permanent. Some of his commissions were associated with his first wife, Anne of Burgundy, sister of Philip the Good, who died in 1432; others perhaps resulted from Bedford's second marriage in 1433 to Jacquetta of Luxembourg, niece of Louis of Luxembourg, chancellor of France for the English.

Bedford's building works in Rouen, as well as his tomb in the cathedral, have all perished, as have the plate and nearly all the other luxury goods he commissioned from Rouen craftsmen. The exceptions are a few secular illuminated manuscripts made in Rouen, which are securely associated with Bedford and Anne of Burgundy and with their court. This group of manuscripts does not include the three liturgical manuscripts completed or begun for Bedford in Paris: the Bedford Hours, the Salisbury Breviary in the Bibliothèque nationale, and the lost Benedictional, the so-called 'Pontifical of Poitiers'.[2] The only piece of Bedford's plate known to survive is the Royal Gold Cup in the British Museum, which is Paris not Rouen work. It serves as a reminder of the value and beauty of Bedford's possessions, and also of the way in which as regent he was able to acquire so much from the French royal collections.[3]

The visual sources for the lost buildings in Rouen associated with Bedford are limited to early views and plans. They demand careful interpretation.[4] The 'Livre des Fontaines', a remarkable topographical manuscript in the Bibliothèque municipale, Rouen (Pls XXVIIIA, B, XXIXA),[5] was made for a Rouen councillor and échevin, Jacques Le Lieur in 1524 to 1525, with additions in 1530 to 1531. It was dedicated to Georges d'Amboise, as cardinal archbishop of Rouen, and describes the conduits and fountains of Renaissance Rouen, which the archbishop had helped to endow. Plans of the fountains and of the streets through which the water courses passed were executed in pencil, ink and coloured wash. The hatched blue ribbons of the water-conduits appear in many of these views.

Hoefnagel's view of 1574 (Pl. XXIXB), was taken from the Mont-Sainte-Catherine.[6] From this standpoint, the north-eastern sector of the city walls is in the foreground, the area once occupied by Bedford's manor of Joyeux Repos, and later by the Celestines (Pl. XXIX). Many differences can be seen in the plan of 1575 by Belleforest, and its derivatives (Pls XXVII, XXIXC).[7] The plan of 1655 by the cartographer, Jacques Gomboust, belongs to another world (Pls XXVIIIC, XXIXD). Besides an accurate plan of the city, Gomboust represented many buildings, now destroyed. His plan was copied within a year in a reduced format for *Topographia Galliae* (Pl. XXVI). The 19th-century facsimile of Gomboust's

1655 plan, produced for the Société rouennaise des bibliophiles, is an accurate copy of the original.[8]

The archival collections in Rouen are a rich source of written evidence, especially the ecclesiastical records, series G, and the notarial registers, the *registres du tabellionage*, series E. Some of the relevant documents were published in the 19th century, others before the Second World War, in the invaluable calendars and collections of Charles de Beaurepaire and of Paul Le Cacheux.[9] De Beaurepaire used some of the material relating to Bedford's religious foundations in an article published in 1873 in the *Bibliothèque de l'Ecole des Chartes*.[10] The Rouen *registres du tabellionage*, the official records of the *tabellion*, a notary public who entered details of property sales and many other kinds of transaction, have survived as an unusually rich series for both the Valois and Lancastrian periods; they are extant for much of the English occupation to 1445, shortly before the reconquest of Rouen by Charles VII in 1449, with a significant gap during Bedford's regency from October 1428 to April 1430.[11] Documents in Rouen can be supplemented by the Bedford inventories in the Public Record Office, London, and by other related documents in London and Paris.[12]

As regent of France, Bedford divided much of his time between Paris and Normandy, although it is difficult to estimate exactly how much time he spent in Rouen itself. During October 1427, for example, when chronicle sources might suggest Bedford was in Rouen, the riding household moved between Domfront, Argentan, Falaise, Alençon and Bedford's castle at Harcourt. And this is recorded only because a few details were copied from the sole account of Bedford's household known to have survived until it was burnt in 1871. No one has attempted to construct an itinerary for Bedford; it would have many gaps.[13]

During the regency, Bedford returned twice to England, between late December 1425 and March 1427, and again between midsummer 1433 and July 1434. In spite of the nearly complete loss of his personal archive, enough information survives to make it clear that his building works, his religious foundations and his acquisitions of luxury objects were in tune with these peripatetic circumstances. In England, Bedford undertook building works at Penshurst and at Fulbrook, in Paris at the Hôtels des Tournelles and de Bourbon. He bought plate, jewels and textiles in both England and France, in London, in Paris and in Rouen. Bedford's state as regent was on a fitting scale; the Rouen works should not be thought of in isolation from those in Paris or in England.[14]

Bedford's building works in Rouen cannot be entirely divorced from the king's works. First of all, where did he live? The new royal palace on a site commanding the Seine at the south-west angle of the city walls (Pl. XXVI), is not in question.[15] It was known at first simply as the Palais, but by the end of the 15th century, after the Palais de Justice was built, as the Vieux-Palais. Building works were begun by Henry V after the siege and surrender of Rouen in 1418–19. Between 1422, the death of Henry V, and 1436, the year after Bedford's death, few works on the Palais are documented. These years are sometimes thought to have seen a pause in the construction work, but the apparent gap may be the result of the loss of the relevant records.[16] Nevertheless, the Palais, occupied by a garrison by 1439, was still unfinished several years after Bedford died. Edmund Beaufort, duke of Somerset, the last English governor-general of Normandy, was living there when Rouen was retaken, but minor works continued to 1449.[17]

The castle built by Philip Augustus in the north-west of the city after the capture of Rouen in 1204 (Pl. XXVI), was, on the contrary, often occupied by Bedford and by his immediate household. Bedford himself, his lieutenant or deputy as captain of Rouen (the effective commander of the Rouen garrison), his bastard daughter, the chaplains and clerks of his chapel, were among those allotted chambers in the castle. Many other officers of the regent's large household, as well as his household troops (a force of 400 in a city with a population estimated at between 10,000 and 15,000), may have been lodged there.[18] Today, the only part of the castle still standing is the Donjon Philippe Auguste, once at the north-east of the castle wall. The 'Livres des Fontaines', in a view from the north (Pl. XXVIIIA), depicts this tower in the foreground. Joan of Arc was held captive in the north-west curtain tower from December 1430 until her execution in May 1431. Until recently, Joan's captivity was the main impulse for investigation of the castle, and the inspiration for the 1931 plan by the Commandant Quenedey.

Quenedey's reconstruction of the castle has often been republished. It depicts the regent's apartments and chapel in a wing south of the north curtain wall, between the Donjon and the tower where Joan of Arc was imprisoned. This is speculative. The plan published by Bernard Gauthiez and Dominique Pitte, following rescue excavations of the western sector of the courtyard in 1983–4, indicates clearly the towers, the sections of curtain wall and the very few elements within the courtyard confirmed by archaeological evidence.[19]

Some works undertaken at the castle in the king's name and at crown expense during the 1420s and 1430s were to fit the regent's needs. In June 1429, two short flights of broad stone steps were cut to and from the chamber where the goods and vessels of Bedford's chapel were kept.[20] From other sources, it is clear how rich and valuable the regent's chapel goods were. The date the work for the storeroom was put in hand suggests that better access was first needed in 1429, a date significant in the history of English occupation. The reverses following the siege of Orléans meant a shift in the centre of English power from Paris to Rouen. Bedford visited Paris, undertook building works and ordered luxury goods there until 1435, the last year of his life, but in 1429, when he relinquished the captaincy of Paris, he probably moved to Rouen his chapel goods and the great Louvre library he had acquired from the French royal collections.[21]

In early April 1433, just before Bedford's second marriage to the seventeen-year-old Jacquetta of Luxembourg, other works were undertaken at the castle affecting Bedford and his household. A carpenter worked on the windows of the castle library. This document has long been thought to relate to the place where the Louvre library was kept. The 843 books of the Louvre library of Charles V and Charles VI, acquired by Bedford in 1425, were removed from Paris in 1429. A scrap of additional evidence supports the theory that the books were kept in Rouen Castle before they were taken to England. The keeper of the Louvre library in Paris handed them over to John Salvain, *bailli* of Rouen.[22]

The same *quittance* of 1433 lists repairs to the windows of Bedford's own chamber, to the door of his chaplains' chamber, and new arrangements for the regent's altar hangings. In October 1434, a *serrurier* supplied locks, bolts and fittings for the bedchamber of Bedford's bastard daughter, Mary, for the adjacent latrine, and for a great bench in the regent's wardrobe. Other minor works, ordered by Bedford himself in December 1434, were carried out by March 1435. New fireplaces were built in the regent's own chamber, in his artillery storeroom and in the chamber of his great officer, Nicolas Burdet, then lieutenant of Rouen and captain of the castle garrison. Rubble had to be removed from these works, from a newly built staircase and from a broad, glazed casement window pierced in the courtyard wall of the captain's chamber, 'pour donner une vue'. In the king's small chapel, panes of stained glass with the arms of the duke of Gloucester and the duke of Burgundy were washed and releaded on Bedford's orders.[23] From these few details, taken from documents which happened to survive, it is clear that Rouen Castle, where Bedford died in September 1435, and where his considerable stores of artillery, ordnance and jousting equipment were kept,[24] was fitted up to receive not only the regent and his household, but also to house his wardrobe, his chapel goods and his library.

Across Rouen to the east, was Bedford's manor of Joyeux Repos, afterwards the Celestine priory (Pls XXVI, XXIX).[25] Joyeux Repos was in the north-east of the city, the last area to be brought within the medieval walls. It occupied a site of about 3 ½ acres in the large parish of Saint-Vivien (the Vieux-Palais occupied about 3 acres).[26] But in Bedford's time, its dependencies also embraced lands in the small sector of the parish of Saint-Hilaire within the walls.[27] At the east and south-east, the boundaries ran close to the ramparts, from near the Porte Saint-Hilaire, past the rising ground of the Tour du Colombier and towards the Porte Martainville; the other boundaries are more problematic. Gomboust's plan shows the Celestine enclosure in the 17th century, bounded by the Eau-de-Robec, the road along the walls and the Bureau des Pauvres Valides, founded in 1534 (Pl. XXIXD), the approximate area occupied today by the hospital. Bedford's property also continued north of the Robec. The site has never been excavated, and the loss of the *tabellionage* register for 1428–30 leaves a key gap in the records.

In 1429 or 1430, Bedford and Anne of Burgundy bought the houses and gardens lying between the Robec and the Tour du Colombier, which formed the nucleus of Joyeux Repos. They changed the name of the manor from Chantereine (according to the early historians of Rouen, a 'maison de plaisance' of the dukes of Normandy). Bedford bought adjacent houses, plots, gardens and stables on five further occasions to October 1433.[28] He began to pour money into Joyeux Repos following the shift in the centre of English government from Paris to Rouen in 1429. His acquisitions continued during 1430–1, his period of longest residence in Rouen, when Henry VI and his household were occupying the castle.

On Easter Sunday 1430, Bedford bought 1 ½ acres of an adjacent garden, La Lavanderie, near the walls, planted with trees and stocked with fishponds, belonging to the monks of Saint-Ouen. In October, he paid handsomely for three houses, a garden and a stable near the Porte Saint-Hilaire, perhaps also housing his treasury. Both these additions were in the parish of Saint-Hilaire. The boundaries of the first plot were the road along the ramparts, the rue Chantereine (the easternmost street between the rues Eau-de-Robec and Saint-Hilaire visible in the Gomboust detail), and the rest of the garden belonging to Saint-Ouen; the second bordered the duke's property, the rampart road, the rue Chantereine and land of Saint-Ouen.[29] Between September 1431 and March 1433, Bedford bought three further plots adjoining Joyeux Repos in the parish of Saint-Vivien. The first, near the walls, consisted of over half an acre of garden with a building, belonging to Roger Mustel, *vicomte de l'eau* of Rouen; it extended to the corner of the fifth 'crenel de la garde des murs' in the direction of the Porte Martainville, no doubt one of the turrets visible in the Belleforest view (Pl. XXIXc). The other plots abutted on the duke's land and the residue of Mustel's garden; the third, a little piece of garden, was 'in the place called Chantereine'.[30]

Bedford's final acquisition was a small road, the rue des Célestins (Pl. XXIXA, D). The Celestines dated this purchase to 1 December 1433, but William Worcester (secretary of Bedford's executor, Sir John Fastolf), recorded that Bedford's executors spent 35 *livres tournois* in buying the passageway running from the rue Saint-Vivien (an alternative name for the rue Saint-Hilaire), to Joyeux Repos, in return for perpetual prayers for the duke. The statements can be reconciled if a debt remained from Bedford's lifetime purchase. The Robec was used nearer the city centre for public latrines; the purchase would have protected Bedford from nuisance.[31]

According to William Worcester, Bedford spent 4,500 marks sterling or £3,000 building Joyeux Repos, the equivalent of about 27,000 *livres tournois*, at a time when the wages of a mason or skilled building worker in Rouen were 5 *sous tournois* per day, and those of building labourers around 3 *sous* 4 *deniers* a day. Plenty of fine building stone was available to be shipped to Rouen; the regent himself held Elbeuf and other great forests in Normandy.

But almost nothing is known of the fabric or structure of Joyeux Repos. No building accounts have survived from Bedford's lifetime. The gardens were varied and well-wooded. Besides the fishponds essential to the late medieval diet, there was probably at least one fountain (as recorded in post-medieval descriptions). Water was an important element in a pleasure garden, and there is good evidence of Bedford's interest in gardens.[32] There was also a tennis court. After Bedford's death, Louis of Luxembourg, chancellor of France for the English, archbishop of Rouen and uncle of Jacquetta, Bedford's second wife, occupied Joyeux Repos, probably until his death at Hatfield in 1443. The *jeu de paume* was repaired in 1438–9. Other minor works were undertaken for Louis in the following year.[33]

There was a household chapel at Joyeux Repos in Bedford's time, but Farin's statement, repeated by de Beaurepaire, that Bedford built a chapel for the Celestines, is questionable. The lands and income derived from Bedford's succession, but the household chapel was being rebuilt for the Celestines in 1448, when Edmund Beaufort was governor-general of Normandy.[34] The church, drawn in the 'Livres des Fontaines' (Pl. XXIXa) from the south, following the direction of the water course from east to west, was completed after 1460.

In 1445, Henry VI relinquished his rights to Joyeux Repos as heir to the property of Bedford and Anne of Burgundy. Similar renunciations were made by Edmund Beaufort, Humphrey, duke of Gloucester, and Jacquetta as heirs. The next year, Henry gave Joyeux Repos to the Celestines, styling himself founder, endowing the house with an annual income of 500 *livres parisis*, and a further 200 *livres tournois* for buildings.[35] Construction work was held up by the opposition of the monks of Saint-Ouen, but Henry and Beaufort (named as joint founders), supported the Celestines in a suit which reached the Exchequer court, the highest court in Normandy. By 1448 the choir had been built and the nave was under construction. Beaufort commissioned stained glass for the windows and endowed an obit in 1449.[36]

With this degree of English royal support, it is not suprising that even before the reconquest of Rouen, Charles VII laid claim to Joyeux Repos in the *Chambre des comptes* of Paris. One of his first political acts in November 1449, immediately after the reconquest, was to regrant the manor to the Celestines, asserting in the donation that Bedford had built it with the revenues of France. In 1451, Charles granted 400 *livres tournois* of annual income as 'first founder'; he gave funds to build a larger church 'selon la forme, deviz et patrons', of his royal officers. The consecration took place in 1458, but the church was still under construction in 1460.[37] Some of the buildings were in disrepair by 1494; a new consecration by Georges d'Amboise took place in 1502. Following the dissolution of the order in the late 18th century. the enclosure bounded by the Robec (but not a plot called 'Cavalier', near the cemetery of the Hôpital général), were sold in 1784 to a Rouen merchant for 120,000 *livres*. In 1820, part of the site was bought for 38,000 francs by the hospital.[38]

The site of the Carmelite house, destroyed at the Revolution, has never been excavated. The drawing in the 'Livres des Fontaines' (Pl. XXVIIIb) is hard to decipher even in the original, but the pointed spire of the church and the portal are both visible. The Gomboust plan shows the site more clearly (Pl. XXVIIIc), near the main north–south axis of Rouen, north of the cathedral and south of Saint-Ouen. The rue de la Chaîne runs directly to the south. Bedford had good claims as the 'founder' of the Rouen Carmelites. The order had been established outside the walls, on a site subject to flooding and poorly defended. By the mid-14th century, they had moved within the walls. In the 1420s, their buildings were unfinished and they were burdened by rents. In August 1425, Bedford undertook to relieve them. The Carmelites were to recognise Bedford and Anne of Burgundy as principal founders, and to celebrate masses and prayers for them in perpetuity.[39] Two stone images,

Bedford on the right, Anne on the left, with their arms carved beneath, were to be erected on the church. The intention seems to have been to set donor figures either side of the portal like the standing figures of Charles V and Jeanne de Bourbon on the Celestine church in Paris, or the kneeling figures on the west door of the church of the Chartreuse de Champmol in Dijon.[40]

Bedford left for England in December 1425 and nothing had been done for the Carmelites before his return in March 1427. In May 1428, he acquired the tithes of Sierville, rich agricultural land about 20 km from Rouen in the pays du Caux, to pay the Carmelites' rents. The earlier provisions for masses and prayers were repeated in 1428. Minor differences in wording may be merely linguistic; the 1425 act is in Latin, the 1428 act in French. In 1425, the figures with their arms were to be on the exterior of the portal, in 1428 on the two sides, 'costés', of the church, and to be kneeling.[41]

By 1431, Bedford had transferred the tithes of Sierville to the cathedral chapter. This freed the Carmelites from the rents they owed to the cathedral; with the excess revenue, two annual masses were founded in the cathedral for Bedford and for Anne, for which detailed and elaborate provisions survive.[42] Nothing was done about the rents the Carmelites owed to others until 1443, about eight years after Bedford's death. The downturn in English fortunes after 1429 affected Bedford's personal revenues and disposable cash. The huge sums he lent to the English crown for the seige of Orléans remained unpaid long after his death and were probably never recovered. In 1443, Bedford's executors were forced to make up the balance of rents still undischarged. The payment was allocated to the construction of a cloister for the Carmelites; in the 18th century, Bedford was remembered as the donor of the cloister.[43]

The portal statues may have been executed, but were almost certainly never erected. The church was still under construction well after 1432, when Anne of Burgundy died. In 1432, the notorious money changer, Jean Marcel, founded masses in the first chapel next to the portal, facing the rue de la Chaîne. They had to be celebrated in the old church, since the new building was incomplete.[44] Bedford was in England from 1433 to 1434 and died only a year after his return to France, without having fully discharged his obligations. Only fragmentary references are known to the Carmelite glass. Given the flourishing stained-glass workshops of Rouen, it is possible that Bedford's donation was recorded in this way. A choir window displayed the arms of Charles VI and Isabeau of Bavaria, earlier donors.[45]

In 1430 to 1431, Bedford strengthened his connections with the cathedral. He transferred to the chapter the tithes of Sierville, bought for the Carmelites in 1428. The tithes were worth far more than the Carmelites' annual dues to the cathedral. With the residue, Bedford founded sung masses for himself and for Anne of Burgundy, for which detailed provisions have survived. Conforming with earlier foundations in Rouen Cathedral for Charles V and Henry V, torches were to burn at twelve choir piers (all except the two piers at the east end behind the high altar); the great bell and all the other bells were to be rung. In 1430, on the feast of St Romain, Bedford was admitted a canon of the cathedral; immediately after the elaborate ceremony, he gave a huge set of vestments and a gold chalice with a paten decorated with a vernicle, a devotional image already found on patens in the 14th century and increasingly popular in the 15th century.[46]

Bedford died in Rouen castle on 14 September 1435 and was buried 'magnificently' in the cathedral on 30 September. His tomb stood on the north side of the choir at the level of the high altar, between the piers facing the chapel of St Peter and St Paul, a position of great honour near the other royal tombs. Masons were brought in to advise on removing the feretory of St Senier and on erecting the tomb in 1437. The base was of black marble and survived to 1732. The effigy was destroyed by the Calvinists in 1562. It was almost certainly of white alabaster or white marble, like the tomb of Anne of Burgundy in the Celestine church in Paris. The wooden cover was removed (as were those on the heart tomb of Charles V and the other royal tombs in the cathedral), only on fifteen major feasts and on a few special occasions: the solemn Entry of Edmund Beaufort as governor-general in 1448, but not the Entry of Margaret of Anjou.[47] The burial was excavated in 1860 by the Abbé Cochet. There is a 'relic' in the Musée des Antiquités, Rouen, a small glass box said to contain fragments of lead and silk from the burial. Cochet concluded that the body had been embalmed. It was well preserved and he found 'mercury' in the tomb.[48]

In 1648, Dugdale drew the copper plate affixed near Bedford's tomb commemorating his chantry foundation; this drawing was reproduced by Sandford. Another is in the Gaignières collection. The plaque belonged to a type current in France by the first quarter of the 15th century. Above the inscription, each side of the garter collar, were the Lancastrian ostrich plumes. Under the garter was Bedford's root device, within the collar a shield with Bedford's arms, possibly in silver, already lost by 1648. The plaque (without the shield) was in the cathedral library c. 1720, but lost by 1752.[49]

When Bedford's executors paid for the masses in 1437, they promised a missal of the Use of Rouen, a silver chalice weighing two marks, a pair of cruets, a pax and two little silver candlesticks together weighing four marks, sets of vestments for two celebrants and altar hangings, all to be marked with the duke's arms. A missal of Rouen Use must logically have been obtained in Rouen, but nothing can be said of the provenance of the other goods. None of the rich bequests Bedford left to the cathedral in his will seem to have been Rouen work. They included a very valuable gold chalice with jewels and a pair of huge silver-gilt censers, both made in Paris, which the chapter never obtained in spite of strenuous efforts, a silver-gilt processional cross from the ransom of Jean, duke of Alençon (captured at Verneuil in 1424), and a full set of vestments and hangings of red velvet embroidered with the root device in gold which Bedford had used in his own chapel, probably also made in Paris. The cross and vestments survived at Rouen to the Revolution, as did a pall, very probably used at Bedford's funeral.[50]

Some of the secular manuscripts made for Bedford in Rouen have survived. They include the French translation of *Les Amphorismes Hippocras*, compiled for the duke and duchess by a member of their medical household, Jean Tourtier. This seems to be the presentation copy and was completed, as the colophon tells us, at Rouen on 1 February 1430. In the margins are the duke's personal device, the root, his supporters, the eagle and yale, as well as the fruitful palm associated with the duchess. The Physiognomy, now in Lisbon, seems to be in the same Rouen style. It is probably also the presentation copy. The Physiognomy was one of at least two works compiled for the duke by his physician and astrologer, Roland of Lisbon. Both these Rouen books were compiled for the duke and duchess by members of their household.[51]

Our knowledge of Bedford's own commissions remains fragmentary. No building accounts, no household or wardrobe books have survived. It is therefore remarkable that there is any evidence at all for goldsmiths' work and for embroideries ordered by Bedford in Rouen. The Bedford inventories describe five great silver chargers, each averaging about three Troy pounds in weight and belonging to Bedford's 'rich cupboard' or plate for state days, made in 'English fashion', but with Rouen marks. The circular Rouen mark incorporated the Agnus Dei, which can be seen in the arms of the city (Pls XXVI, XXVII). A silver-gilt spiceplate is described in some detail in the Bedford inventories. It weighed nearly 3½ Troy pounds and was undoubtedly made for Bedford, since it was engraved with the root, his personal device, and his beast, the yale, was enamelled on the cover. The spiceplate listed in the inventory can be matched with a surviving payment to a Rouen goldsmith and *bourgeois*, Jean Vasse. Vasse was paid in Rouen in November 1431 for this commission.[52]

Evidence for the embroideries is limited but of great interest. After Bedford's death, his executors in England were left with 2,154 root devices embroidered in gold and coloured silks on linen backing, ready to sew on to hangings. These badges were valuable, worth 1s. 6d. each second hand, so the gold was undoubtedly *or de cipre*, the best quality gold thread. William Worcester recorded a payment to an embroiderer in Rouen, Thomas Brydon, for 918 similar roots at a cost of about 3s. 4d. for three. Brydon was an Englishman settled in Rouen by 1421, whose descendants remained Rouen embroiderers. A contract between Brydon and Thomas Montagu, earl of Salisbury, has survived from 1422. Brydon was evidently a talented and skilled specialist. He agreed to embroider two cloths for long robes for Salisbury in gold and coloured silks, following a pattern. One cloth was to be ready before the first of May. Together, they cost the spectacularly large sum of 140 gold nobles or £46 13s. 4d. sterling. Bedford also ordered embroideries in London and in Paris, but in Brydon he was calling on a man of proven skill.[53]

The picture of Bedford's expenditure on building works and on other luxury goods in Rouen (as elsewhere) will always remain incomplete, but enough evidence has survived to suggest the ways in which he maintained his state as regent. Bedford's expenditure in Rouen should be seen against first, his other commissions in England and in Paris, second against the commissions and religious foundations of other Englishmen in Rouen and elsewhere in France. The difference was probably one of scale. There is some slight evidence for a shift of emphasis from Paris to Rouen in about 1429, and for increased expenditure in 1430 to 1431 during Bedford's longest stay in Rouen. During the Lancastrian occupation, Rouen could provide masons, sculptors, stained-glass artisans, goldsmiths, embroiderers, illuminators, and other craftsmen, not necessarily all natives of the city, to satisfy demand.

ACKNOWLEDGEMENTS

For their generous help with this paper, I thank Claude Hohl and his colleagues at the Archives départmentales de la Seine-Maritime, Patrick Périn and Madame L. Flavigny, Musée des Antiquités, Rouen, the staff of the Bibliothèque municipale, Rouen, Peter Barber, Map Room, British Library, Christopher Allmand, Michael K. Jones, Pierre-Yves Le Pogam, and Robert Massey.

REFERENCES

1. See M. Mollat, *Le commerce maritime normand à la fin du Moyen Age* (Paris 1952); *idem*, 'Une expansion différée par la guerre (1382-environ 1475)', *Histoire de Rouen*, ed. M. Mollat (Toulouse 1979), 123–43; C. T. Allmand, *Lancastrian Normandy, 1415–1450: The History of a Medieval Occupation* (Oxford 1983).

2. J. Stratford, 'The Manuscripts of John, duke of Bedford: Library and Chapel', *England in the Fifteenth Century: Proceedings of the 1986 Harlaxton Symposium*, ed. D. Williams (Woodbridge 1987), 329–50; C. Reynolds and J. Stratford, 'Le manuscrit dit "Le Pontifical de Poitiers"', *La Revue de l'Art*, LXXXIV (1989), 61–80; J. Stratford, *The Bedford Inventories: the Worldly Goods of John, Duke of Bedford, Regent of France (1389–1435)* [Society of Antiquaries of London, forthcoming].

3. Stratford, *Bedford Inventories*, 60–1, 319–25.

4. For views and plans of Rouen, see J.-P. Bardet, *Rouen aux XVIIe et XVIIIe siècles: Les mutations d'un espace social*, 2 vols (Paris 1983), 62–7.

5. *Catalogue général des manuscrits des bibliothèques publiques de France*, XLVIII (Paris 1933), 80, no. 742 (Rouen, BM, MS G. 3), see the very high quality facsimile, Jacques Le Lieur, '*Le Livre Enchaîné' ou Livre des Fontaines de Rouen . . .*, 2 vols, ed. V. Sanson (Rouen 1911); see also, L. R. Delsalle, 'Jacques Le Lieur et Le Livre des Fontaines', *Connaître Rouen*, IV (Rouen 1977). The reproductions in T. De Joliment, *Les principaux édifices de la ville de Rouen en 1525 . . .* (Rouen 1845), are heavily 'improved', and are unreliable.

6. G. Hoefnagel, 'Rotomagus vulgo Roan Normandiae Metropolis', G. Braun and F. Hogenberg, *Civitates Orbis Terrarum* (Cologne 1573–1618), I, 9, reproduced here from BL, Map Room, *17380 (1).

7. Detail from bird's-eye view after Belleforest (Paris 1575), reproduced here from 'Rothomagus Galliae Lugdunensis ad Sequanam flu. Opp. vulgo Rouen', *c.* 1590, BL, Map Room, *17380 (2).

8. Gomboust, *Rothomagus-Rouen* (Paris and Rouen 1655), the original is BN, Estampes (6 ff.); reproduced here from *Description des antiquités et singularités de Rouen. Par Jacques Gomboust, 1655* . . . and *Atlas*, 2 vols, ed. J. Adeline (Société rouennaise des bibliophiles, Rouen 1873–5); first reduction for *Topographia Galliae* (1656), reproduced here from [M. Merian?], 'Rothomagus-Rouen', *Topographia Galliae* (Amsterdam: Casper Meriaen and Jan Joesten Appeluer 1662).

9. C. de Robillard de Beaurepaire, *Archives départementales de la Seine-Inférieure. Inventaire sommaire des archives départementales antérieures à 1790. Série G*, 7 vols in 9 (Paris 1868–1912); *idem, Derniers mélanges historiques et archéologiques* (Rouen 1909); P. Le Cacheux, *Actes de la chancellerie d'Henri VI concernant la Normandie sous la domination anglaise (1422–1435)*, 2 vols (SHN, Rouen and Paris 1907–8); *idem, Rouen au temps de Jeanne d'Arc et pendant l'occuptation anglaise (1419–1449)* (SHN, Rouen and Paris 1931).

10. C. de Robillard de Beaurepaire, 'Fondations pieuses du duc de Bedford à Rouen', *Bibliothèque de l'Ecole des Chartes*, XXXIV (1873), 343–86.

11. See A. Dubuc, 'Le tabellionnage rouennais durant l'occupation anglaise (1418–1445)', *Bulletin philologique et historique, 1967* (Paris 1969), 797–808.

12. Stratford, *Bedford Inventories*, for texts and bibliography.

13. BN, MS n.a. fr. 5085, f. 40ᵛ, notes by Vallet de Viriville on the destroyed controller's book of the expenses and liveries of Bedford's household, 1 Oct. 1427–30 Sept. 1428, ex-Bibliothèque du Louvre, MS F 1286. Another set of notes, made in 1835, is PRO, PRO 31/8/135/11.

14. See Stratford, *Bedford Inventories*, 109–13 and *passim*.

15. For works in 1421–2, see 'The King's Works in Normandy 1415–1449', *History of the King's Works: the Middle Ages*, ed. H. M. Colvin, 2 vols (London 1963), I, 461–2; for a comprehensive study with illustrations and bibliography, see P.-Y. Le Pogam, 'Un chantier exemplaire: le palais royal de Rouen', *Bulletin archéologique du Comité des travaux historiques et scientifiques, 1987–8*, n.s. 23–24 (Paris 1991), 213–47.

16. Until the death of Henry V, works were paid for in England, where the documents survive among the Exchequer records; after the death of Charles VI, and in accordance with the provisions of the treaty of Troyes (1420), the Norman *Chambre des comptes* was reunited with the Paris *Chambre*. Most of the Paris documents were lost in the fire which destroyed the *Chambre* in 1737. After the recapture of Paris in 1436, and the English withdrawal to Normandy, the English *Chambre* moved to Rouen. The incomplete debris of its records have survived, divided between the collections of the Bibliothèque nationale, the British Library and the Lenoir collection (microfilms in the Archives nationales, Paris).

17. De Beaurepaire, 'Fondations pieuses', 353–4, 380–2; Stratford, *Bedford Inventories*, 39; Le Pogam, 'Le palais royal de Rouen', 233, suggests construction was largely complete by 1442.

18. This figure is suggested by L. Delsalle, *Rouen et les Rouennais au temps de Jeanne d'Arc, 1400–1470* (Rouen 1982), 22; see further, Robert Massey, 'Lancastrian Rouen: Military Service and Property Holding, 1419–1449', *England and Normandy in the Middle Ages*, ed. David Bates and Anne Curry [forthcoming 1993]. I thank Robert Massey for sending me a draft of this paper before publication.

19. See P. M., 'Notes sur la prison et les lieux, théâtre du procès et du supplice de Jeanne d'Arc à Rouen', *Procès de condamnation de Jeanne d'Arc*, ed. P. Tisset, 3 vols (SHF, Paris 1971), III, 219–35; D. Pitte, B. Gauthiez, *Le château de Philippe Auguste: nouvelles recherches* (Rouen 1987).

20. Le Cacheux, *Rouen*, 153; Stratford, *Bedford Inventories*, 80.

21. Stratford, *Bedford Inventories*, 15, 96.

22. Le Cacheux, *Rouen*, 257–9; Stratford, *Bedford Inventories*, 96; for the construction of the windows, Delsalle, *Rouen*, 37–8.

23. P.-Y. Le Pogam, 'Les œuvres royaux à l'époque de Charles VII d'après les documents de la Chambre des comptes' [unpublished thesis for the Ecole des Chartes, 1989], 131–2, citing BN, MS fr. 26059, no. 2438 (*mandement* of the treasurers-general of Normandy for the works on Bedford's orders, 18 Dec. 1434), no. 2434 (*quittance* of Jean de Senlis, *verrier et peintre*, 16 Jan. 1435), no. 2436 (*quittance* of the carters and labourers, 10 March) and no. 2435 (*quittance* of the tilers, 23 March); see *Ecole des Chartes: Positions des thèses* (Paris 1989), 131–7. I thank P.-Y. Le Pogam for allowing me to use his work on these documents.

24. Partly printed, *Letters and Papers illustrative of the Wars of the English in France during the Reign of King Henry VI*, ed. J. Stevenson, 2 vols in 3 (RS 22, London 1861–4), II (II), 565–74.

25. The Celestine priory, founded in 1445, was suppressed in 1778 and united with the Séminaire Saint-Nicaise in 1784. For the archives, see *Inventaire Sommaire, sér. G*, VII, pt 2 (Rouen 1905). For Saint-Ouen and the surviving *tabellionage* registers, see below. See also, de Beaurepaire, 'Fondations pieuses', 343–4; *idem*, 'Notice sur le monastère des Célestins de Rouen', *Derniers mélanges*, 1–10.

26. ADSM, G 9208, temporal, 1673: church, cloister and other monastic buildings, entrance courtyard, basse-cour and garden within the walls in the parish of Saint-Vivien; visitation, 1771, printed de Beaurepaire, 'Célestins', 9, about 3 acres.

27. For the properties in the Parish of Saint-Hilaire within the walls, see n. 28; Bedford also bought for 500 *liv. t.* from the authorities of the king's hospital in Rouen, a manor with houses, woods and pastures, etc., at Beaurepaire in the parish of Saint-Hilaire, 18 Nov. 1430 (ADSM, 2 E 1/174, f. 129), but this was outside the walls and although conveniently close to Joyeux Repos, cannot have formed part of it.

28. ADSM, G 9192, pp. 1–2, 'Inventaire des titres et papiers des Célestins de Rouen (1735)'; for the change of name, ADSM, G 9195, f. 1 and G 9204, p. 97; F. Farin, *Histoire de la ville de Rouen*, 3rd edn, 6 vols (Rouen 1738), VI, 260; A. Chéruel, *Histoire de Rouen sous la domination anglaise au quinzième siècle*, 2 pts in 1 vol. (Rouen 1840), 117, stating wrongly that Henry V gave Bedford Joyeux Repos; N. Périaux, *Dictionnaire indicateur des rues et places de Rouen* (Rouen 1870), 120.

29. ADSM, 2 E 1/174, ff. 105–105ᵛ, 11 Oct. 1430, for 50 *saluts d'or*, and a rent of 50 *sous t.* p.a. payable to Saint-Ouen, naming Bedford and Pierre Baille, his treasurer and receiver-general in France and Normandy from 1429; ADSM, 14 H 18, p. 442, dated Easter Sunday, 16 April 1430, for 10 *liv. t.* rent p.a. to Saint-Ouen; ADSM, 14 H 465, pp. 472–3, 21 Jan. 1450.

30. ADSM, 2 E 1/175, f. 2ᵛ, 27 Sept. 1431, for 100 *liv. t.*; 2 E 1/176 [unfoliated], 26 Feb. 1433 (n.s.), for 64 *saluts d'or*; 2 E 1/176, 22 March 1433 (n.s.), for 6 *saluts d'or* and 45 *sous t.* I thank Claude Hohl for the references to 2 E 1/176.

31. ADSM, G 9192, p. 2, contested in 1499; *Letters and Papers*, II (II), 558; Le Cacheux, *Rouen*, 274–9. For the rue des Célestins, also known as the rue de la Porche because of the Celestine gateway, see Périaux, *Dictionnaire*, 104–5.

32. *Letters and Papers*, II (II), 558; G. Bois, *The Crisis of Feudalism: Economy and Society In Eastern Normandy, c. 1300–1500* (Cambridge and Paris 1984), 430; R. Quenedey, *L'habitation rouennaise* (Rouen 1926), 122–4; Le Pogam, 'Le palais royal de Rouen', 230. For the gardens, visitation, 1771, see de Beaurepaire, 'Célestins', 8–9; Stratford, *Bedford Inventories*, 110–11.

33. ADSM, G 39, G 40, see *Inventaire sommaire, série G*, I, 14; L. Jouen, *Comptes, devis et inventaires du manoir archiépiscopal de Rouen . . .* (Paris and Rouen 1908), 174, n. 2.

34. Farin, VI, 260; de Beaurepaire, 'Fondations pieuses', 343; *idem*, 'Célestins', 1; ADSM, G 9434, see *Inventaire sommaire, sér. G*, VII, pt 2, 192, 1448, 'certain édiffice de moustier [church] ou chapelle que lesdits Célestins s'estoient efforchiez de vouloir faire et construire de nouvel audit hostel de Joyeux Repos . . .'; BL, Add. MS 11509, ff. 26ᵛ–27.

35. ASDM, G 9192, pp. 2, 3 (summary includes grant for buildings, 1446); G 9195, f. 1, letters patent of Henry VI, 23 May 1445; G 9204 and G 9195, ff. 32ᵛ–33ᵛ [medieval foliation], letters of mortmain, 8 July 1446; BL, Add. MS 11509, f. 27, 200 *liv. t.* to be paid by the *Chambre des comptes* in Rouen, until the buildings and church were in use by the Celestines.

36. ADSM, G 9434, see *Inventaire sommaire, sér. G*, VII, pt 2, 192–3; G 9208, nos 21, 22. For Beaufort, see M. K. Jones, 'The Beaufort Family and the War in France, 1421–1450' (Bristol, Ph.D., 1983).

37. ADSM, G 9192, p. 3, 4, arrests, 23 Aug. 1449, 4 Aug 1451; letters patent of Charles VII, 30 Nov. 1449, and 6 Feb. 1451 (400 *liv.t.* p.a. to a total of 6,000 *écus*), see *Inventaire sommaire, sér. G*, VII, pt 2, under G 9195, 9202, 9204, etc.; see also Le Pogam, thesis, 79–80, for copies of the act of foundation in mémorial L of the *Chambre des comptes*, and for documents concerning lands and revenues for the Celestines in Paris collections. For building works in progress 1460, *Inventaire sommaire*, ibid., 193–4.

38. De Beaurepaire, 'Célestins', 3–10, with text of the visitation of 1771.

39. For this paragraph and the next two, see de Beaurepaire, 'Fondations pieuses', 345–6, 358–63, 367–9; Stratford, *Bedford Inventories*, 35, nn. 63, 65, with references.

40. A. Erlande-Brandenburg, 'Les statues de Charles V et de Jeanne de Bourbon du Musée du Louvre', *Bull. mon.*, CXXVI (1968), 28–36; see further, J. R. Gaborit, 'Les statues de Charles V et de Jeanne de Bourbon du Louvre: une nouvelle hypothèse', *Revue du Louvre*, XXXI (1981), 237–45; K. Morand, *Claus Sluter: Artist at the Court of Burgundy* (London 1991), 315–16, pl. 7–8, 13–17, with bibliography.

41. ADSM, G 3573, 12 Aug. 1425, 'Ponuntur in super in portali exteriori ipsius ecclesie due lapidee ymagines, una a dextris, nostram, et alia a sinistris, dicte consortis nostre, personas representantes, sub quarum ymaginum pedibus erunt arma nostra et illa dicte consortis nostre insculpta . . .'; ibid., 27 May 1428, if they so wish, the duke and duchess may 'faire mettre aux deux costez de la dicte eglise du Carme, les ymages de leurs deux personnes contrepans a genoulx, et dessoubz eulx leurs armes et les ymages eslevez . . .'.

42. Stratford, *Bedford Inventories*, 35, n. 65.

43. ADSM, 2 E 1/183, f. 207ᵛ, 18 June 1443, 600 *liv. t.* to be used 'en la construction et edifficacion d'un cloestre ordonné estre fait en ladicte eglise'; according to the 18th-century Carmelite, Etienne Guéroult, 'le principal et grand côté du clôitre d'une structure admirable, les pilastres étant bien degagez l'un de l'autre à hauteur de 10 pieds outre les chapiteaux et piédestaux', cited by de Beaurepaire, 'Fondations pieuses', 346, from the

H

manuscript in the Bibliothèque municipale, Rouen, see *Cat. gén. des mss. des bibliothèques publiques de France. Départements*, I (Paris 1886), 302, no. 1205.

44. Le Cacheux, *Rouen*, LXXX, from ADSM, 2 E I/175, ff. 139–40; M. Mollat, 'Jehan Marcel, changeur à Rouen', *Annales ESC*, I (1946), 35–42.

45. De Beaurepaire, 'Fondations pieuses', 345.

46. ADSM, G 2126, ff. 60–61, printed by de Beaurepaire, 'Fondations pieuses', 363–6; Stratford, *Bedford Inventories*, 116.

47. ADSM, G 2128, ff. 17–17ᵛ; ADSM, G 3573, 25 Oct. 1448, '. . . celebre monumentum ac speciosa sepultura artificiossime composita . . .', '. . . ipsius monumenti et corporis ymaginem . . .'; ibid., n.d., but datable to May 1449, 'tam magnifice sepultus est'; A. Deville, *Tombeaux de la cathédrale de Rouen* (Rouen 1837) 173–9; de Beaurepaire, 'Fondations pieuses', 351–2, 355–7, 376.

48. J.-B. Cochet, 'Dévouverte du cercueil du duc de Bedford', *Commission départementale des antiquités de la Seine-Inférieure. Procès-verbaux (1816–66)*, 2 vols (Rouen 1864–7), 150–65. Madame Flavigny kindly drew my attention to the box.

49. F. Sandford, *A Genealogical History of the Kings and Queens of England . . .* (London 1707), 314; BN, MS fr. 20077, f. 9, see H. Bouchot, *Inventaire des dessins exécutés pour Roger de Gaignières* (Paris 1891), II, 426; J. Adhémar and G. Dordor, 'Les tombeaux de la collection Gaignières: Dessins d'archéologie du XVIIᵉ siècle', pt ii, *Gazette des Beaux-Arts*, LXXXVIII (1976), 5, no. 1098, both reproduced Stratford, *Bedford Inventories*, pl. XXI; A. C. Ducarel, *Anglo-Norman Antiquities . . .* (London 1767), 13.

50. Stratford, *Bedford Inventories*, 36, 394 and *passim*.

51. BN, MS fr. 24246; Lisbon, Bibl. d'Ajuda, MS 52–XII–18, see n. 2 above.

52. *Bedford Inventories*, B 184, 392.

53. *Bedford Inventories*, B 39; *Letters and Papers*, II (II), 558; ADSM, 2 E I/169, ff. 230ᵛ, 302ᵛ; de Beaurepaire, *Derniers mélanges*, 246–7.

The Shrewsbury Book, British Library, Royal MS 15 E.VI

By Catherine Reynolds

The Shrewsbury Book, a compilation of romances and treatises, was made in Rouen for John Talbot, earl of Shrewsbury, to present to Margaret of Anjou on her marriage to Henry VI in 1445.[1] Despite the general rejoicings at the Anglo-French Truce and the prospect of peace, Talbot used his gift to ensure that Margaret understood her new position as not only Queen of England but also rightful Queen of France, an attitude which would make war inevitable. Not all the texts serve this end and shortage of time may have led Talbot to adapt a collection already being prepared for himself. From the miniatures in this book and in two Books of Hours made for the earl and countess, the predominant style has been named that of the Talbot Master. Other miniatures are by a painter in the Bedford Master's style, working independently of the main workshop based in Paris, and by the master of Lord Hoo's Book of Hours. The Shrewsbury Book is valuable evidence for book production in Rouen in 1444–5 as well as for the political attitudes of one of the leading figures in the English war effort.

Talbot's dedicatory poem, f. 2ᵛ, opens: *Princesse tres excellente/Ce livre cy vous presente/ De schrosbery le conte*, a presentation depicted in the opening miniature where the earl offers a large volume to the Queen, seated beside the King. The book is indeed large with 442 folios, measuring about 50 by 33 cm, trimmed by at least 5 by 3 cm. The kneeling earl is identified by his Talbot dog[2] and by his arms in their simplest yet grandest form with the shield of the Beauchamp earls of Warwick in pretence, by right of his second wife since 1425, Margaret, daughter and co-heiress of Richard Beauchamp, earl of Warwick. Although their claim to Warwick was never abandoned,[3] this arrangement was unusual and does not reappear in the manuscript. The countess of Shrewsbury, not known to have combined the Talbot and Beauchamp arms in this form[4] and not mentioned in the poem, presumably made some other gift. The Queen's arms appear in the miniature and border and on the facing folio, f. 3, beside a genealogical table demonstrating Henry VI's descent from St Louis.[5] Although standard motifs, the numerous daisies (*marguerites*) in the decoration refer to Margaret. Stow's report that her 'badge was the daisy flower'[6] is supported by a gift she made Henry, recorded in 1451, of a salt enamelled with his arms and the flowers called *margaretez*.[7] A *marguerite* and an *agnus dei*, Rouen's emblem, decorated the leather case made for the town's wedding gift to Margaret of twelve *chargeurs*, twelve *plats* and twelve *ecuelles*.[8]

Fifteen texts follow the prefatory matter, each written on an independent gathering or set of gatherings.[9] Ruling, for two columns, and script vary between sections, the ruling sometimes for the different requirements of prose and verse. Each text is preceded by a full border and miniature across both columns, except for *Ogier*, f. 86, the *Arbre des batailles*, f. 293, and the *Régime des princes*, f. 327, with single-column miniatures. There is an additional full-page frontispiece, f. 4ᵛ, for *Alexander* which, like the *Quatre fils Aymon* and *Pontus*, has small miniatures at some chapters, an enrichment perhaps determined by the available models.[10]

The borders to the *Alexander* frontispiece, f. 4ᵛ, the three chansons of Charlemagne, ff. 25, 43 and 70, the *Quatre fils*, f. 155, *Guy de Warwick*, f. 227, and the Garter Statutes,

f. 439 (Pl. XXX), include in the lower margin Talbot's banner in the centre and, at the outer edge, his herald with a banner of Margaret's arms, reversed on f. 4ᵛ as seen from the wrong side. For the first text page of *Alexander*, f. 5, the herald's banner bears the English royal arms and the herald is by the same hand as the miniature, while the other heralds are by the hand of the Alexander frontispiece, f. 4ᵛ. Similar heraldic displays were planned for four further texts: *Ogier*, f. 86, the *Chevalier au cygne*, f. 273 (Pl. XXXI), and the *Chroniques de Normandie*, f. 363, where two grassy mounds have been painted but the spaces originally left for banners and herald have been filled with obtrusively horizontal elements and flowers. The outline of the central banner is still visible and the herald's flagstaff is defined by gold dots. Confusion over the status of the romance of *Heraud d'Ardennes* f. 266ᵛ, considered a part of *Guy*,[11] may help to explain the drastic re-working of its decoration, where a full border and bar with spaces for herald and banners were drawn to be replaced with a partial border and bar to the left text column. Apparently, when the heraldic/figure specialist did not complete his part of the work, the spaces were made good by the border illuminator. The changes at the start of the *Régime des princes*, f. 327, are less clear: a bar was planned but never executed in the central margin, where faint lines might indicate a sketched banner. Three texts remain with no signs that armorial displays were ever intended for their opening borders: Honoré Bouvet's *Arbre des batailles*, f. 293, Alain Chartier's *Bréviaire de noblesse*, f. 403, and Christine de Pisan's *Livre des fais d'armes*, f. 405. Within the miniature on f. 405, probably representing Talbot's appointment as marshal of France, the English royal arms identify Henry VI and a Talbot dog pennon the earl himself.[12]

The impression of haste created by the alterations to the full borders is reinforced by the obvious insertions of omitted text into *Ogier*, f. 153, and the *Quatre fils*, ff. 200–203.[13] The added leaves bear the continuous contemporary red foliation, itself showing signs of speed. Losing concentration after f. *vj xx*, the scribe numbered the next three folios *vij xx*, *viij xx* and *ix.xx*, an error not, however, accounting for the discrepancies in the contemporary list of contents on f. 1ᵛ.[14]

Hurried decoration and careless editing are not surprising since there were only ten months between Margaret's proxy betrothal followed by the Truce of Tours, 24–28 May 1444, and her arrival in Rouen, 22 March 1445.[15] The initial estimate for bringing Margaret to England was two months shorter, perhaps affected by Henry's longing for his wife.[16] The party which left England under Suffolk in November 1444 waited in Nancy, while Charles VII and René of Anjou completed their campaigning and Margaret was fetched from Saumur for the proxy marriage finally celebrated in February 1445.[17] Although not members of her household as was the widow of Shrewsbury's elder brother, Beatrice, Lady Talbot,[18] both earl and countess were paid to attend Margaret to England and probably escorted her from Lorraine.[19]

Whether Talbot intended to make his gift at their first meeting or on Margaret's arrival in English territory, the dedicatory poem shows that presentation was envisaged before Margaret married Henry in person. *Le roy nostre souverain* is referred to as *le vostre affye*, the term applied to Margaret herself by Richard, duke of York, in November 1444: *la princesse affyee, et qui, au plaisir de dieu, sera en bref la femme et espouse du roy nostre souverain*.[20] The presentation miniature, f. 2ᵛ, which shows Margaret as Queen of England, holding Henry's hand, cannot postdate the actual events of personal marriage and coronation. Margaret was treated as Queen of England from her proxy betrothal at Tours;[21] when she passed through Paris, Charles VII instructed the chapter of Notre-Dame to receive her with the ceremonies proper to a reigning queen.[22] There is therefore nothing inappropriate in a miniature which shows her crowned before her coronation and beside a husband she had yet to meet.

Margaret's arrival in England was still in the future for the lines: *Et lorsque parlerez anglois/Que vous n'oubliez le françois*, f. 2ᵛ. Talbot's assumption that Margaret might forget French in favour of English is further evidence for his nationalistic awareness of the vernacular.[23] In addition to the pleasure of her native language, the poet hopes that Margaret will avoid boredom by enjoying tales of heroes who gained honour in France and England (as in the romances, with the English Guy of Warwick and much of *Ogier* and *Pontus* set in England) and that stories of the wisest and most valiant of men will move others to follow their example. A text like Boccaccio's *De mulieribus* in French could have provided more suitable female models;[24] his *De casibus* was later adapted by Chastellain to console Margaret in her misfortunes.[25] The text of the Norman Chronicles offered more heroes and instruction on Anglo-French relations to 1217, through the history of the French territory with the longest connection with England and where English rule was still a reality. The Garter Statutes would also be useful reading, their miniature, f. 439 (Pl. XXX), probably showing Edward III and the founder knights, since Talbot, elected in 1424,[26] would surely have been recognisable if Henry VI and the contemporary knights were intended. His Garter was demonstrably a source of pride: Garters feature in the heraldry of three Books of Hours made for the Talbots[27] and of the Shrewsbury Book, ff. 2ᵛ–3. Garters also ornament Talbot's role on f. 2ᵛ, perhaps reflecting reality since, at some time before 1441, he had presented vestments patterned with Garters to the church of Saint-Sepulchre in Rouen in honour of St George, whose cult had been fostered there by the Archers' Guild of the Cinquantenaire.[28] The prominence in the miniature of the Order's patron, St George, so venerated by Talbot,[29] is unlikely to have been initially so welcome to Margaret: the St George's cross was the distinguishing emblem of the English armies in France.[30]

The texts that best fulfil the objects of the compilation in entertaining or instructing Margaret bear, or were intended to bear, her coats of arms. If a banner were designed for Giles of Rome's treatise, it too would seem appropriate, if heavy, reading for a queen. Of the texts without her arms, only the *Bréviaire des nobles* seems particularly suitable since the other two, dealing exclusively with chivalry and warfare, were not obvious choices for a young lady turning fifteen, albeit a queen.[31] Christine de Pisan prefaced her *Livre des fais d'armes* with an apology for her temerity, as a woman, in writing of chivalry, *chose non acoustumee et hors usage a femme*, f. 405ᵛ, and she omitted the text from the compilation of her works made for Isabel of Bavaria.[32] It would, however, have appealed to a warrior like Talbot, as would the *Arbre des batailles*, on which Christine drew and which was owned by Talbot's opponent, Artur de Richemont.[33] The coincidence between Talbot's own interests and the texts presented to Margaret has led to the suggestion that the Shrewsbury Book was copied from works he already owned,[34] although it is not unreasonable to assume that copies of such popular texts were available to the Rouen booktrade.[35] An alternative interpretation is that these 'masculine' texts with no trace of Margaret's arms were being prepared for Talbot himself when news of the betrothal caused him to expand the collection in a way more appropriate to a young queen. Precious metalwork would have been a more usual gift[36] and Talbot's choice of a book may reflect the Rouen goldsmiths' inability to meet the sudden demand for royal presents or his desire to convey a message too complex for metalwork.

An ostentatious present was in keeping with the splendour with which Margaret was welcomed by her new countrymen. Rouen witnessed the expenditure lavished on her when Suffolk's embassy with the Queen's household and escort made their formal Entry *en route* for Nancy. Even without the Queen, her *chariot*, occupied by the marchioness of Suffolk and the countess of Shrewsbury, and the magnificence of the retinue made sufficient

impression to reach the pages of Matthieu d'Escouchy's chronicle.[37] Talbot could apparently be hardheaded about material ostentation. Watching the entry of Charles VII's troops
into Rouen as a hostage for the fulfilment of the surrender treaty, he was asked if they were
not *bien habillés et armés* to which he replied that *de leur paremens ne tenoit il compte, et
que ce n'estoit pour donner courage et appetit à ceulx qui les combateroient de gaigner.*[38]
For Margaret of Anjou's marriage, however, he played his part in contributing to the
necessary magnificence, wishing the Shrewsbury Book *meilleur/Et plus riche pour son
honneur*', f. 2ᵛ. His honour was inextricably linked to that of his king and kingdom. Henry
had asked for money so that Margaret could be escorted to him 'according to thestat and
worship of him of hir and of this his reaume'[39] and French honour was equally at stake.
Charles VII pointed out that René of Anjou would need time *de preparer sa conduyte et
delivraunce à l'onneur des lieux et maisons ou elle doit aler et dont elle part*,[40] preparations
which included another painted *chariot*.[41]

The marriage seems generally to have been welcomed since it was coupled with a truce
offering hope of peace and prosperity. The advantage to trade was one of the first reasons
given to Parliament for welcoming the Truce[42] and London greeted Margaret with a series
of pageants of which the first at Southwark Bridge was 'pees and plenty', saluting the Queen
as 'the causer of welth, joie and abaundance'.[43] Rouen received news of the Truce with
enthusiasm, welcoming Suffolk as he returned to England[44] and, when he finally escorted
the Queen to the town, bestowing gifts not only on her and the marchioness of Suffolk but
on members of her and Suffolk's households.[45] It has been argued that the chronic problems
of war finance and his losses before Dieppe led Talbot to share this enthusiasm.[46] The
Shrewsbury Book would then be a graceful gesture from the old warrior to the young
Queen. Talbot is not known as a man of empty gestures. Even his motto, f. 2ᵛ: *Mon seul
desir / Au roy et vous / Et (sic) bien servir / Jusqu'au mourir* was fulfilled by his death at
Castillon in 1453, where his herald of forty years, pictured in the Shrewsbury Book,
identified his body.[47] His notion of good service did not preclude blunt speaking. His sword
bore the inscription *sum Talboti pro vincere inimico meo* with the date 1443[48] and the
dedicatory poem makes it clear that anyone denying English sovereignty in France is likely
to be an enemy.

No less than fourteen lines of the poem direct Margaret's attention to the table of descent
opposite, f. 3, demonstrating the legitimacy of Henry's title to the French throne. The
poem's stress on Henry's descent from St Louis in the eighth degree is matched by the
organisation of the table where, unusually, each generation is carefully aligned horizon-
tally.[49] The family tree is well known as an embodiment of the Treaty of Troyes and, more
specifically, a reflection of the trees designed to accompany verses commissioned in 1423 by
the duke of Bedford to publicise his nephew's right to the French crown. It was at the request
of Talbot's father-in-law, the earl of Warwick, that Lydgate produced an English translation in 1426, also intended to be illustrated.[50] Its very familiarity has tended to disguise its
significance in a book made for Margaret of Anjou in 1444–5.[51] Even Talbot appears to
have felt it inappropriate for his verse to follow the original poem in detailing the crimes of
Charles VII, omitted from the tree. Margaret's reaction to the apparent non-existence of her
uncle by marriage who, like her, is said to have been speechless with grief at their parting,[52]
can only be imagined. Other divergences from the original were governed by the passage of
time rather than taste. Both French and English dynasties are supported by English princes:
Humfrey, duke of Gloucester and Richard, duke of York. Originally, the French line was
probably supported by the duke of Burgundy, whose part in the Treaty of Troyes was
stressed in the accompanying poem and who was represented with his affinity supporting
the crown and arms of France in a tableau for Henry VI's Parisian coronation, when York

was one of the English magnates led by the duke of Bedford supporting the English crown and arms on the other side of the King.[53]

Talbot was well aware of the implications for Margaret of maintaining Henry's claim to the French crown. His poem concludes with the prayer that the couple will live long and peacefully with heirs to succeed them in peace. Yet the likelihood of peace is undermined by the wish: *et tousjours ait victoire / Le roy sur tous ses ennemis / Sauver luy plaise vos amis*. The Queen's friends were indeed likely to be the King's enemies while the King claimed her uncle of France's crown, which the house of Anjou had been crucial in preserving, and while his armies occupied parts of her father's duchy of Anjou and her paternal uncle's county of Maine. Margaret cannot have remained unaware of this visual and verbal statement of the English right in France. It did not pass unremarked by the French ambassadors in 1445, for instance, that Henry VI received them in a room hung with French royal tapestries of Charles VI's badges and motto and of the granting of the fleurs-de-lys to Clovis.[54] While Margaret must have registered Talbot's unsubtle message, her active intervention for the surrender of Anjou and Maine shows that she was far from accepting it.[55] Talbot's reappointment as lieutenant in Ireland redeployed a military leader unwanted in France in time of truce and also distanced one apparently unsympathetic to the peace policy.[56]

If the Shrewsbury Book is evidence for Talbot's political views, so his political and military career which based him in Rouen from 1435 to 1445 helps to locate his illuminators. The poem tells Margaret that she will see *les hystoires / Qui bien sont dignes de memoires* but a daughter of René of Anjou, largely brought up by her grandmother Yolande, purchaser of the de Limbourg's *Belles heures*,[57] might have found some of the poorer miniatures memorable for the wrong reasons. The predominant style has been named as that of the Talbot Master, from its presence here (Pls XXX, XXXI, XXXIIA) and in the Book of Hours made for Talbot and Margaret Beauchamp, Cambridge, Fitzwilliam Museum MS 40–1950.[58] A second almost identical Book of Hours made for the couple, Aberdeen, Blairs College, MS 1, also has miniatures in the Talbot style.[59] Postdating Talbot's second marriage in 1425, both Hours are probably of at least the 1430s. Localisation of the Talbot style in Rouen is supported by miniatures in a Book of Hours of Rouen Use and in a collection of treatises made for the *échevinage* of Rouen.[60]

Three other styles are evident in the book. That of the miniatures on ff. 266^v and 293 remains unnamed. The hand of the Alexander frontispiece, f. 4^v, and the heralds was responsible for the miniatures on one bifolium, ff. 22–23 (Pl. XXXIIB), of the final binion of the *Alexander*. He has been identified with the Master of Lord Hoo's Book of Hours, probably also made in Rouen.[61] The other bifolium, ff. 21/24 (Pl. XXXIIC), has miniatures in a style derived from the Bedford Master,[62] which, with the Bedford-style painting in the third Book of Hours made for the earl and countess, Cambridge, Fitzwilliam Museum, MS 41–1950, have been used to argue that the Bedford Master moved to Rouen.[63] The Bedford style must have reached Rouen independently of the main workshop which seems never to have left Paris, where they began the Missal of the Bishops of Paris for the English appointed Jacques du Chatelier who died in 1438 and completed it for his French appointed successor, Denis du Moulin, Bishop from 1439 to 1447.[64] Other loyalist French patrons in the 1440s were two of Talbot's military opponents, the comte de Dunois and the admiral Prigent de Coëtivy.[65]

The Shrewsbury Book constitutes valuable evidence for book production in Rouen under English rule. If Talbot did convert for the Queen a compilation intended for himself, no disrespect should be inferred. Margaret's household was equipped with plate on which her arms replaced those of Louis of Luxembourg[66] and her very wedding ring was made by breaking up Henry's Parisian coronation ring.[67] The unintended symbolism of this most central of wedding gifts came to sum up the subsequent course of Anglo-French relations more accurately than Talbot's deliberate assertion of Henry's right to the crown of France on the opening pages of the Shrewsbury Book.

ACKNOWLEDGEMENTS

I thank the staff of the Department of Manuscripts, British Library; the paper benefited from the comments of members of the BAA and of the Later Medieval France Seminar organised by P. S. Lewis, All Souls College, Oxford: photographs courtesy of the British Library Board.

REFERENCES

1. See G. F. Warner, J. P. Gilson, *Catalogue of Western Manuscripts in the Old Royal and King's Collections* (London 1921), II, 177–9, detailing texts, miniatures and heraldry, IV, pl. 96 reproduces f. 2ᵛ; for the romances, H. Ward, *Catalogue of Romances in the Department of Manuscripts in the British Museum* (London 1883), I, 129–30, 469–70, 487–9, 598–600, 604–10, 615–19, 622–4, 627–9, 708–10; A. G. Watson, *Catalogue of Dated and Datable Manuscripts* c. 700–1600 *in the Department of Manuscripts in the British Library* (London 1979), I, 155–6; Vallet de Viriville, 'Notice de quelques manuscrits précieux', *Gazette des Beaux-Arts*, XX (1866), 453–8.

2. For Talbots on his seals, W. de G. Birch, *Catalogue of the Seals in the Department of Manuscripts in the British Museum* (London 1894), III, 572–3; referred to as 'Talbot our good dogge' in a poem c. 1450, V. J. Scattergood, *Politics and Poetry in the Fifteenth Century* (London 1971), 97–8.

3. See Talbot's will of 1452, H. Talbot, *The English Achilles* (London 1981), 183.

4. Her seals showed her and her husband's arms on separate shields, Birch, *Catalogue of Seals*, III, 574.

5. F. 3 reproduced B. J. H. Rowe, 'King Henry VI's claim to France in picture and poem', *The Library*, 4th ser. XIII (1933), 77–88, and J. W. McKenna, 'Henry VI of England and the dual monarchy: aspects of royal political propaganda', *JWCI*, XXVIII (1965), pl. 27.

6. J. Stow, *Annales, or a Generall Chronicle of England* (1631), 385.

7. F. Palgrave, *The Antient Kalendars and Inventories of the Treasury of His Majesty's Exchequer*, 3 vols (London 1836), II, 215, no. 63.

8. 24 April 1445, Guillaume le Tavernier and Guieffroy Barnisson, *orfevres*, paid for the metalwork; Guillaume Poitevin, *orfevre*, for metal embellishments for the case; Godeffroy de Coulongne, *coffretier*, for the case and Simon le Masurier, *escriptorier*, for the *façon et painture* of the emblems, BL, Add. Ch. 26805–7.

9. Collation: 1 ruled unfoliated, ff. 1–3, 1 ruled unfoliated, f. 4–uncertain; 2⁸–3⁸, 4⁴, 5⁸–6⁸, 7², 8⁸–10⁸, 11⁴⁻ˡᶠ, 12⁸–14⁸, 15⁶, 16⁸–17⁸, 18⁴, 19⁸–22⁸, 23² + f. 153 inserted, 24⁶, 25⁸–28⁸, 29¹² consisting of a quaternion with a binion inserted between the last two leaves, 30⁸–31⁸, 32⁴, 33⁸–37⁸, 38⁶, 39⁸, 40⁶–41⁶, 42⁸–44⁸, 45², 46⁸–49⁸, 50⁴, 51⁸–55⁸, 56², 57⁸–58⁸, 59², 60⁸, 61⁸⁻ˡᶠ⁺(?), 62².

10. For *Alexander* illustrations, D. Ross, *Alexander Historiatus. A Guide to Medieval Illustrated Alexander Translations*, Warburg Institute Surveys (London 1963), 55, and 'Nectanebus in his Palace', *JWCI*, XV (1952), 69–71, pl. 17.

11. With a single-column miniature but structurally linked to *Guy* in the section ff. 227–272 and not separately itemised in the list of contents, f. 1ᵛ.

12. A. J. Pollard, *John Talbot and the War in France, 1427–1453* (London 1983), xi, frontispiece.

13. Ward, *Romances*, I, 623–4.

14. For all texts from *Ogier*, the red foliation and the numbers given in the list of contents fail to agree by inconsistent amounts. The list promises four books of Charlemagne and the three present are headed as one, two and four; the dropping of a planned Charlemagne book could account for *Ogier*'s misnumbering but not for the inconsistency of the subsequent discrepancies.

15. R. A. Griffiths, *The Reign of Henry VI* (London 1981), 486–7.

16. J. Stevenson, *Letters and Papers illustrative of the Wars of the English in France during the Reign of Henry VI of England*, 2 vols (RS 22, London 1861), I, 462–4, II, 467.

17. G. du Fresne de Beaucourt, *Histoire de Charles VII*, 6 vols (Paris 1881–91), IV, 90–4.

18. Stevenson, *Letters and Papers*, I, 451; BL, Add. MS. 23938, ff. 5, 13. Not always clearly distinguished, the countess and his sister-in-law have been confused.

19. 17 August 1444, £100 was paid of the £303 6s. 8d. estimated to Talbot for future attendance on the Queen, representing 91 days at 5 marks a day, a longer period than escort through Normandy would require;

payment to the countess of £133 6s. 8d. specified service in foreign parts, PRO, E 403/753, m10; Pollard, *John Talbot*, 61.

20. S. Luce, *Chronique du Mont-Saint-Michel, 1343–1468*, 2 vols, repr. (New York 1966), II, 177.

21. A. Vallet de Viriville, *Historie de Charles VII*, 3 vols (Paris 1862–5), II, 454.

22. A. Joubert, 'Le mariage de Henry VI et de Marguerite d'Anjou d'après les documents publiés en Angleterre (1444–5)', *Revue historique et archéologique du Maine*, XIII (1883), 322.

23. Pollard, *John Talbot*, 128, n. 27.

24. BL, Royal MS, 16 G. V, *Livre des femmes nobles*, with miniatures in the Shrewsbury Book's predominant style is modelled on BL, Royal MS, 20 C. V, accessible therefore in Rouen c. 1440, C. Reynolds, 'Illustrated Boccaccio Manuscripts in the British Library (London)', *Studi sul Boccaccio*, XVII (1989), 159–64, 171–80.

25. *Le temple Jean Boccace de la ruyne d'alcuns nobles malheureux*, ed. Kervyn de Lettenhove, *Œuvres de Georges Chastellain*, VII (Brussels 1863), 75–143.

26. Pollard, *John Talbot*, 123.

27. Cambridge, Fitzwilliam Museum, MS 40–1950, f. 7ᵛ, and MS 41–1950, f. 2ᵛ, F. Wormald, P. M. Giles, *A Descriptive Catalogue of the Additional Illuminated Manuscripts in the Fitzwilliam Museum Acquired between 1895 and 1979 (excepting the McClean Collection)* (Cambridge 1982), II, pls 48–9, captions reversed; Blairs College MS 1 (Edinburgh, National Library of Scotland, Dep. 221/1), f. 4ᵛ, J. Balfour Paul, *Memorial Catalogue of the Heraldic Exhibition, Edinburgh, MDCCCXCI* (Edinburgh 1892), pl. XLIV.

28. P. Le Cacheux, *Rouen au temps de Jeanne d'Arc* (SHN, Rouen and Paris 1931), li–lii, 36–40, 378–9; E. de la Quérière, *Notice sur l'ancienne église collégiale du Saint-Sepulchre de Rouen, dite la chapelle Saint-Georges* (Rouen 1861).

29. Talbot chose to be shown with St George, not his name patron, in his Books of Hours, see n. 27 above; his funerary chapel was to be dedicated to the Virgin and St George, Talbot, *English Achilles*, 183.

30. By 1452–3, Margaret was paying for glass with escutcheons of St George and St Edward, A. R. Myers, 'The Household of Queen Margaret of Anjou 1452–3', *Bulletin of the John Rylands Library*, XL (1957–8), 423–4.

31. Margaret was born on 23 or 24 March 1430 according to the Calendars of two of René's Hours, C. N. L. Brooke and V. Ortenberg, 'The Birth of Margaret of Anjou', *Bulletin of the Institute of Historical Research*, LXI (1988), 357–8, though she gave Maundy alms to only fourteen poor women in Rouen on 25 March 1445, BL, Add. MS 23938, f. 9.

32. BL, Harley MS 4431, see S. Hindman, 'The composition of the manuscript of Christine de Pisan's collected works in the British Library: a re-assessment', *The British Library Journal*, 9 (1983), 93–123; Christine's authorship was edited out of some manuscripts, presumably as undermining the text's authority, A. T. P. Byles, *The Book of Fayttes of Armes and of Chyvalrye* (Early English Text Society, OS 189, London 1937), xv–xvi; her reference to English treachery was omitted from the Shrewsbury Book, Warner, Gilson, *Catalogue*, II, 178.

33. N. A. R. Wright, '*The Tree of Battles* of Honoré Bouvet and the laws of war', *War, Literature and Politics in the Later Middle Ages*, ed. C. T. Allmand (Liverpool 1976), 12–13.

34. Pollard, *John Talbot*, 123.

35. For the Rouen booktrade, R. Watson, *The Playfair Hours* (London 1984), 23–34; the *Quatre fils Aymon*, BL, Royal MS 16 G. II, Warner, Gilson, *Catalogue*, II, 207, Ward, *Romances*, I, 619–23, is similar in text to the Shrewsbury Book; its miniatures, identical in style, vary in placing and subject matter, suggesting at least two exemplars in Rouen; the *Régime des Princes* was included in BN, MS fr. 126, a compilation made for the *échevinage* of Rouen c. 1450 with a frontispiece in the same style but completely different in content, suggesting the availability of more than one model, C. Rabel, 'Artiste et clientèle à la fin du Moyen Age: les manuscrits profanes du Maître de l'échevinage de Rouen', *Revue de l'Art*, 84 (1989), 49, 59 n. 24.

36. For gifts to Isabel of France when she married Richard II, L. Douët d'Arcq, *Choix des pièces inédites relatives au règne de Charles VI*, 2 vols (SHF, Paris 1863–4), II, 273–9, listing one book, an Hours, ornamented with gold and precious stones, 277.

37. A scribal error must have joined the Entry of the escort in 1444 onto the aftermath of Margaret's own Entry in 1445, ed. G. du Fresne de Beaucourt, *Chronique de Matthieu d'Escouchy*, 3 vols (SHF, Paris 1863–4), I, 86–90. The whole description has been taken to refer to 1445, leaving historians to explain Margaret's apparent absence, e.g. J. H. Ramsey, *Lancaster and York* (Oxford 1892), II, 63; she was, not suprisingly, present for her own Entry, L. Fallue, *Histoire politique et religieuse de l'église métropolitaine et du Diocèse de Rouen*, 4 vols (Rouen 1850–1), II, 459, for her visit to the cathedral.

38. P. S. Lewis, *Ecrits politiques de Jean Juvenal des Ursins*, 2 vols (SHF, Paris 1985), II, 247–8.

39. N. H. Nicolas, *Proceedings and Ordinances of the Privy Council of England*, 6 vols (London 1834–7), VI, 323.

40. J. B. Sheppard, *Litterae Cantuarienses* 3 vols (RS, London 1889), III, 186.

41. N. Reynaud, 'Barthélemy d'Eyck avant 1450', *Revue de l'Art*, 84 (1989), 35, 43 n. 60.

42. *Rotuli Parliamentorum*, 6 vols (1767–77), V, 73.

43. C. Brown, 'Lydgate's verses on Queen Margaret's entry into London', *Modern Language Review*, VII (1912), 226; R. Withington, 'Queen Margaret's Entry into London 1445', *Modern Philology*, XIII (1915–16), 53–7.
44. C. de Beaurepaire, *Les États de Normandie sous la domination anglaise* (Evreux 1859), 83.
45. BL, Add. Ch. 26808.
46. Pollard, *John Talbot*, 61.
47. De Beaucourt, *Chronique de Matthieu d'Escouchy*, II, 42–3.
48. A. Thevet, *Les vrais pourtraits et vies des hommes illustres* (Paris 1584), IV, 284.
49. The generations are linked by horizontal lines in two English versions of this tree, so losing the fleur-de-lys shape, BL, Add. MS 39236, f. 147ᵛ, contrasting with the more typically confusing arrangement of the Holy Kindred, f. 140ᵛ, and Cambridge University Library, MS Ll V 20, f. 34, McKenna, *JWCI*, 28 (1965), 152, pl. 28b.
50. Rowe, *The Library*, 4th ser. XIII (1933), 77–88.
51. London did not repeat for Margaret the *tableau vivant* version staged for Henry VI in 1432, *The Great Chronicle of London*, ed. A. H. Thomas, I. D. Thornley (London 1938), 166–7; P. Durrieu, 'Les souvenirs historiques dans les manuscrits à miniatures de la domination anglaise en France au temps de Jeanne d'Arc', *Annuaire-Bulletin de la Société de l'Histoire de France* (1905), 21, pointed out Talbot's desire to turn a French princess into an English sovereign.
52. H. Courteault, L. Celier, eds, *Les chroniques du roi Charles VII par Gilles le Bouvier dit le héraut Berry* (SHF, Paris 1979), 440.
53. B. Guenée, F. Lehoux, *Les entrées royales françaises de 1328 à 1515*, Sources d'histoire médiévale publiées par l'Institut de Recherche et d'Histoire des Textes, 5 (Paris 1968), 68.
54. Stevenson, *Letters and Papers*, I, 103; J. Guiffrey, 'Inventaire des tapisseries du roi Charles VI, vendues par les anglais en 1442', *BEC*, XLVIII (1887), for Clovis 86, nos 136 and 401, for Charles VI's badges 74–5, nos 1–5, 77, no. 26, 401, 410; O. Millar, *The Inventories and Valuations of the King's Goods, 1649–1651*, Walpole Society, XLIII (1970–2), for Clovis 292 no. 193, for 'flower de luces', no further details given, 159 no. 17, 343 no. 244.
55. Stevenson, *Letters and Papers*, I, 164–7; II, 640–1.
56. Pollard, *John Talbot*, 61.
57. For René's patronage, F. Robin, *La cour d'Anjou-Provence. La vie artistique sous le règne de René* (Paris 1985); for Yolande and Margaret, A. Lecoy de la Marche, *Le roi René* (Paris 1875), 231; for the *Belles heures*, M. Meiss, *French Painting in the time of Jean de Berry. The Limbourgs and their contemporaries* (New York 1974), 80.
58. L. L. Williams, 'A Rouen Book of Hours of the Sarum Use *c*. 1444, belonging to Thomas, Lord Hoo, Chancellor of Normandy and France', *Proceedings of the Royal Irish Academy*, LXXV section C (1975), 191; J. Plummer, *The Last Flowering: French Painting in Manuscripts 1420–1530 from American Collections* (New York and London 1982), 17.
59. N. R. Ker, *Medieval Manuscripts in British Libraries*, II (Oxford 1977), 113–18.
60. C. Gaspar, F. Lyna, *Les principaux manuscrits à peintures de la Bibliothèque royale de Belgique*, Société française de reproduction des manuscrits à peintures (re-issued Brussels 1987), II, 40: Hours of Rouen Use, Paris, BN, MS lat. 13283, V. Leroquais, *Les livres d'heures manuscrits de la Bibliothèque Nationale* (Paris 1927), II, 85, IV, pls XXXVI–XXXVII; compilation, BN, MS fr. 126, see n. 35 above.
61. Dublin, Royal Irish Academy, MS 12 R 31, Williams, *Proceedings of the Royal Irish Academy*, 75, section C (1975), 189–212.
62. For the Bedford Master, see Plummer, *Last Flowering*, 2–4 with refs.
63. J. J. G. Alexander, 'Painting and Manuscript Illumination for Royal Patrons in the Later Middle Ages', *English Court Culture in the Later Middle Ages*, ed. V. J. Scattergood, J. W. Sherborne (London 1983), 151; Fitzwilliam Museum MS 41–1950 traditionally known as the Hours of Margaret Beauchamp, H. Yates Thompson, *A Descriptive Catalogue of the Second Series of Fifty Manuscripts (mss 51–100) in the Collection of Henry Yates Thompson* (Cambridge 1902), 232–8, perhaps because only two Talbot Hours, those now in Cambridge, were then discussed as a 'his and hers' pair, 'hers' being slightly smaller and with greater prominence given to daisies below the opening miniature.
64. Paris, Bibliothèque de l'Arsenal, MS 621, V. Leroquais, *Les missels et sacramentaires manuscrits des bibliothèques publiques de France*, 4 vols (Paris 1924), III, 37–88.
65. BL, Yates Thompson MS 3; Dublin, Chester Beatty Library; D. Byrne, 'The Hours of Admiral Prigent de Coëtivy', *Scriptorium*, XXVII (1974), 284–61, with refs.
66. Stevenson, *Letters and Papers*, I, 450.
67. T. Rymer, *Foedera Conventiones, Literae*, etc., 3rd edn, 10 vols (The Hague, 1739–45), IX, 139.

THE PLATES

IA.   Saint-Gervais avant 1846 par E. Charpentier *Rouen, BM*

IB.   Saint-Gervais: intérieur de la crypte, par T. de Jolimont (1820) *Rouen, BM*

IC.   Saint-Gervais: vue extérieure de l'abside en 1823 par Villeneuve. Litho. d'Engelmann

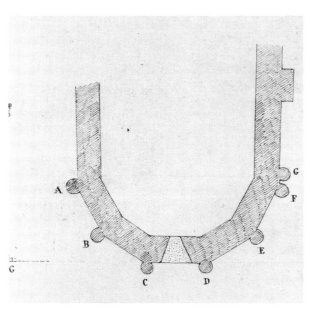

IIA. Saint-Gervais: plan de l'abside par
H. Langlois (1818) *ADSM*

IIB. Saint-Gervais: vue intérieure de la crypte

IIc. Saint-Gervais: chapiteau de l'abside

IID. Saint-Gervais: chapiteaux de l'abside par
H. Langlois (1818) *ADSM*

IIIA.   Montivilliers, abbey church: sculpted arch in south transept

IIIB.   Montivilliers, abbey church: south transept, east wall

IIIC.   Montivilliers, abbey church: groin-vaulted bay, south transept chapel looking north, showing angle roll (S. Heywood)

B

A

IVA, B. Montivilliers, abbey church: sculpted arch in
south transept, details

C

IVc. (*far left and left*). Montivilliers, abbey church:
detail of sculpted arch; David presenting Goliath's head
to Saul

VA.   The Werden Psalter: Berlin, Staatsbibliothek, Preuss. Kulturbesitz, MS theol. lat fol. 358, f. 74ʳ (Rheinisches Bildarchiv)

VB.   Sarcophagus from Marseille. *From R. Garrucci, Storia dell'arte cristiana* (Prato 1879)

VC.   Sarcophagus from Reims. *From R. Garrucci, Storia dell'arte cristiana* (Prato 1879)

VI.   Saint-Georges-de-Boscherville: chapterhouse arcade from north-west,
by E. Langlois, 1822
Rouen, ADSM

VIIA.   Saint-Georges-de-Boscherville: chapterhouse capitals 1–2, sacrifice of
Isaac/unidentified scenes, by E. Langlos
Rouen, ADSM

VIIB.   Saint-Georges-de-Boscherville: chapterhouse capitals 15, 6 and 7, Joshua
commanding the sun to stand still/Passage over Jordan, by E. Langlois
Rouen, ADSM

VIIc.   Saint-Georges-de-Boscherville, chapterhouse capitals 8 and 10, the fall of
Jericho/the conversion of St Eustace, by E. Langlois
Rouen, ADSM

A

B

C

D

E

VIII. Saint-Georges-de-Boscherville, chapterhouse. (A) Capitals 11 and 12,
unidentified subjects/Samson. (B) Capital 14, 'Constantine' figure. (C) Capital 19,
unidentified subjects (King David?). (D) Capital 24, the brazen serpent. (E) Capital 28,
unidentified subjects. All by E. Langlois
Rouen, ADSM

IXA.   Petit-Quevilly, Saint-Julien: view of
interior, looking eastwards
Photo J. M. Culerrier

IXB.   East compartment of choir vault
Photo J. M. Culerrier

IXc.   Watercolour of the interior, looking eastwards, signed Polyclès
Langlois, 1833
Photo Archives départementales

XA. Petit-Quevilly: head
of a king, from the Journey
of the Magi
*Photo Jean Taralon (before
restoration)*

XB. Petit-Quevilly: heads
of two kings, from the
Journey of the Magi
*Photo author (after
restoration)*

XIA. Petit-Quevilly: detail of drapery of a king, from the Journey of the Magi
Photo Jean Taralon (before restoration)

XIB. Petit-Quevilly: head of Joseph, from the Flight into Egypt
Photo author (after restoration)

XIIA.   Petit-Quevilly: Herod
Photo author (after restoration)

XIIB.   Petit-Quevilly: angel, from the Dream of the Magi
Photo author (after restoration)

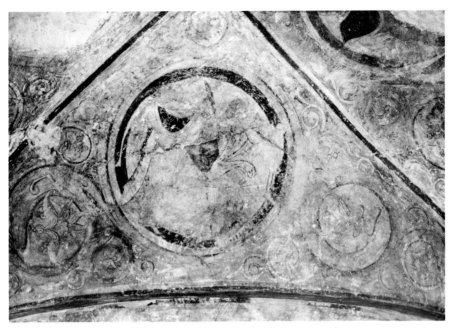

XIIIA.   Ely Cathedral: south aisle, groin vault
Photo RCHME

XIIIB.   Petit-Quevilly:
blossom
*Photo Eilebé, Rouen (after
restoration)*

XIIIC.   Zacharias of
Besançon, *In Unum ex
Quatuor* (Colln J. Paul
Getty, Jr), f. 81
Photo Christie's

XIIIF.   Saint David's Cathedral
Treasury: gilt copper-alloy crosier
from an anonymous bishop's
tomb
Photo National Museum of Wales

XIIID.   Winchester Bible,
f. 131ʳ, detail of Isaiah
initial
Photo Warburg Institute

XIIIE.   Paris, BN, MS Latin
8846, f. 15ᵛ, detail of initial to
Psalm 9
Photo Bibliothèque nationale

XIVA. (*far left*) Petit-Quevilly: Journey of the Magi
Photo Eilebé, Rouen (before restoration)

XIVB. (*left*) Petit-Quevilly: Adoration of the Magi
Photo Eilebé, Rouen (before restoration)

XIVc. BL, Cotton MS Nero C.IV, f. 12^r, detail, Journey of the Magi
Photo British Library

XIVD. BL, Cotton MS Nero C.IV, f. 6^r, detail, Saul
Photo British Library

XIVE. Winchester Bible, f. 350^v, detail of Maccabees, by the 'Master of the Apocrypha drawings'
Photo Warburg Institute

XIVF. Winchester Bible, f. 430^v, detail of St Peter enthroned, by the 'Master of the Leaping Figures'
Photo Warburg Institute

XV.   Rouen Cathedral: nave; looking north-east
Photo Conway Library, Courtauld Institute

XVIA.   Rouen Cathedral: nave, south aisle, west bay
Photo Conway Library, Courtauld Institute

XVIB.   Rouen Cathedral: nave, north aisle, west bay
looking north-west
Photo Conway Library, Courtauld Institute

XVIC.   Rouen Cathedral: nave, north aisle, looking
east
Photo Conway Library, Courtauld Institute

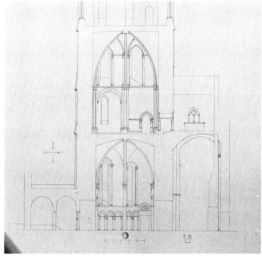

XVIIA. Rouen Cathedral: Tour Saint-Romain, section
Photo Conway Library, Courtauld Institute

XVIIB. Rouen Cathedral: bridge passage, door to first floor of Tour Saint-Romain
Photo Conway Library, Courtauld Institute

XVIIC. Rouen Cathedral: nave, west bays, looking south-east from north aisle
Photo Conway Library, Courtauld Institute

XVIID. Abbey of Bonport: south-east crossing pier from north
Photo Conway Library, Courtauld Institute

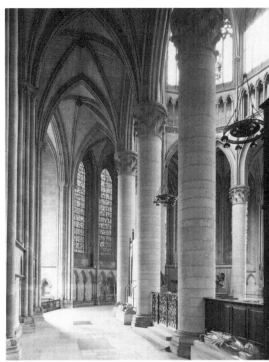

XVIIIA. Saint-Laurent, Eu: nave, north aisle,
looking west
Photo Conway Library, Courtauld Institute

XVIIIB. Rouen Cathedral: choir, north aisle,
looking east
Photo Conway Library, Courtauld Institute

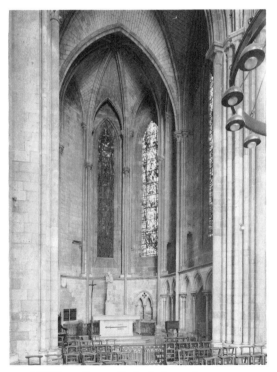

XVIIIc. Rouen Cathedral: south transept
chapel
Photo Conway Library, Courtauld Institute

XVIIID. Lisieux Cathedral: choir, ambulatory
chapel
Photo Conway Library, Courtauld Institute

XIXA.   Rouen Cathedral: Portail des Libraires. From
d'Allemagne (1943)

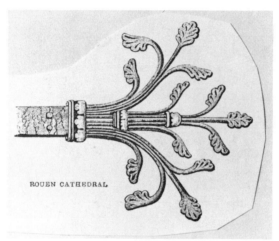

ROUEN CATHEDRAL

XIXB.   Rouen Cathedral: Portail des
Libraires. From Parker (1850)

XIXC.   Rouen Cathedral: unknown location. From
Digby Wyatt (1852)

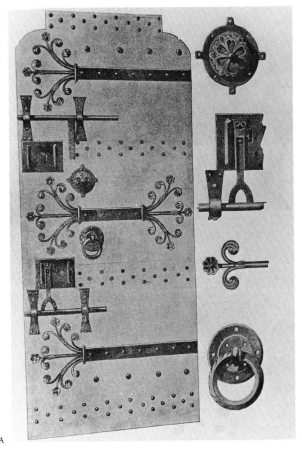

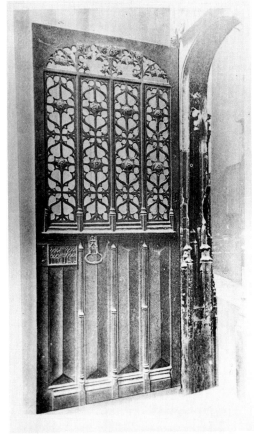

XXA.   Rouen Cathedral: door in sacristy. From Labarata (1902)

XXB.   Rouen Cathedral: door to sacristy from ambulatory. From d'Allemagne (1943)

XXC.   Rouen Cathedral: west doors
Photo J. Geddes

A

B

C

XXIA.   Rouen Cathedral: fragments
from choir screen. Now in Musée des
Antiquités, Rouen

XXIB.   Plaster casts of stamped
terminals in Beauvais group
From top: CL 9323/6064; CL 19962;
Beauvais Cathedral; Saint-Germer-de-
Fly; Vand A 4830–1875; Troyes

XXIC.   Beauvais Cathedral:
ambulatory chapel, north side

XXID.   Saint-Germer-de-Fly:
screen around choir

Photos J. Geddes

XXIIA.   Musée de Cluny, Paris: part of chest, Cl. 9323/6064
Photo J. Geddes
XXIIB.   Troyes Cathedral: post from screen across east chapel,
ambulatory
Photo J. Geddes
XXIIC.   Musée de Cluny, Paris: part of screen, Cl. 19962
Photo J. Geddes
XXIID.   Victoria and Albert Museum, London: fragment, 4830–1875
Photo J. Geddes

XXIIIA.   Rouen Cathedral: Lady Chapel,
window 5-a-b
*Photo Thierry Leroy ©1992, Inventaire
Général/Spadem*

XXIIIB.   Rouen Cathedral: Lady
Chapel, window 7-c

XXIIIC.   (*left*) Rouen Cathedral: Lady
Chapel, window 7-d
*Photo Thierry Leroy ©1992, Inventaire Général/
Spadem*
XXIIID.   (*below*) Rouen Cathedral: Lady
Chapel, window 6-c-d
*Photo Thierry Leroy ©1992, Inventaire Général/
Spadem*

XXIVA.   (*left*) Rouen Cathedral: Lady Chapel, window 8-b
Photo Thierry Leroy ©1992, Inventaire Général/Spadem

XXIVB.   (*below*) Rouen, Saint-Ouen: tomb slab of an anonymous architect. *c.* 1340

XXIVD.   (*above*) Rouen, Saint-Ouen: window 26
Photo Thierry Leroy ©1992, Inventaire Général/Spadem

XXIVC.   (*left*) Strasbourg, Saint-Thomas: window nVI, *c.* 1340
Photo Thierry Leroy ©1992, Inventaire Général/Spadem

XXVA. Rouen, Saint-Ouen: window 36-a-b-c
Photo Thierry Leroy ©1992, Inventaire Général/Spadem

XXVB. Rouen, Saint-Ouen:
window 23-a-b
*Photo Thierry Leroy ©1992,
Inventaire Général/Spadem*

XXVC. (*left*) Rouen, Saint-Ouen: window
34-a-b-c
*Photo Thierry Leroy ©1992, Inventaire Général/
Spadem*

XXVD. (*below*) Evreux Cathedral: anonymous
tomb slab, 1344

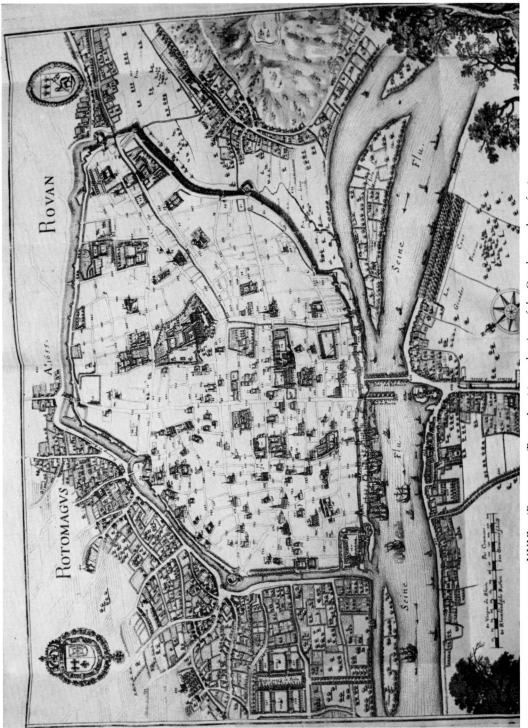

XXVI. 'Rotomagus/Rouen', 1662: reduction of the Gomboust plan of 1655
Photo British Library

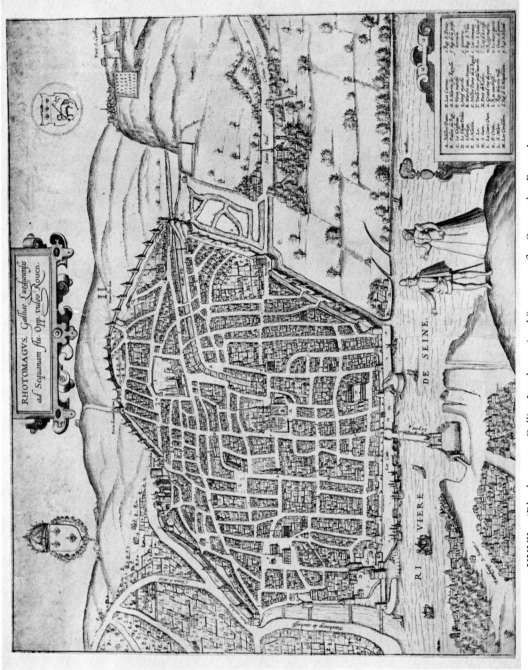

XXVII. 'Rhothomagus Galliae Lugdunensis ad Sequanum flu. Opp. vulgo Rouen', *c.* 1590: bird's-eye view after Belleforest, 1575

Photo British Library

XXVIIIA. Rouen castle, *c.* 1525: after the 'Livre des Fontaines'

XXVIIIB. Rouen, the Carmelite church, *c.* 1525: after the 'Livre des Fontaines'

XXVIIIC. Rouen, rue des Carmes: detail after Gomboust, 1655

A

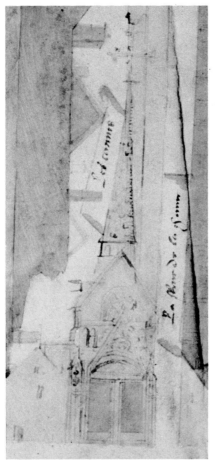

B

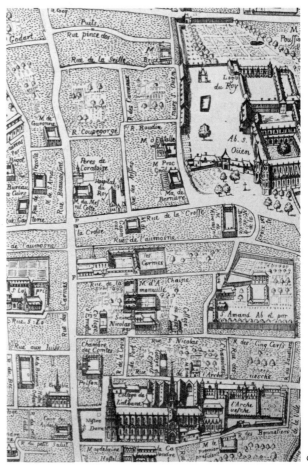

C

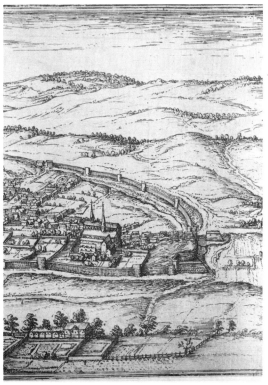

XXIXA.   Rouen, the Celestine church,
c. 1525: west end and portal after the 'Livre
des Fontaines'

XXIXB.   G. Hoefnagel, view of Rouen,
1574: detail
Photo British Library

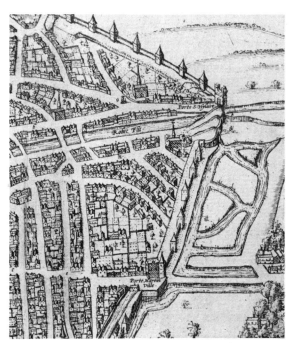

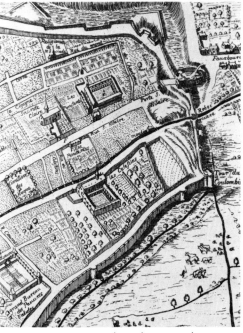

XXIXC.   Plan of Rouen, c. 1590, after
Belleforest, 1575: detail
Photo British Library

XXIXD.   Rouen, the Celestine enclosure:
detail after Gomboust, 1655

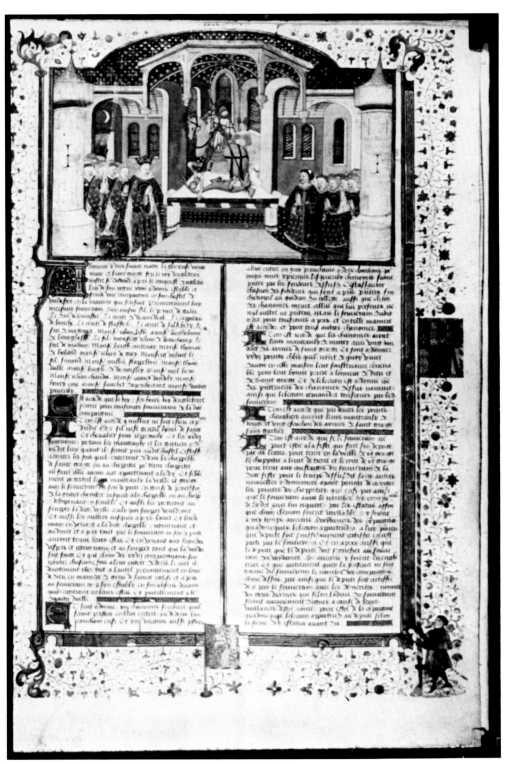

XXX.　London, BL, Royal MS 15 E.VI, f. 439, Statutes of the Order of the Garter
Photo British Library

XXXI.   London, BL, Royal MS 15 E.VI, f. 273, *Chevalier au Cygne*
Photo British Library

XXXIIA.   London, BL, Royal MS 15 E.VI, f. 25, detail, *Simon de Pouille* (first book of Charlemagne)

XXXIIB.   London, BL, Royal MS 15 E.VI,
f. 22ᵛ, detail, *Alexander*

XXXIIC.   London, BL, Royal MS 15 E.VI, f. 21ᵛ,
detail, *Alexander*

Photos British Library